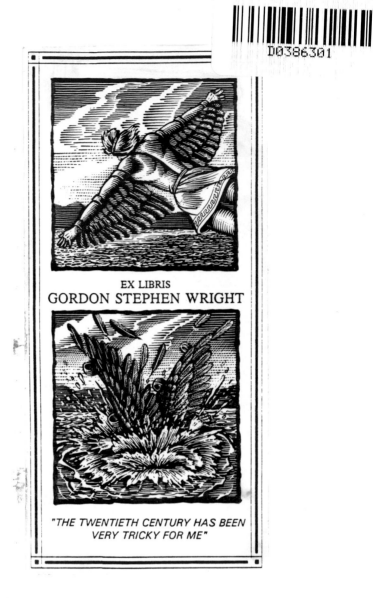

EX LIBRIS
GORDON STEPHEN WRIGHT

"THE TWENTIETH CENTURY HAS BEEN
VERY TRICKY FOR ME"

IN MORMON CIRCLES

IN MORMON CIRCLES

Gentiles, Jack Mormons, and Latter-day Saints

James Coates

Addison-Wesley Publishing Company, Inc.
Reading, Massachusetts • Menlo Park, California
New York • Don Mills, Ontario • Wokingham, England
Amsterdam • Bonn • Sydney • Singapore
Tokyo • Madrid • San Juan

All photographs reprinted courtesy of George Frey, except as noted. Used by permission.

Many of the designations used by manufacturers and sellers to distinguish their products are claimed as trademarks. Where those designations appear in this book and Addison-Wesley was aware of a trademark claim, the designations have been printed in initial capital letters (e.g., Band-Aids).

Library of Congress Cataloging-in-Publication Data

Coates, James, 1943–
    In Mormon circles : gentiles, jack Mormons, and Latter-day Saints / James Coates.
        p.   cm.
    Includes bibliographical references and index.
    ISBN 0–201–51758–2
    1. Mormons. 2. Mormon Church—Doctrines. 3. Church of Jesus Christ of Latter-day Saints—Doctrines. I. Title.
BX8635.2.C63 1990
289.3′32—dc20   90–42231
                                            CIP

Cover design by Richard Rossiter
Text design by Wilson Graphics & Design (Kenneth J. Wilson)
Set in 10-point Century Schoolbook by WorldComp, Sterling, Va.

ABCDEFGHIJ-MW-943210
First printing, December 1990

In Memory of Dale Lee Genz

There would never be a moment, in war or in peace, when I wouldn't trade all the patriots in the country for one tolerant man.

E. B. White

Contents

Preface

This book flows from a lifelong fascination with Mormondom. I don't share the church's beliefs and even my political inclinations are out of step with much of my Mormon neighbors' secular style. Their down-home brand of Republican-type civic boosterism—locker-room camaraderie for the men and sewing-circle sweetness for the women—is overseen by fifteen stern-faced but loving elders at their magnificent Salt Lake City Temple.

I do, however, have an intense appreciation for the people living in that world of clean-scrubbed white children at play behind immaculate picket fences, of mommy in the kitchen clattering pots and pans, and daddy off to earn the bacon from 9 to 5. I admire how, after supper, Mormon families trot out the church-supplied materials for Family Home Evening, during which the kids put on skits telling *Book of Mormon* stories, sing hymns, or play "pretend missionary" games in which each child imagines ringing a door bell in a far-away land to offer to whomever answers the restored Gospel of the Church of Jesus Christ of Latter-day Saints.

Family Home Evening is just one of many Mormon activities that pepper each Saint's weekly calendar assuring repeated contact with a church that is far more than just a Sunday-only affair. Mormonism is a day-in and day-out proposition. Dating men and women are provided social activities with groups called Young Men and Young Women—dances, ice cream socials, Bible readings, just plain gabfests. The two groups often join adults working on "welfare farms" where food is grown and canned for needy members, or on volunteer projects such as mowing lawns and making home repairs for elderly or disabled members.

Fathers are summoned to Priesthood meetings where they are required to perform duties like visiting Mormon families in the neighborhood. Married women have similar meetings and visitation duties as members of Women's Relief, that peculiarly Mormon sorority that insures that no family will ever taste death without a covered-dish meal to accompany it. Mormons sometimes joke that the "ladies" Relief starts baking the chicken and making the potato salad even before tragedy strikes.

By the same token, teens attend "seminaries" and "LDS institutes" near their high schools and college campuses where intermediate instruction is given in Mormon theology. For the very young, each Sunday includes Primary, an hour and a half of Catechism in which these youngest of Mormons learn a most peculiar set of rules, traditions, and legends. A treasured moment for Mormon parents is the day their children receive their patriarchal blessing, a one-page prophecy written by an elder designated by each congregation as its patriarch. He gives a revelation ("Thus saith the Lord. . . .") from God about each child's coming church life and salvation. Most Latter-day Saints (LDS) members can quote their personal blessing verbatim even decades later.

Thus, day in and day out, Mormons participate in what they like to call "faith-promoting" activities that leave precious little time for dabbling in the affairs of the Gentiles who surround Saintly circles.

Despite their church's demand for clannishness, the Mormons who live around me have been my good friends ever since childhood, and today they are fine neighbors. Observing the Mormon way of life makes me want to be a better family member, a more worthwhile citizen, or simply a friendlier person. But to be a Mormon is also to be an enigma.

Behind the friendly Saintly facade is a strict and regimented social order where unquestioning obedience to the church's elders is demanded. Above all, Mormon tradition demands that those inside church circles see to the needs and interests of their brethren before dealing with outsiders. And much of what goes on inside those circles is rarely, if ever, glimpsed by outsiders. While Catholic and Protestant missionaries invite prospective converts to attend services, the most important Mormon ceremonies, called Temple Endowments and Ordinances, are considered so secret that even discussing their content with an outsider carries substantial risk of excommunication.

This book is intended as a glimpse inside Mormon circles to

reveal the people and the institution who together make up America's fastest growing religion. Mormonism today is a movement that enjoys social and political power far greater than its substantial membership might be expected to wield. Much of this power is a direct result of Mormons' robust tithing, an all-but-ironclad requirement that every family plow back at least 10 percent of its earnings to support the church treasury.

Amazingly enough, that tithing seems only to make LDS numbers grow. There now are more Mormons than Episcopalians, Lutherans, or Methodists in this country. The church counts its assets in the many billions of dollars and holds stock portfolios so large that they are managed by computer trading techniques like those favored by America's major brokerage houses. Mormons have been cabinet members, titans of commerce, writers, poets, ranking White House officials; Mormons make up a substantial portion of the middle management of the United States government.

Despite its robust growth and institutional strengths, however, Mormonism today is beset by crisis. To understand that crisis is to understand something important about Mormondom. It is a crisis of turmoil among the church's mainstream brought on by bloodletting at the fringes, outbreaks of violence that have received national media attention and have caused many rank-and-file members to agonize over their beliefs if not their very way of life.

As a child I grew up happily surrounded by Mormons. I mowed their lawns, played sports with their sons, and went to school dances with their daughters. Now as a journalist I have reported much of their trauma, the polygamy killings, the ritual "blood atonement," the armed standoffs with police, and other headline grabbers. Some of their trauma I have shared as I have seen it hurt friends; some of it I respect but cannot share. All of it has fascinated me. But always, mine has been the fascination of an outsider looking in, peeking through the cracks in the walls thrown up between initiates within the Church of Jesus Christ of Latter-day Saints and outsiders like me, non-Mormons who are identified as "Gentiles" by the Mormon world.

Calling themselves "God's chosen people" and the rest of the world, including the Jews, "Gentiles," is emblematic of the Mormons. In Mormondom, it is always "us" versus "them." A legacy of the long and bloody persecution that the seminal Mormons experienced was the lesson that one way to keep your neighbors from harassing you was to convert them to your way of life. No religion works harder or more lovingly to bring outsiders within the fold. But those who refuse to come inside ultimately are all but shunned. Close childhood friendships between Mormons and Gentiles often become polite but cool acquaintanceships in adulthood. Outsiders living among Mormons often are simply left alone or ignored once they reject efforts to convert them. In areas of Utah, Idaho, and parts of California, where members of the church wield influence over such matters as who gets jobs, who gets bank loans, even who qualifies for auto insurance and food stamps, being left alone means far more than just loneliness for any Gentile.

Incredibly enough, even within the ranks of practicing Mormons there are degrees of inclusion and exclusion, degrees of us versus them. On one side within the church there are the apathetic church members whom LDS slang calls "Jack Mormons." On the other side are the ardent fundamentalists or "polygs," oftentimes believers in polygamy, "blood atonement," and other now-outlawed practices that are remnants from a past when Mormons fought to survive in a world of unfriendly Gentiles. In the middle is a growing congregation of mainstream Mormons that now approaches seven million members.

The Jack Mormons reveal what holds these tightly knit people together and what makes them special. Just as a jackrabbit looks like a rabbit but isn't truly a hare, a Jack Mormon is a man or woman whose ardor has waned. A Jack Mormon is a Mormon by birth or conversion, but a backslider by nature. Smoke a cigarette, start the morning with a strong cup of coffee, or sleep in on Sunday and you're a Jack Mormon. A Jack Mormon is not unlike an Easter Catholic or a bacon-lettuce-and-tomato Jew. More so than most theological strays, however, Jack Mormons are the object of much discussion by fellow Mormons who stream into the neighborhood churches or ward houses for the three hours of prescribed Sunday worship and community planning. At these meetings plans are laid to have members of the ward's Women's Relief Society visit the "lady of the house" in hopes of straightening things out. Or a priest is selected—all male church members are priests—to drop by on a church-required "Home Teaching Visit" to urge a return to the "Word of Wisdom," as the church calls its strict codes regarding everything from caffeine intake to underwear. Although their church never forgets them, Jack Mormons are at the low end of the pecking order among non-Gentiles.

At the opposite end of the Jack Mormons are the fundamentalists. An estimated fifty thousand Mormons living in Utah, Montana, Idaho, Wyoming, and California practice polygamy and adhere to other fundamentalist beliefs which mainstream Mormons long ago abandoned. Church dogma requires that polygamists be excommunicated. Many of the people interviewed for this book describe how they were "disfellowshipped" after ward meetings and other church gatherings where they raised questions about taboo topics, such as whether the ban on polygamy was more political compromise by the pioneer church than genuine divine revelation. Mormons who raise such questions face stern admonitions from the elderly leaders to adhere to the inflexible words of the prophet, seer, and revelator in Salt Lake. "Follow the Living Prophet," Mormons urge one another.

Addam Swapp, the polygamist who was arrested in a bloody shootout after he barricaded himself, his wives and children, complained that he was excommunicated merely for asking questions about polygamy long before he actually engaged in "The Principle," as the practice was called by founder Joseph Smith.

Such confrontations with authority demonstrate that Mormons are great builders of hierarchy. While all Mormon men are priests, the best-connected soon become bishops. Bishops from several wards (parishes) convene at stake houses (dioceses) where they spend much time deliberating on the devotion of individual priests and their wives to the "United Effort," Brigham Young's term for the uniquely Mormon approach to community affairs. Priests tend to be blue-collar workers, clerks, farmers, computer programmers, or school teachers, while bishops tend to be auto dealers, chiropractors, store owners, plant managers, school principals, and, of course, doctors and lawyers. Priests are Jaycees, while bishops belong to the Chamber of

Commerce. Priests work for people who belong to the Chamber of Commerce.

Bishops move up by aspiring to a place on the Quorum of Seventy, the body of elders who manage the Mormon empire's assets, handle its massive stock trading, administer its vast news and entertainment media assets, oversee its many agribusiness operations, real estate holdings, and other ventures. Within the Quorum, seventy aging men vie for openings on the Council of Twelve Apostles, the dozen old men who move according to strict seniority onto the three-member First Presidency—patterned after the Holy Trinity—and, ultimately, to the Presidency itself, the role of Mormondom's "prophet, seer, and revelator." The church teaches that the President receives direct revelations from God and is not to be questioned on matters of belief.

The Mormon hierarchy is patterned after that of the early settlers in the Salt Lake Valley. They were led by Brigham Young, one of Joseph Smith's "Twelve Apostles" who maintained tight-fisted control over the Saints well into his seventies, all the while keeping a harem of dozens of wives. Young was aided by seventy of the valley's most powerful ranchers and businessmen. These geriatric Mormon hierarchial systems have been oppressive and intolerant of those who raise only the mildest of questions. In politics rule by seniority is dangerous enough, but in religion it can become disastrous.

A common belief among Mormons, both within the mainstream and without, is that ordinary Mormon men can seek revelations on important family matters, such as whether to approve a son's or daughter's marriage, which college a child should attend, whether to change jobs.

As the teachings on personal direct revelation from God make clear, even mainstream Mormon beliefs differ significantly from those held by other adherents of Judeo-Christian religions. Mormons use the nomenclature of other Christian denominations, but oftentimes these terms mean something quite different in Mormon circles. The Mormon Trinity, for example, consists of two "exalted" physical men and a third individual who is "pure spirit." Our Father in Heaven lives with Heavenly Mother. The best Mormons will be elevated in the next world until they too are Gods.

Beliefs such as these brought to early church members persecution and scorn that hasn't abated despite substantial Mormon efforts to co-exist. These efforts have included the decision in 1890 to outlaw polygamy and the decision in 1978 to allow black males to join the church as priests. Both changes were announced as direct revelations by the prophet of the time.

Today one must wonder whether the excommunicated fundamentalists and their bizarre crimes threaten mainstream Mormons with a return of the rejection and persecution that the church has worked so hard to overcome. Temple-going Mormons reject the "polygs" but it is a distinction often lost on those outside the church. Worse still, mainstream Mormons cannot help but question themselves about whether all the bloodletting on the fringes, as outsiders so often suggest, is indeed a symptom that something is wrong at the core. As the Church of Jesus Christ of Latter-day Saints continues to grow both in political power and in numbers, the questions the Saints wrestle with become important for non-Mormons as well as for those within the fold.

Acknowledgments

This book could not have been written without the help of LDS friends, ordinary men and women who love living the Mormon way but who all too often will speak about it to Gentiles only when promised anonymity. I thank these helpful souls and acknowledge as well that the LDS church's own press secretaries, particularly Jerry Cahill and Don LeFevre, have been extraordinarily tolerant in answering my often ignorant and sometimes insulting questions.

A good reporter works both sides of the street, and so I must acknowledge as well Sandra and Jerald Tanner, two tireless anti-Mormons whose scholarship, investigative reporting, and zeal for ferreting out the dark side of LDS lore have done so much to give us Gentiles our few clear snapshots of the core LDS mysteries, glimpses of the garments, the Temple rituals, the recommend forms, and so on.

Even farther across the street from One Temple Square than the Tanners are the polygs who helped me, particularly Ross LeBaron, the elder brother of the deceased "Prophet of Blood" Ervil LeBaron, and Roger Bates, brother-in-law of gun-happy Addam Swapp, who spent much time patiently explaining such bizarre concepts as the One Mighty and Strong and the Principle as I stood in the sub-zero cold watching the tragic high-country siege that took Fred House's life.

Likewise, many journalist colleagues in Utah and elsewhere provided facts and insights that greatly focused these pages. I extend particular collegial thanks to Dawn House, Mike Carter, Mike Gorrell, Lance Gurwell, George Frey, Bob Unger, and R. R. Reid.

The book owes a particular debt to my editors at the Chicago *Tribune,* who devoted substantial resources and patience to keep me in the field to cover the major stories unfolding in the western United States, including the church's recent traumas everywhere from the most humble back porch to the boardroom at One Temple Square.

Peggy Fletcher, the founding light behind *Sunstone,* not only helped me by giving interviews but, more important my buying up back issues and subscribing to her magnificent magazine gave me insights into the hopes, fears, and doubts of devout thinking Mormons in ways that their own church's hierarchy simply cannot.

I also must acknowledge the staff in the rare book department at Sam Weller's Zion's Book Store in Salt Lake, where I found much needed and very hard to acquire original source material written by Fundamentalists and polygamists. Among Weller's dusty archives in a second-story loft one can shop for everything from antique patriarchal blessings scrawled in pencil across mid-nineteenth century foolscap to the latest revelations run off on laser printers by a new generation of zealots using the latest desktop publishing software. I find a strange comfort in the fact that, half a century from now, you probably will be able to find a copy of this book in Sam's upstairs treasure trove.

At Addison-Wesley, Senior Editor Martha Moutray honed a bulky original manuscript into a lean and coherent final product with deft strokes that eliminated verbiage but retained the voice I tried mightily to bring to telling the complex story of the always peculiar and sometimes wonderful people who dwell in Mormon circles.

My wife Kay never complained through all the word processing weekends, lost vacations, and lonely evenings I spent staring at a computer screen. I can only say to Paul, my son and my fondest hope, that I regret the time I didn't spend with him while this book was being written. The Mormon people taught me just how important a family is even as I traded time with my own family trying to understand theirs.

Introduction

Historical Circles

*God never introduced the patriarchal order of marriage
with a view to please man in his carnal desires, but He
introduced it for the express purpose of raising up to His
name a royal priesthood, [a] peculiar people.*

— Brigham Young

The peculiar people who dwell in Mormon circles don't just
debate their history. They die over it.

Mormons die like Kathy Sheets died, slaughtered in 1985 by
a pipe bomb in the Salt Lake City suburbs. They die like polygamous patriarch Joel LeBaron, gunned down in a ritualistic
shooting in Mexico in 1972, or as Daniel Ben Jordan died, shot
to death in 1987 in a hunting camp he had pitched with six of
his wives and forty of his children in a Utah national forest.

Death came hard for a kindly old doctor named Rulon Allred,
shot "blood atonement" style by rival polygamists in 1977. Polyg
John Singer was gunned down in 1979 by a Utah sheriff for
refusing to let his children study Gentile history.

Sometimes the carnage is particularly senseless as in the tragedy of Brenda Lafferty and her infant daughter, Erica, whose
throats were slit in 1984 by two men who claimed to be acting
under divine orders from a uniquely Mormon God who ordered
them to restore Mormon history by shedding the blood of heretics.

Another little noted and bizarre tragedy occurred when Rachal David and her seven children jumped to their deaths from
the eleventh story of a downtown Salt Lake City hotel in 1978
after her husband, who claimed to be rewriting Mormon history
with the aid of God-given golden plates, called them "home" to
heaven. The most celebrated recent mayhem in Mormon circles
has been the case of Mark Hofmann, convicted of killing two
people in brutal pipe bombings on the streets of Salt Lake and
its suburbs in the mid-1980's. Authorities ultimately linked the

1

1985 murders of Steven Christensen, a wealthy Mormon bishop, and Kathy Sheets, wife of Christensen's one-time business partner, Mark Sheets, to a bizarre Hofmann scheme to blackmail Mormon leaders with bogus historical documents that Hofmann had concocted to discredit the church's official accounts of its own past. Exploiting Mormondom's preoccupation with history, Hofmann's forgeries tended to bolster anti-Mormon theories about early church history. Hofmann faked a letter that seemed to prove that the church's founders were obsessed with folk magic when they claimed to be receiving direct revelations from God. Hofmann sold several forgeries to top church authorities who placed them in the confidential archives rather than making them public. Hofmann murdered Christensen because he told Hofmann that he was going to report the forgery scheme. Mrs. Sheets was murdered in an effort to fool investigators into concluding that the bombings were related to the two men's business dealings rather than to their religious principles.

Suffering death for their beliefs is nothing new to Mormons, who have been lynched in Missouri, shot in Illinois (including the church's founding prophet Joseph Smith, Jr. and his brother, Hyrum), and tarred and feathered in Ohio. Rarely has a people cared so deeply about their history or paid such a price for it as have individual members of the Church of Jesus Christ of Latter-day Saints. Perhaps only the Jews have suffered so much persecution over their history as have these ill-starred and uniquely American people who call themselves Saints.

Mormon teachings call for special efforts to record the church's history as it unfolds and as church leaders continue to receive direct instructions from God in the form of revelations to the church's head prophet, which are written down and carefully preserved. Mormons are taught to keep history sacred hoping to avoid the confusion about the past that exists with far older religions like Catholicism and Protestantism. A Mormon founding principal was that competing Christian churches had become corrupted by a clergy that rewrote the Gospels and church history to maintain unfettered power; the prophet Joseph Smith restored the rewritten record to its original state. Only by preserving the historical record can the Latter-day Saints keep the restored testament intact.

Another LDS tenet on the subject holds that the ignorant savages whom European settlers encountered when they subdued the New World actually were a lost tribe of Israelites called Lamanites who degenerated because they lost their sense of history. Yet another belief is that the faithful must compile extensive genealogies of their families in order to perform proxy baptisms for all ancestors, a "gathering of Saints" that the faithful believe must be completed before humanity can find its ultimate purpose. Genealogy, it is said, provides the sentences with which the book of history is written.

The obsession with keeping a detailed historical record to foster Mormon solidarity against the surrounding Gentile world has had a down side that the founders probably didn't anticipate. As the late Fawn Brodie noted in the preface to *No Man Knows My History,* her acclaimed biography of Mormonism's founding prophet: "Joseph Smith dared to found a new religion in the age of printing. When he said 'Thus saith the Lord!' the words were copied down by secretaries and congealed forever into print."

Brodie notes that this LDS paper trail provides a wealth of ammunition for those in unfriendly circles even as it gives those within the fold much to peruse when they question their own faith, as virtually all thinking people must—whether they be Saint or Gentile.

Brodie writes of her own quest for Mormon roots that led to her excommunication:

> The task of assembling these documents—of sifting first-hand account from third-hand plagiarism, of fitting Mormon and non-Mormon narratives into a mosaic that makes credible history, absorbing all the while the long-forgotten realities of religion and politics between 1805 and 1844—is not a dull one. It is exciting and enlightening to see a religion born. And Joseph Smith's was no mere dissenting sect. It was a real religious creation, one intended to be to Christianity as Christianity was to Judaism: that is, a reform and a consummation.

Both foes on the outside and Saints going through their dark night of the soul within the church's inner precincts use the materials that so compelled Brodie to confront instinctive doubts about Mormondom's official account of the strange events surrounding Joseph Smith, Jr., the charismatic farm boy who claimed to "restore" Christianity to its proper form by following instructions etched into solid gold plates that only he could read and then only by using a set of sacred spectacles called the Urim and the Thummim. To church foes, the Urim and Thummim as described in the *Book of Mormon* sound suspiciously like the "seer stones" that early nineteenth-century folk magicians used to hunt for buried treasure. The description of finding golden plates on a hill called Cumorah near Palmyra, New York, sounds very much like other accounts of post–Revolutionary War farmers digging through the ancient Indian burial mounds of New York and the Ohio River Valley hoping to find hoards of pre-Columbian gold. To the faithful, the same account is held as their most sacred mystery, much as mainstream Christians regard the story of the Resurrection.

The Mormon canon holds that much of the material written on the plates that Smith claimed to unearth and translate had been written by people who had had absolutely no contact with the Old World since 600 B.C.. However, the similarity between the *Book of Mormon* and many New Testament passages is a disturbing anachronism for the spiritually belabored. The suspicion that surfaces is simply that Joseph Smith used his family Bible for inspiration in those long winter nights at Palmyra as he composed a fictitious book and claimed that the manuscript was nothing less than the direct words of God.

During the 1980s, the battle was joined with particular zeal. Several monographs were published linking Smith to folk magic; essays questioned whether the Mormon liturgy was copied from rituals at Masonic Lodges, studies cast doubt on claims that the "reformed Egyptian" characters Smith claimed to translate were actual writing, and anti-Mormon attacks like Jerald and Sandra Tanner's *Mormonism—Shadow or Reality?* listed hundreds of parallel phrases between the King James Bible and the *Book of Mormon*.

Adding to the crisis has been a renewed tendency by the Mormon establishment to severely discipline growing numbers within the pale who voice questions about whether the rampant strangeness on the fringes and intense scholarship by what is usually called "the Mormon Underground" points to weaknesses inherent in their faith. In 1985, Elder James E. Faust, a member of the ruling Council of the Twelve Apostles, put questioning Mormons on notice at the church's General Conference by saying,

> When a member expresses his private doubts or unbelief as a public chastisement of the leadership or the doctrine of the church, or a confrontation with those seeking eternal light, he has entered upon sacred ground. Those who complain about the doctrine or leadership of the church but who lack the faith or desire to keep God's commandments risk separating themselves from the divine source of learning.

Faust closed his hard-nosed admonition to the Doubting Thomases of Mormondom by starkly saying, "Nothing is mandatory in this church. The only punishment for serious transgression or apostasy is the removal of members from the society and fellowship of the church, nothing more."

Such a cracking of the whip dramatized the fact that a crisis of belief is bothering the Mormon elite mightily. It is also clear that even as the once-faithful fall into crises of faith over new developments in Mormondom, ardent new converts happily accept this powerful and robust religion. It is difficult to quarrel with church adherents who point out that the clamor of skepticism from the outside seems to rise in volume and bile as a function of rising worldwide LDS conversion rates. That trend is as old as Mormon history.

Mark Hofmann, the infamous "Mormon forger-bomber," was just one in a long string of the church's enemies who have used its strange and turbulent history to promote violence and anti-Mormon sentiments. Fights over Mormon history have raged ever since Smith first told his rural neighbors about receiving the new religion via the golden plates and magic glasses.

The strange and tragic violence that has blazed forth in recent Mormon history has given the world an intimate look at the birth pains of the world's fastest-growing religious movement.

Even as their numbers grow, the turmoil raging in Mormon circles frequently plays itself out across the headlines of America, and one is tempted to write the Saints off as bizarre anomalies. To do so, however, is to miss one of the most extraordinary spiritual and intellectual experiences in human history. It also would be to ignore a major secular force with which all Americans must contend as these Saints accumulate ever growing political power and social influence.

Chapter 1

Joseph and the Gentiles

*Behold there are save two churches only; the one is the
church of the Lamb of God, and the other is the church of
the devil; wherefore, whoso belongeth not to the church of
the Lamb of God belongeth to that great church which is
the mother of abominations; and she is the whore of all the
earth.*

—The Book of Nephi (1:14) in the *Book of Mormon*

Establishment Mormon historians love to quote Josiah
Quincy, the Gentile mayor of Boston, who wrote of the Latter-day Saints (LDS) prophet, Joseph Smith, circa 1840, "Born
in the lowest ranks of poverty, without book-learning and with
the homeliest of all human names, he had made himself by the
age of 39 a power upon earth. Of the multitudinous family of
Smith . . . none had so won human hearts and shaped human
lives as this Joseph. His influence, whether for good or for evil,
is potent today, and the end is not yet."

Mormon critics, in turn, love to quote Fawn Brodie, who wrote
a quite different assessment of the same American giant: "[He]
was not an adolescent mystic brooding over visions, but a likable
ne'er do well who was notorious for tall tales and necromantic
arts and who spent his leisure leading a band of idlers in digging
for buried treasure."

Although they agree on little else, Mormons and their critics
concur that Joseph Smith, Jr., was born in Sharon, Vermont, on
December 23, 1805, to Joseph and Lucy Mack Smith. A few
years before Joseph was born, Lucy and Joseph, Sr., themselves
children of relatively well-to-do New Englanders, had fallen into
poverty through a series of bungled real estate deals. The family
made frequent moves westward to escape irate creditors, a pattern common to many people who settled the then western fron-

tier around the time of the War of 1812. The Smith family, with its eight children, eventually settled at Palmyra, New York—crammed into a well-chinked four-room cabin. Lucy taught each child to read and do a bit of arithmetic. But the demand for incessant manual labor in the spring and summer, and weather-enforced isolation in winter made it impossible for Joseph and his siblings to get an education outside the home.

Like many of the ill-educated Americans who had left the cities of the eastern seaboard to settle western New York and Ohio, the Smiths followed the way of what was called "Seekers," people without any sectarian religious affiliation who sampled the offerings of all groups.

Lucy Mack Smith taught her children not only to read and to add, but to seek answers to questions that had long troubled her. Was God a Presbyterian? A Baptist? A Methodist? A Shaker? God forbid, a Roman Catholic? In 1820, when Joseph was 14, Mother Smith, as the family called her, announced that her seeking days were at an end. She persuaded three of her children, Hyrum, Sophronia, and Samuel to join the Presbyterian church along with her.

Alvin, the eldest son, refused outright as did Joseph, Sr., who by this time had been telling his brood that he received many visions at night in his sleep in which God advised him on spiritual matters so that he needed no formal churching. Joseph, Jr., said he was inclined toward the Methodist religion and promised his mother he would decide soon.

In the spring of 1820 Joseph Smith, Jr., retired to a secluded grove of trees and said a prayer for guidance about whether to join the Presbyterians as his mother demanded, whether to cleave to the credo of Baptists, take up the faith of Methodists, or follow some other of the contending sects in his humble but confusing frontier world. Virtually every Mormon knows by heart Joseph's account of what happened next:

> I saw a pillar of light exactly over my head, above the brightness of the sun, which descended gradually until it fell upon me . . . I saw two Personages, whose brightness and glory defy all description, standing above me in the air. One of them spake unto me, calling me by name and said, pointing to the other—This is My Beloved Son. Hear Him.

> My object in going to inquire of the Lord was to know which
> of all the sects was right, that I might know which to join ...
> I was answered that I must join none of them, for they were
> all wrong; and the Personage who addressed me said that all
> their creeds were an abomination in his sight; that those pro-
> fessors were all corrupt; that: "they draw near to me with their
> lips, but their hearts are far from me, they teach for doctrines
> the commandments of men, having a form of godliness, but
> they deny the power thereof."

This was the "First Vision," the theophany that seven million
Mormons around the globe treasure. To Mormons Joseph's divine
encounter marked the start of what continues today as the ongoing, frequent contact between God and humans. Saints see this
contact through divine revelation as a "restoration" of relations
between God and humanity to what they were in Old Testament
times and through the days when Jesus Christ walked on earth.

A belief in ongoing divine revelation not just to church elders
but to rank-and-file men and women is an essential component
of Mormonism and one of many key tenets that differentiates
the church from mainstream Christianity. Mormons believe that
their entire religion was founded through direct revelation and
that even today it is evolving through one-on-one contact with
God.

Joseph's next theophany occurred three years later, on September 21, 1823, as he lay in bed praying again for guidance.
This time the prayer was answered by the appearance of an
angel named Moroni (pronounced more-own-eye), a resurrected
inhabitant of the Americas. Moroni, Joseph was to learn, was
the last of a once great race called Nephites who had been utterly destroyed by an evil, dark-skinned race called Lamanites
just before the fourth century A.D.

Joseph Smith later wrote of Moroni,

> He said there was a book deposited, written upon gold plates,
> giving an account of the former inhabitants of this continent,
> and the source from whence they sprang ... Also that there
> were two stones in silver bows—and these stones, fastened to
> a breastplate, constituted what is called the Urim and Thum-
> mim—deposited with the plates; and the possession and use of

these stones were what constituted Seers in ancient or former times; and that God had prepared them for the purpose of translating the book.

Joseph reported that he saw the vision three times that night, complete with a picture of the place in a hill, actually a gigantic Indian burial mound, named Cumorah, near Palmyra where the holy items awaited him.

Anti-Mormons have noted that a common tenet of Appalachian folk magic was that a dream that repeats itself three times in a single night always comes true. The fact that Joseph's vision occurred on the night of the equinox, a favored time for witches' Sabbaths and other occult dabblings, raises the issue of folk magic in the minds of many skeptics.

The day after encountering Moroni, an exhausted Joseph went to his father and told him of the vision. The elder Smith believed Joseph's experience was "of God," and he sent the boy to seek out the golden plates on the hill Cumorah about four miles from the Smith farm.

Joseph quickly found the sacred cache and pried off its stone lid. Mormons are taught that he found a biblical warrior's breastplate like the one described in the Old Testament Book of Exodus upon which was inscribed the names of God's chosen people. Laying on that breastplate were the Urim and Thummim, the sacred objects that had allowed Aaron to read the names of the saved from the breastplate.

Alongside these treasures of the ancient "Book of Exodus," Joseph said he found the plates of Lehi, the plates of Nephi, the plates of Mormon, and the plates of Ether, all in gold upon which each author had inscribed in "reformed Egyptian characters," a portion of the saga of the Nephites and Lamanites, two tribes who came to the Americas from Jerusalem and settled there in a state of periodic feuding. Also in the stone box were the plates of Laban, made of brass, which contained a copy of the Old and New Testaments in their original forms before they were defiled by the corrupt Church of Rome.

As the saga is told, a spirit—usually said to be Moroni, although sometimes described as a demon in reptilian form—appeared to Joseph to tell him that he couldn't yet take the relics.

Instead he was ordered to return again at the next autumnal equinox and on each subsequent September 22 until the time was right for him to take possession and spread the restored word of God to the world.

In 1827, when the spirit guarding the sacred treasure finally allowed him to take custody of God's golden Bible, Joseph, now 22, was accompanied by his new wife, the former Emma Hale of Harmony, Pennsylvania, who had eloped with him in spite of her father's angry objections.

Millions of Mormons today believe that on the tree-covered flanks of the hill Cumorah a crude backwoods farm boy was anointed by God to restore his pilgrim church on earth and to usher in the "Dispensation of the Fulness of Times," the final phase in human history before the arrival of the Millennium.

The above account is how the Mormon church tells the story of its founding. There are many people, however, who take a much different view of these reported events.

Mormon critics describe Joseph Smith as a necromancer, money digger, and folk magician who used divining rods and "seer stones," a superstitious backwoods rustic who clung to magical charms and whispered incantations to summon bad spirits to do his bidding.

These critics are quick to point out that the book which Smith claimed to translate from the golden plates adopted a later-disputed explanation of the hundreds of bodies buried in the ubiquitous Indian mounds in the lake country around the Smith farm. The book, according to Smith, said that they were victims of a great war in which the aboriginal inhabitants of North America were wiped out, as they are in the *Book of Mormon,* following a clash by two tribes of transplanted Israelites, which Smith dubbed the Lamanites and the Nephites. The earthworks represent a massive human effort in which millions of cubic yards of dirt and stone were moved to create artificial hills as high as one hundred feet. Today, a few unplundered mounds still exist at Cahokia in southern Illinois and at Marietta in Ohio. Anthropologists attribute the bone piles in these mounds to Native American customs of reburying their dead in fortified compounds protected by characteristic terraced battlements rather than to battles of the sort that rage in the pages of the *Book of Mormon.*

These mysterious mounds were particularly intriguing to Joseph Smith and his contemporaries who would dream of the gold and treasures buried there and build hopes of escaping a lifelong burden of debts. Stories abounded about how somebody somewhere had found the gold-filled grave of an Indian war chief, a rich store of loot tucked away by Spaniards returning from the fabled Seven Cities of Cibola, or some other fabulous trove.

These tall tales stirred the juices of destitute farmers scratching puny crops out of the rocky New England soil. Treasure hunts were often led by folk magicians equipped with divining rods, seer stones, crystals, stuffed toads, and other cabalistic paraphernalia.

Treasure hunting was common among backwoods farmers in Vermont when the Smiths lived there. A widely quoted passage from a weekly Vermont newspaper reprinted in July of 1822 in the Palmyra *Herald* reads: "We could name, if we pleased, at least five hundred respectable men who do in the simplicity and sincerity of their hearts believe that immense treasures lie concealed upon our Green Mountains, many of whom have been for a number of years industriously and perseveringly engaged in digging it up." The article reported that one man near Lake Champlain had dug a treasure valued at "the enormous sum of fifty thousand dollars!"

Predictably, books on the riddle of the mounds were popular during Joseph Smith's formative years. Much as the discovery of the tomb of Tutankhamen by Howard Carter and Lord Carnarvon led to the Egyptian fad of the 1920s, discoveries of the Indian mounds sparked a fascination during Joseph Smith's life.

The best-selling book of 1833, with sales exceeding 22,000 copies, was *American Antiquities and Discoveries in the West,* which, just as the *Book of Mormon* would later do, speculated that the Indians encountered in the New World are the remnants of the ten lost tribes of Israel which disappeared in the sixth century A.D. just before the time of the Babylonian Captivity of the Jews.

Skeptical historians who would like to discredit the Mormon credo have proposed that Joseph spent those long winters in upstate New York reading about the Indian mounds and dreaming how he would crack their riddle with folk magic and thus break his own dismal poverty by writing a book. Adherents like Brigham Young University's revered antiquarian Hugh Nibley respond with voluminous scholarship that bolsters the view that Joseph's history was foretold in ancient scripture. Nibley, like the church's most effective apologists, scorns critics for their selective emphasis of sensational facts such as those first surfaced in Brodie's *No Man Knows My History,* which Nibley rebutted in a widely distributed essay with the chauvinistic title, *No, Ma'am, That's Not History.*

The Mormon canon cannot help but raise questions about Joseph's use of folk magic even as it tells a stirring tale of mystic revelations and human courage on a par with the hagiography of great Catholic saints. Fueling the speculation about Smith's necromancy is the strong historical evidence that Smith once was charged with fraud as a result of a money digging project financed by another New York upstater, Josiah Stoal (sometimes spelled Stowell), who hired Joseph and members of his family to help search the countryside for silver that he believed had been buried by the Spanish Conquistadors.

The records of Joseph's court appearance in 1826 in Bainbridge, New York, on civil charges of defrauding Stoal in the ostensible treasure hunt indicated that the trial led either to Smith's conviction as a "disorderly person and an imposter" or a decision by the justice of the peace to simply order the twenty-one-year-old first offender to get out of town—"leg bail" in the slang of the time.

In that trial, relatives of Stoal charged that Smith was paid after convincing the elderly Josiah that he could find buried money, salt mines, and other things of value by placing his seer stone in a hat and then looking into the hat. Later witnesses to Mormondom's foundation, including Emma Hale Smith and Joseph's confidant, Oliver Cowdery, told how the prophet dictated the *Book of Mormon* to them by gazing into a stone he kept in his hat and reading aloud the words he saw on the sacred plates.

As early as 1838, Smith's enemies used these charges to attack Mormons in general and Joseph in particular. Joseph denied the charges in a passage in the Mormon holy book *Pearl of Great Price* where he writes in History 1:53:

In the year 1823 my father's family met with a great affliction by the death of my eldest brother, Alvin. In the month of October, 1825, I hired with an old gentleman by the name of Josiah Stoal, who lived in Chenango county, State of New York. He had heard something of a silver mine having been opened by the Spaniards in Harmony, Susquehanna county, State of Pennsylvania: and had, previous to my hiring to him, been digging, in order, if possible, to discover the mine. After I went to live with him, he took me, with the rest of his hands, to dig for the silver mine, at which I continued to work for nearly a month, without success in our undertaking, and finally I prevailed with the old gentleman to cease digging after it. Hence arose the very prevalent story of my having been a money digger.

Predictably, LDS apologists have devoted impressive amounts of scholarship trying to explain away the damaging allegations that their prophet was a bone-tossing necromancer, literary hustler, and cynical fake rather than God's anointed messenger.

Nevertheless, in Mormondom's founding hours, treasure was very much on all the players' minds. The very day that the newly married couple brought their find home, other treasure hunters were lying in wait to claim the sheets of gold. Mormon lore holds that Joseph anticipated that his hard-up neighbors would stop at nothing to relieve him of the gold plates, and so en route home he hid them in a hollowed birch log.

An old foe and possibly a former partner of Joseph's in a few money digging schemes, Willard Chase and his sister, Sally, apparently led a mob of a dozen townspeople on several efforts to wrest the plates away from the Smiths. Chase later signed an affidavit in which he claimed that he had loaned Joseph the seer stone that the prophet used to find the plates and therefore deserved a share in the treasure. Loyal LDS historian Richard L. Bushman wrote that Joseph did, in fact, have a chocolate colored seer stone about the size of a hen's egg which was consecrated by Brigham Young's successor, Willard Woodruff, during the opening of a Mormon temple in Manti, Utah, in 1888. That stone is widely believed to be kept today in the Elders' Vault of the First Presidency along with other sensitive items.

Brigham Young, Joseph's successor and inarguably the second

most influential force in the formation of Mormondom, himself described Smith's magical stone which he said Joseph showed to his Council of Twelve Apostles in 1841. Brigham wrote that "every man who lived on earth was entitled to a seer stone and should have one, but they are kept from them in consequence of their wickedness . . ."

To the devout, of course, these events are part of the bold saga of the birth of God's chosen church in the midst of adversity. To skeptics the tale is a farce of superstitious dolts vying for a nonexistent treasure which the feckless Joseph had claimed to find as part of a scheme to write and sell a book. Fawn Brodie's analysis is simply that, "Perhaps, in the beginning, Joseph never intended his stories of the golden plates to be taken so seriously, but once the masquerade had begun, there was no point at which he could call a halt."

To escape the harassment, Joseph and Emma left New York and went hat-in-hand to live with her father in Harmony, Pennsylvania. In subsequent months, Joseph and Emma worked to produce the first translations while Isaac Hale hectored his son-in-law about his lack of visible means of support. But friends and foes alike agree that Smith, in fact, was working toward winning the financial support of Martin Harris, a rich and credulous farmer saddled with a nagging wife named Lucy who enjoys the dubious distinction of having been the world's first anti-Mormon. Harris wanted to publish the *Book of Mormon* both as a money-making proposition and as a means of promoting his own anti-Catholic views. Lucy Harris was disgusted that her husband gave up his farm to finance what she considered a fool's errand.

As a first order of business, Joseph and Emma produced what they explained to Harris were several pages of the reformed Egyptian characters that Moroni, Nephi, Laban, Ether, and others had scratched onto the plates telling the history of the great American civilizations that had unfolded out of the sight of European historians between the Babylonian Captivity and A.D. 400.

Harris took these transcriptions to New York where he showed them to a distinguished antiquarian, Professor Charles

Anthon, who, at least according to Harris, at first said they were accurate renditions from the Egyptian, Chaldean, Assyrian, and Arabic written languages.

Harris told how Anthon then asked to see the original etchings and, when told it was impossible to show him, Anthon retorted, "I cannot read a sealed book," and snatched away a certificate he had written attesting to the validity of the "reformed Egyptian" alphabet Joseph claimed to read.

While the Anthon story appears today as an inconsequential sidebar to the Mormon saga, it is faithfully retold by virtually every Mormon historian because it became a key part of Joseph Smith's efforts to confirm his claim of having found real plates with actual writing on them.

Due to this thirst for authentication, the *Book of Mormon,* unlike the Old and New Testaments, is issued with a certification of veracity. Every edition from its first publication to this day opens with two affidavits, one called "The Testimony of Three Witnesses" and the other "The Testimony of Eight Witnesses."

The first, signed by Martin Harris, Oliver Cowdery, and David Whitmer, said that the signators had physically seen the plates and engravings and had been commanded by God to attest to their truth. The eight witnesses swear that they had been allowed to "handle with our hands" the plates and had "hefted" them. These eight included four members of the Whitmer family, Christian Whitmer, Jacob Whitmer, Peter Whitmer, Jr., and John Whitmer as well as Joseph Smith, Sr., his sons Hyrum and Samuel, and Hiram Page, the husband of a Whitmer daughter. Mormondom's critics note with satisfaction that such testimonials were commonplace on the labels of patent medicines, bottles of snake oil, and other questionable commodities. Furthermore, the certification is shaken somewhat by the fact that all three of the most important witnesses, Cowdery, Harris, and David Whitmer later left the church, and three of the eight witnesses left as well. But as Elder Gordon Hinckley notes in his small book, *Truth Restored,* not one of the men who left the fold ever denied his testimony about having seen or "hefted" the sacred plates. Their departures from the church came over conflicts with the strong-willed Joseph and others in the inner circle that quickly rose up around the self-proclaimed prophet.

Clearly, Joseph Smith worried that his work would be discredited by his opponents if they could convince the public that his claims were fraudulent. That point emerges with another tangential tale of the Mormon epic—the story of the missing 116 pages.

When Martin Harris returned from his encounter with Professor Anthon, Lucy Harris responded by making her husband sleep in a separate room. She also made a show of copying the characters Joseph had written and told her husband that she would find someone to read them and prove once and for all that Joseph Smith was a fraud.

Undaunted, Martin Harris, energized by Anthon's reply, traveled to Harmony, Pennsylvania, where he replaced Emma Smith as Joseph's chief scribe.

As had Emma before him, the poorly educated farmer worked on the other side of a blanket stretched across the room, writing down the words that Joseph said he was reading from the plates using the Urim and Thummim. In about two months the two men produced the "Book of Lehi," composing the first 116 pages from the plates of Mormon. Harris decided that if he showed the material to his wife, she would be converted, and after days of pleading he persuaded Joseph to let him take the first 116 pages back to Palmyra to show Lucy.

Harris returned a few weeks later weeping and distraught with the story of how the pages had disappeared from his house and simply could not be recovered. Joseph faced perhaps the biggest challenge in his religious odyssey as a result. He could redo the missing pages, but he suspected that Lucy Harris was waiting with the first draft so she could triumphantly produce it and show that the first and second versions were quite different and therefore couldn't be accurate translations from the plates. That would be a blow to the project that all the witnesses in the world would be unable to deflect.

Joseph's solution was to incorporate the story of the lost 116 pages into the preface to the *Book of Mormon* and explain that God was so outraged that Smith had let Harris carry away the first translation that He had taken away the Urim and Thummim. Later God allowed Joseph to continue the translations but required him to recover the material in the purloined 116 pages not from the "Book of Lehi," but from the accompanying plates of Nephi which tell the same story from a different viewpoint. Thus the LDS holy book starts with the book of Nephi, and not with Lehi.

Again critics see a patently obvious ploy to escape Lucy Harris's trap while believers see confirmation that God watched most closely indeed as their special scriptures were produced in Isaac Hale's Pennsylvania cabin and then were finished up at the Whitmer farm near Fayette, New York, before being sent to the printer in Palmyra.

In April of 1829 Oliver Cowdery, a schoolmaster who became captivated by talk of divinely inspired Joseph dictating the words of God in a rustic Pennsylvania cabin, took over the job of scribe from Martin Harris. Cowdery was trained in the craft of penmanship, and the compilation of the holy book went much more quickly. One of Cowdery's friends, David Whitmer, who was to become one of the "three witnesses" cited in the front of the book testimonials, later described the process of transcribing the plates at the Harmony cabin:

> Joseph Smith would put the seer stone into a hat, and put his face in the hat, drawing it closely around his face to exclude the light; and in the darkness the spiritual light would shine. A piece of something resembling parchment would appear, and on that appeared the writing. One character at a time would appear, and under it was the interpretation in English. Brother Joseph would read off the English to Oliver Cowdery who was his principal scribe, and when it was written down and repeated to Brother Joseph to see if it was correct, then it would disappear, and another character with the interpretation would appear. Thus the Book of Mormon was translated by the gift and power of God, and not by any power of man.

Blessed now with a capable scribe, Joseph's work took off like a rocket sled. While it had taken two years to squeeze the lost 116 pages from the plates, Joseph and Cowdery started on April 7, 1829, and by early July had completed a 275,000-word manuscript. Brodie notes that to produce such a work in 75 working days, the scribe and revelator duo would have to have averaged about 3,700 words a day.

Once again the contrast between how friend and foe view this phenomenon is striking. Critics cite the parallels to biblical usage and story line and charge that Joseph was simply spinning yarns starting with his well-thumbed King James Bible. Adherents argue that the scope, power, and complexity of the *Book of Mormon* could never have sprung from an ignorant farm boy without the aid of divine revelation.

The very words, cadence, and syntax of the *Book of Mormon* seem to many critics more likely a parody of New Testament writings than original revelation. The suspicion arises that Joseph Smith was more a plagiarizer than a prophet and simply used his family Bible for inspiration as he composed a fictitious book and claimed that it was nothing less than the direct word of God.

Brodie noted one of the chief irritations most new readers encounter while wading through Joseph's immense and strange book—the continual mimicry of biblical phraseology and style— the material that church critics like Jerald and Sandra Tanner call "parallelisms." By Brodie's count no fewer than 2,000 sentences begin, "And it came to pass . . ." Mark Twain claimed to have read the *Book of Mormon* and pronounced it "chloroform in print." Twain, one of the earliest of a breed of critics who employ ridicule to attack LDS tenets, has been dubbed a "Mormon-eater" by Wallace Stegner, a sympathetic non-Mormon.

Nonetheless, literary quality is not what is at stake here; the birth of a religion is the issue. By the middle of 1829, Joseph Smith had produced not only a finished manuscript, but an entire theology. By April of 1830, the book was published and the Church of Jesus Christ of Latter-day Saints was founded.

The first review of Joseph's new book set the tone for much of what was to follow. The Rochester *Advertiser* wrote under the headline "Blasphemy—*Book of Mormon*, Alias the Golden Bible":

> The *Book of Mormon* has been placed in our hands. A viler imposition was never practiced. It is an evidence of fraud, blasphemy and credulity, shocking both to Christians and moral-

ists. The author and proprietor is Joseph Smith, Jr., a fellow who by some hocus pocus acquired such influence over a wealthy farmer of Wayne county that the latter mortgaged his farm for $3,000, which he paid for printing and binding five thousand copies of the blasphemous work.

Bad reviews didn't stop Joseph Smith from launching a sequel. He promptly set to work on his next epic, the second volume in his trilogy of holy books which today is called *Doctrine and Covenants*.

D & C (or "Dee and Cee" as most LDS students call it at Sunday school) records the formation of the church starting with another theophany in 1829 when John the Baptist appeared to Smith and Cowdery and showed them how to baptize one another with total immersion as God requires instead of the half-hearted sprinklings instituted by apostate Catholic priests. First Joseph dunked Oliver; then Oliver dunked Joseph and both men merged as the first humans in twenty centuries to hold "the Priesthood of Aaron," which, according to D & C Section 13, "holds the keys of the ministering of angels, and of the gospel of repentance, and of baptism by immersion for the remission of sins."

Divided into 138 "sections" and two "Declarations," D & C is the official compilation by the church of every revelation God has given to Joseph and his successors as "Prophet, Seer, and Revelator," the title Smith assumed and that each President of the LDS church takes today. The first revelation in D & C, given in 1823 to seventeen-year-old Joseph by the angel Moroni promises that all white males in the church will be elevated to the priesthood of God. The last passage, "Declaration 2," given 155 years later in 1978, finally allowed black males to join that same priesthood.

The young prophet ruled his flock through revelations. Thus when the decision was made to pull up roots and head for Ohio, Joseph was told to do so in a revelation. Later revelations told the prophet everything from how to lay out the streets of one of his towns and who would own which lots, to whether an army should run away or fight and even, at one point, that Emma, apparently distraught over Joseph's embracing of polygamy, should be more obedient to her husband and stop her "murmuring."

Joseph's D & C also recorded his persecutions. The torment started early. When the Mormons numbered only forty they built a dam across a Palmyra stream to make a pool deep enough for their immersion baptisms. An angry mob came in the night and tore down the dam. At church meetings, the new Saints often huddled inside while mobs circled Hyrum's house and shouted obscenities. Later, mobs fired pistols and rifles as well as epithets at the huddled Saints.

Joseph responded to these pressures by sending members of his inner circle west on missionary trips to scout out possible locations for the building of a new Zion. One of these parties, led by Cowdery and a fresh convert named Parley Pratt, stopped at the town of Kirtland just outside Cleveland, Ohio, and worked to convert the local minister, the legendary Sidney Rigdon, himself one of the most celebrated Revivalist stump preachers and a recently disaffected partner of the great Disciples. of Christ founder, Alexander Campbell.

These "Campbellites" who numbered in the thousands taught the creed of the New Dispensation, that the New Testament was given as a replacement and not a supplement to the Old Testament. Joseph told the Campbellites that his was an even newer Dispensation, as many Protestants refer to various biblical epochs such as the Dispensation of Adam or the Dispensation of Jesus Christ. Joseph promised the Campbellites that he brought the Dispensation of the Fulness of Times, the last epoch before the long-awaited Millennium. To this day Mormons retain the archaic spelling of fullness in referring to the dispensation.

Perhaps the most fundamentalist of gospelers, Campbellites allowed no music in their churches because there is no mention of music associated with worship in the New Testament's Dispensation. They celebrated The Lord's Day but didn't say the word Sabbath because that was an Old Testament term. All members were part of the ministry, and none could be called "reverend" or "priest." Baptism was by immersion only; each congregation was considered autonomous and there was no hierarchy because none was mentioned in the New Testament.

Rigdon had established a communal group in Kirtland striving to restore what he perceived as the cooperative lifestyle of sharing practiced by the early Christians in accordance with the

New Testament "Acts of the Apostles," which describes the early Christians as a group wherein members "had all things common; and sold their possessions and goods, and parted them to all men as every man has need."

Rigdon had broken with Campbell because Campbell didn't approve of Rigdon's plan to set up a communistic colony separated from society as a whole. Like many leaders, Campbell realized that by separating a church group from its neighbors into an exclusive commune, those neighbors would become intolerant and unfriendly. It was a lesson the Mormons would learn even though their teachings and tradition of "gathering" for the Millennium have made such assimilation into Centile society all but impossible. That idea of gathering appealed to Rigdon's communal inclinations even as it appalled Campbell.

After reading the *Book of Mormon* and hearing at length from Pratt and Cowdery about the Prophet of Palmyra, Rigdon agreed to be baptized and quickly persuaded 127 of his followers to join him.

Thanks to Rigdon's subsequent help, when the Mormon missionaries left Kirtland to start another settlement in Jackson County, Missouri, in December of 1830, they already had recruited one thousand members for the Ohio branch, far more than Joseph and his colleagues had gleaned in all of New York.

Meanwhile, to escape persecution in Palmyra, Joseph led his people to Kirtland the next summer, and with the resulting gathering of Saints from New York, Pennsylvania, and Ohio, the June, 1831 General Conference, as the church to this day calls each of two annual meetings open to all Mormons, included two thousand members. That same summer several hundred Mormons who had left Colesville, New York, and briefly settled at Kirtland moved on to Missouri's Jackson County. It was here, according to Joseph's revelation, that the site of the Garden of Eden was located. This was where he should build the Temple of Zion, the mystical city where at the end of time all God's chosen people will flock for the millennarian gathering of Saints.

Joseph announced at the Ohio General Conference that he had spent much of the winter translating new words of God which amounted to rewriting the King James Bible to restore scripture to its original form. The early "restorations" included the "Book of Moses" and the "Book of Enoch" which described a style of cooperative living in line with Rigdon's tastes.

That communistic lifestyle, adopted first at Kirtland and then at other settlements, was called the Law of Enoch or the United Order. Under it, all property was owned by the church but each member was given a farm, a tract of land, or a business to operate to the best of his ability with the requirement that all surplus goods and services produced be turned over to church stores. Typically in Mormon history groups of Saints operated under this Law of Enoch while establishing a new colony, and once things were running smoothly, divided the assets and returned to a system of private ownership, albeit with strict rules of tithing.

The King James revisions that outlined the United Order and other writings that Joseph claimed as divine revelation were collected into the final volume of Mormondom's sacred trilogy, *The Pearl of Great Price.*

The *Pearl* ends with Mormondom's thirteen Articles of Faith, the sixth of which calls for the sort of New Testament Christian communal style Rigdon advocated: "We believe in the same organization that existed in the Primitive Church, namely, apostles, prophets, pastors, teachers, evangelists, and so forth."

Another of those thirteen articles, however, quickly enraged thousands of the non-Campbellite, non-Mormon residents around Cleveland. It reads simply and starkly: "We believe the Bible to be the word of God as far as it is translated correctly; we also believe the *Book of Mormon* to be the word of God."

Even as the assembled thousands of freshly minted LDS zealots laid out their Ohio Utopia at Kirtland with Mormondom's first glorious temple at its center, their new neighbors on the Western Reserve were grumbling mightily. The Mormons did much to bring that grumbling down on themselves. The gathering Saints often drove up land prices for their Gentile neighbors by their very eagerness to buy plots near the Kirtland commune. Church members likewise tended to shun Gentile businesses and do all their buying from enterprises run by kindred folk. They voted in blocks as ordered by Joseph, a fact that made even opportunistic politicos less than eager to try to court votes from individual Mormons. And, of course, their beliefs were an affront to their frontier neighbors.

Mainstream Mormon historians Leonard Arrington and Davis Britton, in *The Mormon Experience,* acknowledge, "Clearly there were ample reasons for the unpopularity of the Mormons. The appeal the new faith had for some does not negate the fact that the common reaction to it, almost everywhere, was distaste and antipathy."

The antipathy was clear indeed. In March of 1832 Joseph was seized in his own bed by a mob who broke into the house and carted the prophet away. He was stripped and the mob ordered a participating doctor to perform a castration on the spot. When the physician demurred, a burly Ohioan fell on the naked Joseph, kicking and scratching him. "Goddamn you," shouted this attacker, "that's how the Holy Ghost falls on folks!" A second tormentor jammed a vial filled with an unknown liquid into Smith's mouth, but he spit it out. Then they covered his body with steaming tar and jammed the tar paddle cruelly into his mouth. For reasons unknown the mob scattered before the feathers arrived, and the bloodied, burned, and terrified prophet managed to crawl home. When Emma answered the door, she thought the dripping tar was blood and fainted on the spot. The same night the mob seized Sidney Rigdon, then a man in his early forties, and dragged him along the hard frozen ground. Rigdon nearly died from a fractured skull and other injuries.

Nonetheless Joseph and his Saints would remain in Ohio for five years before being driven out. During those five years, they would create the Mormon Way as it exists today. In Ohio came the early revelations that Joseph used to justify the practice of polygamy. Also in Ohio, the Mormons refined the communistic United Order that later allowed Smith's successor, the legendary Brigham Young, to get his people to work together and wrest a Mormon Mecca from the harsh desert surrounding the Great Salt Lake.

In Ohio, Joseph wrote the Word of Wisdom, perhaps the best known of all tenets of Mormonism, the far-sighted ban on the use of coffee, tobacco, red meat, and alcohol which has left the still-practicing descendants of the LDS pioneers among the healthiest people on earth—so healthy, in fact, that they often are used for medical research targeting the extent to which these practices are killing Gentiles.

It also was during the Ohio sojourn that Joseph created much of the Mormon hierarchical structure that exists today, with a prophet at the top of the three-man Council of the First Presidency, followed by a Council of the Twelve Apostles, and finally a Quorum of the Seventy in which is invested the authority to administer the entire LDS empire.

In Ohio Joseph built the first of Mormondom's Old Testament–style temples wherein the faithful, certified as such with "endowments" or "Temple recommends," performed secret rituals of anointing, proxy baptism, and "celestial marriage" that goes on to this day. That first temple was the site of many rousing, even orgiastic religious meetings during the brief Kirtland years. In its inner precincts, Joseph and his followers claimed to receive repeated visits from bands of angels. The day the building was consecrated, the men inside launched into a two-day-long meeting that featured priests, deacons, and bishops flopping about on the floor in religious bliss, speaking in tongues, and exhibiting other manifestations of divine rapture. Joseph wrote in his Seventh Article of Faith, "We believe in the gift of tongues, prophecy, revelation, visions, healing, interpretation of tongues and so forth." At the end of the two days, Oliver Cowdery and Joseph Smith told the assembled Saints that God the Father, Moses, and Elijah had appeared to them. The prophet Elijah, according to Joseph, proclaimed, "Therefore the keys of this dispensation are committed into your hands, and by this ye may know that the great and dreadful day of the Lord is near, even at the doors."

After this "Mormon Pentecost," a group of Saints, including Heber C. Kimball, Orson Hyde, and Joseph Fielding were sent to Great Britain where they became the first globe-trotting Mormon missionaries. Church historians have concluded that their work among hardscrabble factory workers and others of marginal income in the British Isles brought thousands of converts to Mormon settlements in Ohio and later in Missouri and Illinois. Thus the Ohio period marked the beginning of the church's unique commitment to missionary work.

During the Ohio settlement, the church won grudging respect from Gentiles in direct proportion to the wealth that Saints accumulated along with other lakefront property owners in the great land boom of the 1830s. In fact, the great misfortune of Mormondom in Ohio proved to be that the New York dirt farmer's son became a big time banker as well as a prophet because of that land boom. Almost as soon as the Saints from New York arrived at Kirtland, the land along the south shore of Lake Erie from Buffalo past Kirtland to Cleveland was swept up in a speculation craze brought on by the throngs of settlers heading west. Real estate in Buffalo that had sold for $500 an acre in 1835 was subdivided and then subdivided again until the lots were bringing $40 a foot or $10,000 per acre by 1837. The land-rich Saints were part of a westward migration during which the frontier populations leapt 62 percent in 1830 alone, a massive spurt even when compared to a prodigious national growth rate of 32 percent for that decade.

The boom brought easy credit, and land banks sprung up everywhere, financed by real estate–backed paper money accepted by the U.S. Treasury. At Kirtland, lots jumped from $50 to $2,000, and the farms on the edge of town exploded in value from $10 to $15 an acre to $150 per acre. Joseph's own holdings, including a 140-acre farm and several parcels in town, soared in value until the land alone was worth $300,000, an enormous sum at that time.

For $70,000 the Saints built their three-story white stone Kirtland Temple with its dozens of expansively ornate pulpits and a system of giant velvet draperies that could be moved about by hidden pulleys that allowed division of the building for the numerous complex religious rites that Joseph invented and performed there.

Just as the church was running smoothly, the land rush that brought the Mormons such sudden prosperity sparked a national financial crisis, the Panic of 1837, which raged after President Andrew Jackson ordered the U.S. Treasury to stop accepting payment for public lands in anything but gold. Overnight much of the land-backed paper money produced by private land banks was worthless.

In coming months the failure of Joseph's Kirtland Safety Society Bank Company sparked dozens of lawsuits against the prophet and earned the Mormons even more hatred among their Gentile neighbors who had been financed by the institution and who complained the bank took care of church members first and ignored Gentile claims.

Dissension erupted within Saintly circles as well. Joseph had forced his flock to use the now-foundering bank by claiming that he had been ordered by a revelation to set up an LDS financial institution which, God had promised, would grow until it swallowed up all competing banks in Ohio. Instead it was among the first to fail in the panic.

At stormy sessions inside the deeply hocked temple many Saints displayed open rebellion. At one point the three men named as witnesses in the *Book of Mormon* testimonials, Cowdery, Harris, and David Whitmer, defected. Fistfights were reported in the holy building itself. A warrant was issued for Joseph's arrest on bank fraud charges. Ultimately, Joseph and Rigdon fled Kirtland in the middle of the night on horseback and headed for Missouri, where the same pattern of colony building, prosperity, persecution, and collapse would repeat itself. In Missouri, however, the persecution was to be much bloodier and far crueler than it had been in Ohio.

Chapter 2

From Missouri to Martyrdom

"Nits will make lice!"

—A Missouri state militiaman's explanation of why he fatally shot
a nine-year-old Mormon boy during an 1838 raid ordered
by Governor Lilburn W. Boggs.

In Search of the New Eden

When the Saints fled oppression a second time, pulled up stakes in Ohio and headed for Missouri, it turned out to be an unfriendly and inconvenient choice. But Missouri was sacred: Adam was born there. One of the more startling Mormon beliefs is that the site of the biblical Garden of Eden is in the center of North America. It was from the banks of the Missouri and not the Euphrates that humanity fanned out to populate the Old Testament world.

Thus, while the prophet and most of the church's elite had taken up residence in Kirtland after being driven from New York in 1831, a substantial number of his followers, led at first by Oliver Cowdery, now endowed with the title of Second Elder to Joseph's First Elder, had settled in Missouri, twelve miles west of Independence, a place they called Zion and known today as Kansas City.

The Saints were drawn to Missouri for another reason: Independence was close to the edge of Indian country and thus offered a chance to convert the Lamanite infidels. Moroni had explained that the aboriginal Americans were descendants of the American patriarch Lehi's evil son, Laman, and that they bore their red skins as a punishment for such savageries as having wiped out the Nephites—the descendants of Lehi's good son, Nephi—who was "white, and exceeding fair and beautiful" (1 Nephi 15). Thus, restoring these heathens to the gospel has been a prime Mormon goal from the beginning, and Missouri seemed an excellent place to start.

When the Missouri Saints built a cabin in what is now Kansas City, Joseph told them it probably rested on the precise spot where Cain had killed Abel. Later they established a town about forty miles to the north which the prophet called Adam-ondi-Ahman because he said it was where Adam and Eve moved to start the human race after being expelled from the Kansas City Eden.

From the start, the Missouri Saints were greatly outnumbered by rugged and bigoted frontier folk who scorned their new neighbors for virtually everything they did or said. Called the "old settlers" by LDS historians, these intolerant people really were as mean as their legendary Missouri mules. The old settlers held such intense pro-slavery and anti-Indian sentiments that a white man would be flogged if he were caught trying to teach a black man to read. "Hunting parties" ranged across the nearby Indian Territory border where they shot the Indians like they were game animals. Blacks who killed whites were lynched, or sometimes burned at the stake.

Mormon lore recalls how when members of a vigilante group that had burned a black man accused of murdering a white were brought to trial the year the Saints arrived, the judge instructed the jury that the burning, although clearly murder, was nevertheless justified because it was the will of a majority of Missourians. The decision to immolate the murdered black man "is beyond the reach of human law," said the judge.

In such a climate, the generally abolitionist Mormons from the Northeast who went among the Indians, not to shoot them but to convert them, were deeply distrusted from the day they arrived. On the other hand, the Saints did much to alienate themselves from the old settlers. For example, while an outsider might assume that the migration of Saints to Independence meant welcome trade for the frontier city's merchants, in fact, the Mormons traded exclusively with stores owned by church members like Sidney Gilbert, whose Independence general store quickly became the town's biggest. It didn't matter in the least that most Gentiles refused to trade with Gilbert. He flourished and contributed his share to the general treasury, allowing the Mormons to buy more farms to establish their Zion.

The continual Mormon efforts to buy land for their holy city forced prices up for old settlers who wanted to expand their holdings. The settlers saw their own ranks shrink as their neighbors sold to the Saints and moved on, a development that, in turn, tended to increase the political power of the Mormon minority as it grew toward majority status. That political prospect dismayed Missouri's establishment of clergymen, lawyers, merchants, and editors who realized that the Mormon bloc soon would be a powerful voice in local affairs that they would have to heed.

Anti-Mormon sentiments erupted into violence after W. W. Phelps, the editor of the Mormon-owned newspaper, *The Evening and Morning Star,* published an editorial warning Mormons around the country not to send free blacks associated with the church to Missouri unless they could prove they were "free people of color." Stunned to see the old settlers misinterpret his editorial as a conspiracy to show blacks how to move to Missouri as nonslaves, Phelps issued an "Extra" edition of the paper in which he noted that Mormons considered black skin to be the mark of Cain and forbade blacks to live with the white children of Adam. He added that his reason for writing the offending piece was "not only to stop free people of color from emigrating to this state, but to prevent them from being admitted as members of the Church."

It is ironic that Mormons should have been attacked for being "nigger lovers,"—their nickname in Missouri—when in fact the church itself was one of the most racist institutions ever to appear on the American scene. Until 1978 Mormons taught that blacks were cursed with the "mark of Ham" in the form of skin color and therefore unworthy of salvation.

The first mob action in Missouri against Mormons occurred in July of 1833 when an angry group of 500 men met in Independence and issued a "Manifesto" demanding that: 1) no Mormon settle in Jackson County in the future; 2) those Mormons already settled must promise to sell their lands and leave; 3) the Mormon businesses and storehouses be shut immediately; 4) leaders stop all future immigration by Ohio Mormons anywhere in Missouri. The document ended with the warning that any Mormon who didn't know what failure to meet the four demands would mean should "be referred to those of their brethren who have the gifts of divination, and of unknown tongues, to inform them of the lot that awaits them."

After drafting the manifesto the mob destroyed the offices and press of the Mormon-owned newspaper, *The Evening and Morning Star,* burned Mormon literature, and then tarred and feathered two Missouri Elders, Edward Partridge and Charles Allen.

In the next few days the mob made repeated raids on Mormon towns, routing women and children into the surrounding forests and beating the men. Haystacks were burned and shots fired into Mormon houses by roving bands of men on horseback.

There was no relief for the Mormons in the courts. When a group of Saints captured a man who had helped sack one of the church's United Order storehouses and took him before a justice of the peace, the justice freed the man and at the man's request jailed his captors for false arrest.

Tragedy was inevitable and on November 4, 1833, a gunfight broke out in which two non-Mormons and one Mormon were killed. Missouri's lieutenant governor, a notorious anti-Mormon named Lilburn Boggs, called out the militia, who persuaded the Mormons to hand over their weapons as a sign that they wanted peace in exchange for a similar voluntary disarming of the old settlers. But after disarming the Mormons, the militia left without collecting the mob's arsenal. That night every Mormon community in Missouri was attacked, the men beaten, and the women and children herded away in a blizzard. More than 1,200 people were left homeless.

While contemporary accounts report that no one was killed outright, the Mormons were forced to spend the winter months without proper shelter, and many died from exposure.

In response to the plight of these persecuted Saints, Joseph, who was still living in Kirtland, raised an army of about two hundred men called Zion's Camp, and in May of 1834, headed to Missouri, a distance of nearly a thousand miles. It was as ragtag a bunch of Christian soldiers as ever assembled and the march south was marked by frequent arguments among the undisciplined troops. Later accounts describe how Joseph lost the respect of his own people when he was unable to stop the carping and defiance in the ranks.

Food was scarce, and by the time the Saintly force arrived at the front lines in late June, they were in the first stages of an outbreak of cholera. Anti-Mormon forces of at least five hundred men waited on the other side, armed with better weapons and in much better health.

Worse still when the Missourians had learned that a Mormon army was en route from Ohio, the old settlers attacked and burned to the ground the roughly 150 Mormon-owned homes in Jackson county that still were standing after the earlier razing.

Adding to the outrage, Daniel Dunklin, the governor of Missouri, warned that if Joseph's two-hundred-member force invaded Jackson County he would call out the militia and send Zion's Camp packing. After a stand off of a few weeks the confrontation calmed, largely through the efforts of the Missouri establishment that persuaded the displaced Mormons to move forty miles to the north and establish a new colony called Far West in a newly created Caldwell County which would be set aside for Mormons by the state legislature.

The Missouri War had never taken place and although the Saints lost all that they had dreamed of and built in Jackson County, they were given what seemed a credible promise that they could build yet another Zion near the sacred place Joseph had named Adam-ondi-Ahman. It turned out to be a false promise, as Joseph learned when he led his persecuted followers from the shambles of Kirtland to Far West and the promised Caldwell County in 1838.

Three-and-a-half years after the Zion's Camp affair, the Missouri Saints had risen in true phoenix fashion in Caldwell County. Shortly after Joseph's party arrived broke and depressed from Kirtland, Far West had a population of "five thousand people with two hotels, a printing office, blacksmith shops, stores and 150 houses" according to Gordon Hinckley's official church history, *Truth Restored*.

Far West had been laid out according to Joseph's own inspired notions of urban planning in a pattern that had been used first at Kirtland and later at Zion (Jackson County). Ultimately, the prophet's urban design would be implemented after the terminal exodus to Salt Lake City. The object was to avoid both the blighted slums that appear in cities and the isolation from society that is the lot of the country farmer.

Mormon cities were laid out over one square mile and divided into blocks of ten acres divided by streets 132 feet wide. The blocks in the center were reserved for public buildings including the LDS temple. Each saint was to have a house in town and the farms were to be on lands surrounding the city.

Recalling the bitter and stultifying isolation of his own farm roots, Joseph said that

> the tiller of the soil as well as the merchant and mechanic will live in the city. The farmer and his family, therefore, will enjoy all the advantages of schools, public lectures and other meetings. His home will no longer be isolated and his family denied the benefits of society, which has been, and always will be, the great educator of the human race, but they will enjoy the same privileges of society, and can surround their homes with the same intellectual life, the same social refinement as will be found in the home of the merchant or banker or professional man.

If this ideal sounds appealing even in the age of cable television and satellite dishes, it was compelling indeed when presented to the working poor of Europe by the bands of missionaries Joseph had sent abroad from the first days at Kirtland. Converts, especially from the ranks of English factory workers, were coming in at a bumper rate, and soon Missouri's "Mormon County" of Caldwell was too small to hold all the Saints.

As the English immigrants and the Kirtland refugees broke ground to start farms in the unplowed prairies to the west, north, and east of Far West, Mormon holdings quickly expanded beyond Caldwell County into Daviess, Carroll, and Ray counties. Once again bitter and suspicious old settlers watched the Mormon prosperity with unfriendly eyes. But this time the Saints weren't all that Saintly. The bitter experiences of the past had toughened them and made them wary of their neighbors as the LDS plows broke sod further and further into anti-Mormon Missouri.

Sampson Avard, a particularly bellicose Saint, suggested that a secret army be raised among LDS men, who would be taught to communicate by secret signs and passwords, and be prepared always to take up arms against any foe. Avard's secret army, organized in several units called "tens" and "fifties," also would act as bodyguards for the prophet and function as secret police to ferret out dissenters among Mormon ranks.

They called themselves Danites after the tribe of Dan described in Judges 18 who invaded the city of Laish, killed the population, and then burned down the buildings to establish their own city on the same spot. The Missouri Danites were the first of a long string of self-proclaimed "avenging angels" who have been on the Mormon scene ever since. They brought "blood atonement," a ritualized form of murder in which the victim's blood must mingle with the soil, to those within Mormon circles and to those without who threatened harm.

The early blood-atoning Danites were to take a fair share of Missouri lives in the confrontation that was building, but more importantly, they were to establish a Mormon tradition for blood atonement and a reputation for ruthless fighting. The legacy of blood atonement still was being played out in the late 1980s as members of a violent polygamy cult called "The Church of the Firstborn in the Fulness of Time," was linked to more than twenty murders, all in which blood had been spilled in ritualistic fashion.

It can be argued that the pioneer Saints endured much before they stopped turning the other cheek, but once they unleashed the secret army they suffered the loss of sympathy from many Americans who had supported them precisely because their neighbors so persecuted them.

One of the most hotly debated issues in Mormon history is whether the persecutions would have continued longer in Missouri and beyond if the Danites hadn't started attacking their old settler neighbors just as public sympathy was swinging in favor of the Mormons. The Missouri state legislature had voted to set aside Mormondom's Caldwell County because of public opinion in support of the persecuted church. The violence against Saints in western Missouri was condemned strongly by newspapers in St. Louis and New York even as the Danites gathered for their first raid.

From the beginning, the church's leadership realized how badly the specter of a Mormon revenging army would be viewed in Gentile circles. Joseph Smith's own *History of the Church* quotes the following chilling set of anti-Gentile instructions which the prophet claimed to have learned about long after Alvard issued them to his secret army in 1838:

> Know ye not, brethren, that it will soon be your privilege to take your respective companies and go out on a scout on the borders of the settlements, and take to yourselves spoils of the goods of the ungodly Gentiles? for it is written, the riches of the Gentiles shall be consecrated to my people, the house of Israel; and thus you will waste away the Gentiles by robbing and plundering them of their property; and in this way will we build up the kingdom of God ... and if one of this Danite society reveals any of these things, I will put him where the dogs cannot bite him.

Although Joseph excommunicated Alvard in 1839, the prophet apparently valued the Danites as a defense force for a time. A less friendly view of the situation notes that Joseph addressed at least one Danite meeting and that he may have been particularly gratified because one of the sins for which Alvard wanted to extract blood atonement was heresy against the church Presidency.

While pro- and anti-Mormon scholars debate the extent of Joseph's knowledge of or role in the Danites, the avenging angels clearly pleased Sidney Rigdon, who had grown increasingly intolerant over the years. While Joseph preached about a relatively pleasant hereafter for all people, Rigdon hewed more to his Calvinist roots and urged the Saints toward Puritan severity. He spoke dourly against gaiety, scorned good living, and chastized the Saints for showing any taint of independent thinking. While Joseph said abstaining from strong drink and other vices was a "Word of Wisdom" to keep Saints healthy, Rigdon saw the ban as another way of mortifying the flesh and separating Saints from sinners.

Rigdon saw the Danites as a force to ensure orthodoxy in Mormon circles as well as to strike at enemies outside them. In a firey June 17 sermon Rigdon thundered at potential LDS backsliders. "Ye are the salt of the earth, but if the salt hath lost its savor, wherewith shall the earth be salted? It is henceforth good for nothing but to be cast out and trodden under foot of men." To this day many Mormon fundamentalists warn their neighbors that their "salt hath lost its savor."

The Danites lashed out against Gentiles on election day, August 6, 1838, in front of the court house in Gallatin, Missouri, seat of Daviess County. One of the "fifties" had congregated to vote for county officers in an election where the count between LDS and old settlers was expected to be close.

When the first Mormon attempted to enter the building, a Missourian stiff-armed him and taunted, "Daviess County don't allow Mormons to vote no more than niggers." With that he punched the Danite to the ground and the melee erupted. Although outnumbered four to one, the Danites were equipped with four-foot-long oaken clubs, and they waded into the Gentiles with ruthless efficiency. Once again no one died, but nine Gentiles were beaten unconscious and roughly twenty others crawled away bleeding, according to the contemporary report of John Lee, one of the Mormon leaders and a future defector from the inner circle who later disclosed Danite secrets.

The fragile Mormon–Gentile peace that had survived almost four shaky years collapsed in the wake of the court-house brawl. Joseph led a small force of Saints to visit a justice of the peace named Adam Black and demand that he sign a peace agreement with the Saints on behalf of Daviess County. The JP signed such a paper, but after Smith left, the justice issued intimidation charges against the prophet. Six companies of state militia joined forces and quickly arrested him. Joseph stood trial, but he did so with a Mormon army facing the militia men to assure he wouldn't be lynched. He was placed under a $500 peace bond by a judge clearly wary of the army waiting outside.

Coming days brought a repeat of the harassments of 1833.

Armed bands of Missourians prowled the countryside burning haystacks and granaries, stealing livestock, and whipping Mormons whenever encountered. The Saints were driven into the town of DeWitt, which was the Mormons' river port, and Adam-ondi-Ahman, where they were confined by the roving Gentiles during weeks of siege. The townsfolk lived by slaughtering their dairy herd and eating from dwindling grain stores. Word was sent to them that land agents would buy their properties back for the same prices they paid for them before building houses.

Joseph evacuated the DeWitt settlement to Far West, but once there, he learned that a mob of eight-hundred Missourians had ringed Adam-ondi-Ahman. He made a fateful speech in the Far West town square on October 14:

> If the people will let us alone we will preach the gospel in peace. But if they come on us to molest us, we will establish our religion by the sword. We will trample down our enemies and make it one gore of blood from the Rocky Mountains to the Atlantic Ocean. I will be to this generation a second Mohammed, whose motto in treating for peace was "the Alcoran [Koran] or the Sword." So shall it eventually be with us— "Joseph Smith or the Sword!"

After what historians call Joseph's "Mohammed speech," the Saints went to war. Mormon horsemen raided Gentile farms and carted away "consecreted" items, more properly described as plunder. Later participants lamented in their diaries about having forced pregnant Gentile women and children to leave their homes and then looting and burning the houses. Gentiles caught in the countryside were beaten and robbed just as Mormons once had been. Some church members left in disgust after watching Danite soldiers arrive in Far West and Adam-ondi-Ahman with booty-filled wagons from raids on Gentile farms and stores. A pitched gun battle erupted between a force of Danites and a company of state militia near Crooked River in Daviess County. Two Mormons and a single militiaman died, but reports reaching the governor greatly exaggerated the carnage.

The governor, Lilburn Boggs, who had set the militia on the Saints in 1833, also was shown a copy of Sidney Rigdon's Fourth of July sermon in which he had shouted,

But from this day and this hour we will suffer it no more . . . And that mob that comes on us to disturb us, it shall be between us and them a war of extermination; for we will follow them until the last drop of their blood is spilled, or else they will have to exterminate us; for we will carry the seat of war to their own houses and their own families and one party or the other shall be utterly destroyed.

Boggs used the same term—*extermination*—in his response, a set of infamous instructions for the state militia that read:

Your orders are to hasten your operations and endeavor to reach Richmond, in Ray County with all possible speed. The Mormons must be treated as enemies and must be exterminated or driven from the state, if necessary for the public good. Their outrages are beyond all description.

This infamous "extermination order" led to the bloodiest and most tragic atrocity yet visited on the Saints. On October 30, 1839 a force of 240 Missouri state militiamen attacked the small LDS community of Haun's Mill near Far West where about thirty Mormon families, including a dozen or so converts freshly arrived from the east, had congregated. The troops rode into the middle of the milling crowd and began firing. A few fell in the onslaught but most fled into Haun's blacksmith shop which seemed like a fort but which had such wide spaces in the logs that the troopers were able to spend the afternoon picking off those inside with terrible accuracy. The men inside sent their women fleeing and, while the militia fired a few shots at them in derision, all survived. Finally with seventeen Mormon men dead, the troops broke through the smitty doors and found nine-year-old Sardius Smith—no relation to Joseph—huddled under the bellows.

"Don't shoot," shouted one militiaman, "It's just a boy."

"It's best to hive them when we can. Nits will make lice," shouted another trooper who placed his rifle against the child's head and pulled the trigger.

There was tremendous anguish in Mormon circles when word reached Far West of the tragedy at Haun's Mill, but even as the Saints gathered behind their fortifications and spoke bravely of striking out at their oppressors, it was already clear that the war was lost. Within days a force estimated both by the popular press and Mormons at ten thousand armed and trained Missouri militia had ringed Far West. Joseph made a few game speeches saying things like "I care not a fig for the coming of the troops" and "[let's] fight like angels for angels can whip devils." But he had no real choice but to surrender or face a massacre far worse than the travesty at Haun's Mill. He sued for peace.

The terms could hardly have been more cruel. Joseph must stand trial for treason along with his fellow elders. Second, all Mormon property would be confiscated on the spot, Third, all surviving Mormons must immediately leave the state. Fourth, all arms must be surrendered to the militia.

Joseph ordered his Saints to collect all the plunder they had taken in the Danite raids and place it in an abandoned house so that none of his people might later face the noose for stealing a foe's saddle or blanket. He then told the assembled Saints, "You are good and brave men, but there are ten-thousand men approaching Far West, and unless you were angels themselves you could not withstand so formidable a host." Then he surrendered along with Parley Pratt, Sidney Rigdon, and a few other elders.

In coming days the Mormons suffered greatly at the hands of their captors. Pratt, Smith, Rigdon, and company were ordered to be shot at dawn but escaped that fate when a militia general named Alexander Doniphan refused to convene a firing squad for what he called "cold-blooded murder." While the elders were saved from the ultimate penalty, their following still suffered.

Under the threatening muskets of the militia, the Mormon men filed into the town square at Far West, each depositing his pistols and rifles in a common pile. Each man then was herded to a table where he was forced to sign away his land holding.

Members of the militia roved about Far West for more than a week replaying the role of pillaging biblical armies. They entered houses and took what they wanted. They rode through the streets and countryside shooting hogs, pigs, and sheep for sport, which quickly forced the Mormons to live off hominy, their only remaining grain. An undetermined number of men, thought to be Mormon elders, were shot. In a particularly galling series of attacks, several girls were tied to the benches in the Mormon schoolhouse and gang raped by an estimated twenty men. In a single week it was estimated that six-thousand militiamen came to Far West to extract the bitter spoils of war.

Missouri River Mormons

With their prophet a ward of the hated State of Missouri, the Saints organized their next exodus under Brigham Young—this time to the Illinois of Abraham Lincoln and Stephen Douglas. During that move Smith, Rigdon, and the others languished for months in the Liberty, Missouri jail, where Joseph wrote some of his most moving epistles to Emma and some of his most desperate entreaties to his LDS henchmen for aid. Like a character in a Camus nightmare, Joseph was continually told by his jailers that he would be executed within hours—sometimes within minutes. Each time another reprieve materialized to preserve his life but to drain his spirit.

It was at Liberty jail that Joseph pondered his own mortality even as his guards taunted him by boasting about how they had raped and pillaged during the sack of Far West and the raid at Haun's Mill. The torment toughened the young man who had persuaded thousands to move to his utopian dream towns on the Ohio and Missouri frontiers. Joseph's experience in Liberty jail transformed him into the ruthless lawgiver who catapulted Mormonism from its status as a strange cult of backwoods Seekers and dream-driven foreign converts into a major force on the American political, social, and cultural scene.

In early 1839, Smith, with Sidney Rigdon at his side, escaped the jail and made his way to Illinois. The time was ripe for the prophet to found the City of Joseph, the fabulous Zion on the banks of the Mississippi that would be his last stopover on the road to his Celestial Kingdom. Brigham Young called the new settlement Commerce, Illinois. Joseph later named it Nauvoo, a Hebrew word he translated as "beautiful plantation." Soon all America would know it as "Nauvoo the Beautiful."

Much of the story of Nauvoo is a repeat of the experience at Kirtland and in Missouri. The Saints picked a spot for their modern-day Zion, this time alongside the Mississippi River sixty miles north of Quincy, Illinois, and brought forth yet another of their model cities with the spacious lots, wide streets, and a soaring temple at the center. The prophet worked hard to raise that city and to record the final revelations and policies that were to shape the Church of Jesus Christ of Latter-day Saints into its present form.

It was in Nauvoo that the Mormons first entered into widespread polygamy, the "Law of Jacob" that Joseph taught along with the promise that marriages sealed in this life continue forever in the hereafter. Likewise, it was in Nauvoo that the prophet unveiled many of the church's still secret temple ceremonies, the sealings, anointings, endowments, and oaths that outsiders believe are derived from the rites of small-town Masons with their secret handshakes, blood oaths, and ritualistic garments. At Nauvoo the Mormons first declared that the faithful must always wear sacred underwear, "garments" hauntingly similar to the aprons and robes worn for ceremonies in the most orthodox of Masonic temples. The early Mormon temple garments resembled frontier-era long johns but were emblazoned in strategic points with ritualistic markings like a slash over the belly to remind the wearer that those who disclose hidden rituals face evisceration.

Anti-Mormons today take delight in listing the parallels between LDS inner temple rituals and similar Masonic ceremonies. They note, as well, that during the Nauvoo years Joseph established a Masonic Lodge for his Mormons and that it soon became the largest lodge in Illinois. Smith said that the original builders of the Temple of Solomon had inspired the Free Masonry movement. Like Solomon, he noted, Mormons are great builders of temples. He added that some LDS ceremonies are simply a restored version of the Masonic rituals as they existed before being corrupted by the same evil forces that polluted the Gospel of Jesus Christ. To skeptics such claims do little to dilute the suspicion that the elaborate Masonic rites proved a handy text from which to copy when Joseph needed to draft quickly a wholly unique liturgy for his new religion in the splendid temple at Nauvoo.

In Nauvoo, Joseph's longstanding investments in the foreign missions paid off handsomely. Thousands of Europeans made the dangerous Atlantic crossing and trekked across half the American continent to join ranks with their brethren in Illinois. These hordes of immigrants soon established Joseph Smith as an even bigger political threat to the Illinois establishment than he had been to the Missouri power elite.

Almost from the beginning the Nauvoo bloc held enough votes to determine any statewide election, and Smith found himself courted by Democrats, Whigs, and other parties across Illinois. When the Mormons announced that they wanted to form their own militia, the governor and state legislature quickly approved the Nauvoo Legion as a unit of the Illinois State Militia, and at Joseph's request, installed the prophet with the rank of lieutenant general even as Illinois supplied cannons and muskets to arm this new force. Smith relished his military role and often staged parades in the Nauvoo streets where, bedecked in golden braids and a hat topped Napoleon-style with ostrich feathers, he could lead his troops before throngs of admiring onlookers.

His enemies ultimately swayed public opinion against the Mormons by claiming that they had created this army with the intention either of overthrowing the United States Constitution or invading Mexico to establish a Mormon colony there. At its peak the Nauvoo Legion boasted four-thousand troops who drilled until they were better prepared than any militia among the Gentiles.

At Nauvoo the prophet and his Saints were at the apex of their secular power. They even basked for a while in the light of unfamiliar popularity among Gentiles as newspapers in New York and Chicago reported the atrocities they had endured in the name of their religion. The New York *Herald* and the Chicago *Democrat* ran frequent accounts of how the brave Mormons, their spirits shaken by persecution and their bodies broken by the long winter's march north from Missouri, had set to work and claimed their "Nauvoo the Beautiful" from the malarial swamps alongside the Mississippi, north of Quincy and just across from Keokuk in Iowa.

Nauvoo was laid out along the urban planning lines of other Mormon gathering places, topped by a golden-spired white marble temple surrounded by a checkerboard of houses on expansive lots, businesses, and light factories. The adjoining countryside was filled with lush farms all deeded to worthy Saints by the prophet who held the office of Trustee-of-Trusts in the municipal government as well as that of mayor.

By 1841 there were more than three-hundred houses in Nauvoo as well as two large steam-driven sawmills, a steam-driven flour mill, a foundry, and even a chinaware factory run by converts from the potteries in Britain's Staffordshire. Ultimately, Joseph's power base would boast a population of ten-thousand in Nauvoo and perhaps another thirty-thousand in outlying towns and farms.

The prophet and his church gained greater wealth in Nauvoo than they had had in either Kirtland or Far West. Many of the converts signed on under an arrangement whereby they deeded over their farms, homes, and other property in the East or in Europe and then were given a similar property in or near Nauvoo. The church either operated the new holdings acquired from the converts or sold them. Such deals were particularly common with converts from Great Britain where the Missionary Saints were particularly successful recruiting tradesmen with small property holdings as well as droves of homeless factory workers. Many of these business dealings were based on divine revelations to the prophet. Often God's words were about the most mundane of matters. For example, a revelation recorded as *Doctrine and Covenants* Section 124 Verse 56 instructs Joseph and his followers about how to build a hotel for the many curious visitors who were dropping by Nauvoo to witness the Mormon Miracle firsthand:

> And now I say unto you, as pertaining to my boarding house which I have commanded you to build for the boarding of strangers, let it be built unto my name, and let my name be named upon it. . . . Therefore, let my servant Joseph and his seed after him have place in that house, from generation to generation, forever and ever, saith the Lord. And let the name of that house be called Nauvoo House, and let it be a delightful habitation for man, and a resting-place for the weary traveler, that he may contemplate the glory of Zion, and the glory of this the corner stone there of.

With that revelation providing Joseph and his seed free lodging for all time in the Nauvoo House, the word of God continues with such mundane messages as naming one George Miller as president of the company that would build the hotel. God even set stock prices. He told Joseph this about investors in the hostelry: "And they shall not receive less than fifty dollars for a share of stock in that house, and they shall be permitted to receive fifteen thousand dollars from any one man for stock in that house." Other parts of the revelation commanded numerous Mormon men by name in the town to buy stock in the enterprise.

This rule by revelation enabled the prophet to quickly implement the single most controversial aspect of Mormonism, polygamy, which Saints came to call simply "The Principle."

In Section 132 of D & C God tells Joseph that Mormon men should have the same conjugal powers as did Abraham, Jacob, Isaac, and David of the Old Testament. They should take plural wives as Jacob did rather than concubines as had Abraham. Thus the practice was known as the Law of Jacob. Women later were told they should emulate the stoic Sarah, wife of Abraham, who after years of infertility bore him a single son, Isaac, and then allowed her husband to take Isaac to the top of the Mountain Moriah and offer him as a sacrifice to God.

Afterwards God spared Isaac and gave Abraham many concubines to produce the children of Israel, and Sarah accepted His will without question. For Mormon women, then, the Principle was known as the Law of Sarah even as their menfolk followed the Law of Jacob.

Emma Smith was appalled when she first heard of the Law of Sarah. Joseph enlisted God Himself to win over Emma. Revelation number 132 has God saying,

> "And let mine handmaid, Emma Smith, receive all those
> that have been given unto my servant Joseph, and who are
> virtuous and pure before me; and those who are not pure,
> and have said they were pure, shall be destroyed, saith the
> Lord God . . . And again, verily I say, let mine handmaid for-
> give my servant Joseph his trespasses; and then shall she be
> forgiven her trespasses, wherein she has trespassed against
> me; and I, the Lord thy God will bless her, and multiply her,
> and make her heart to rejoice."

Fawn Brodie notes that Mormondom's first wife had little choice but to bow before her husband's version of God's words. "Emma," wrote Brodie, "was ridden with the helpless jealousy that comes to a woman growing unlovely with illness and childbearing while her husband remains maddeningly young."

Although the prophet's well-known zest for temporal delights surely came into play with polygamy, indications are strong that the major reason for instituting the Principle was to shore up Joseph's power with his own men. In Mormondom the prophet alone could decide which comely virgin went to which man, how many brides each follower could have and other key matters. In turn, the power he gained among his own flock by controlling such things enabled him to order often reluctant daughters and their fathers to agree to being "sealed" to a given man. The doling out of wives was a key to Joseph's later power, just as it helped Brigham Young maintain iron-fisted control over the Saints in rough-and-tumble Utah.

Critics point out that the fact that Joseph "sealed" himself to more than forty women—including the wives of some of his inner circle whom the prophet co-opted while their husbands were overseas on missions—suggests that the pleasure principle was at work in the Law of Jacob if not in the Law of Sarah. Joseph himself had a favored expression that must have been on his mind during scores of conjugal visits among his many wives: "A prophet is a prophet only when he is acting as such."

Predictably it was disclosures of polygamy that brought the prophet's downfall. Those disclosures were made by a former friend, John Cook Bennett, the Mormon Judas. Bennett had joined the Mormons shortly after Joseph and Sidney Rigdon arrived in Nauvoo from Missouri. He quickly won favor because he provided quinine to combat the malaria that was killing Saints as they labored to wrest a new Zion from the stinking river swamps. As a marginally educated frontier physician, Bennett was drawn to the fertile Mormon colony to practice his specialty, midwifery. He turned out to be a rogue who had abandoned a wife and children in Ohio to take up the Principle at Nauvoo. Joseph later learned that Bennett had seduced many LDS women by falsely telling them that Joseph had ordered their sealing. Others he seduced with promises of painless abortions should an unwanted pregnancy occur.

But outside the rough-hewn Mormon boudoirs, Bennett proved a strong business manager and a clever political operative for Joseph. By playing Whigs against Democrats at the state capital Bennett won many legislative favors for the Saints including the creation of Joseph's precious Nauvoo Legion. He likewise obtained official approval for the Nauvoo city government. The official state charter allowed the Saints to establish a court system of their own that largely spared the leadership from the type of harassment they suffered in Missouri.

Bennett helped Joseph start the Nauvoo Masonic Lodge and headed the agriculture college that the Mormons established to train converts in the farming techniques of the American Midwest. Joseph elevated his friend to the title of "second President" of the church. But by 1842 so many fathers and daughters had come forth with tales of Bennett's callous seductions, abortions, and other outrages that the Mormon elders voted to expel Bennett even after Joseph made a plea on his behalf.

Bennett responded by a series of letters to the Sangamon *Journal* in Springfield, the first of which began, "I write you now from the Mormon Zion, the city of the Saints where I am threatened with death by the Holy Joe, and his Danite band of murderers." Subsequent letters told of Smith and Bennett approaching many Mormon women, including Sidney Rigdon's teen-aged daughter, seeking sexual liaisons citing direct orders from God. Other Bennett charges dealt with allegations of theft, counterfeiting, and assaults against outsiders which, he said, Joseph called "milking the Gentiles." He alleged that besides plural marriages, the Mormons were greatly involved in harlotry to the extent that prostitutes in Nauvoo operated at three levels—street whores called Cyprian Saints; Chambered Sisters of Charity who bestowed their favors during house calls; and Cloistered Saints who went through temple ceremonies, including sex in the pews, which made them "spiritual wives" of their men. These accounts, which even among today's anti-Mormon scholars are considered overblown and sometimes outright lies, were collected in one of the most widely quoted early Mormon-eater books, *The History of the Saints: or, An Exposé of Joe Smith and Mormonism.* Bennett even sought out former Missouri Governor Boggs and volunteered to testify that Smith sent Porter Rockwell to shoot Boggs in the head. Joseph Smith was arrested on the strength of Bennett's testimony. Ironically, however, the Mormon founder won in the same court system which Bennett had done so much to set up.

The day that he was freed by his own court Joseph arrived at Nauvoo aboard his private steamship, the *Maid of Iowa,* and triumphantly addressed a crowd of ten-thousand admirers in the open air. The time had come, he said, to think of national politics, of making the almost autonomous city-state of Nauvoo a U.S. territory and incorporating the four-thousand-member Nauvoo Legion into the United States Army.

In early 1844 Joseph announced his campaign for the presidency of the United States. It was perhaps the strangest presidential candidacy in history.

The Mormons were a minority of fewer than 30,000 but they claimed to have a membership of between 100,000 and 200,000. Joseph unleashed his mighty missionary corps to move among the American electorate, and using the same techniques they used to win souls, they worked to win votes instead. Joseph pointedly let the major candidates know that he controlled enough votes to tip the balance either way even if his own bid was doomed from the start.

His platform was stunning. Eliminate the political party system and establish a "Theodemocracy." Reduce Congress by two thirds. Reform prisons like the hated Liberty jail and turn them into seminaries of learning. Make criminals work on public building projects and empty the debtors' prisons like the one his father was committed to in the early New York days. Free all the slaves owned by private parties after buying them with federal money that would be raised by selling surplus federal lands. Bring Texas into the Union and, if necessary, send Joseph Smith with 100,000 troops to wrest the Lone Star State from Mexico.

Joseph relished the attention he gained in the national press as a candidate. But that same heady spring, the seeds were sown for his destruction.

While both Whigs and Democrats paid the strange prophet lip service, it was clear that he planned to endorse a candidate in exchange for major concessions. This plan alienated him from both parties' elite, neither of which could fathom which way the Mormons would go. Talk of freeing slaves estranged him from thousands in Illinois, and still others were repelled by his scorning of the tradition of separation of church and state. Illinois' substantial Masonic membership didn't like the competition they were getting from the Nauvoo Lodge, and entrenched anti-Mormons continued pressing for Joseph's extradition to Missouri. American nativist sentiments were offended at the great influx of European immigrants being routed to Illinois by the Mormon missions even if they weren't of the hated Catholic variety.

Likewise, there were many enemies among Illinois' old settlers who had the same trouble with Mormon clannishness that their Missouri neighbors had. The Illinois Gentiles like the Missourians before them disliked the immigrants because they drove up land prices and added nothing to anybody's economy except that of Mormon-owned businesses. The town of Carthage resented the way nearby Nauvoo was taking away much of its Gentile retail trade, and in the river port of Warsaw locals were angry that Nauvoo's deeper port was taking much of the steamboat traffic that had built Warsaw. And it always was easy to whip up a crowd to anti-Mormon fervor simply by railing at the sect's now-admitted practice of polygamy.

While his inner circle was campaigning for Joseph's presidential bid that fatal spring, the prophet was confronted by a new newspaper published within the city limits of Nauvoo by a group of new apostates. The seer and revelator made the short-sighted move of ordering the destruction of this newspaper, the Nauvoo *Expositor*.

The paper accurately described the settlement's rampant polygamy and was particularly adept at exposing some of Joseph's more tangled financial transactions including the misuse of city council funds set aside for building the temple. A close Smith friend, William Marks, later wrote that Joseph had told him that the disclosure of polygamy in such a newspaper published on the very streets of Nauvoo was devastating. "This doctrine of polygamy, or spiritual wife-system, that has been taught and practiced among us, will prove our destruction and overthrow. I have been deceived; it is a curse to mankind . . . ," Marks quoted Smith.

Joseph had the city council issue an order declaring the *Expositor* a municipal nuisance and he sent the town marshal to destroy the press and burn all back copies. The publishers, including the apostate William Law, fled to Carthage where they continued to publish anti-Mormon material in local papers and launched a criminal case against Joseph Smith for illegally destroying their press in violation of Illinois' riot statutes.

As the publicity continued, an old nemesis returned to plague the Saints. Once again anti-Mormon mobs were riding the countryside at night forcing families off their outlying farms. A tense period followed when Joseph and his brother, Hyrum, started to flee Illinois but then decided to take a chance with the state's courts on the riot charge and on promises that the governor, Thomas Ford, would protect the brothers from both the mob and from hotheads in the Illinois state militia who were grumbling murderously against Mormons.

Joseph and Hyrum wound up in the two story Carthage jail with mobs milling about and sullen anti-Mormon militiamen standing guard under the direct command of Governor Ford. On June 27, 1844, Ford left Carthage to travel to Nauvoo, fifteen miles away, and address the Mormons. When he left the brothers under the guard of a unit called the Carthage Greys, the inevitable happened.

A group of militia from the competing river port of Warsaw stormed the jail and met no resistance from the Carthage Greys. Joseph emptied a six-shooter at his attackers, maiming three of them. Hyrum was struck repeatedly by bullets in the face and chest and fell dead. The prophet then leapt to a window sill and stood there glaring down at a crowd of men below with their bayonets at the ready. Some reports say he tried a final ploy with the Gentiles, giving the Masonic hand signal of distress and uttering the accompanying code, "Is there no help for the widow's son?" There probably were Masons in that crowd, but there was no mercy. As he teetered on the windowsill, a rifle ball fired from upstairs slammed into Joseph's back, sending him to the ground below as he shouted, "Oh Lord, My God."

Joseph landed on his shoulder with a snap of cartilage. A disguised militiaman with his face painted black dragged the wounded Joseph across the yard and propped him up against the side of a well. An officer ordered a firing squad, and four men sent rifle balls into the prophet killing him at last. Thus did the mob deliver Mormondom its finest martyr.

Thus too did the murdering mob pave the way to power for Brigham Young, the one-time New Hampshire cabinet builder who would now become the Mormon Moses.

Chapter 3

Brigham Young and the New Zion

The time will come when this gathering host of religious fanatics will make this country shake to its centre. A western empire is certain!

—Letter to the editor of the New York *Herald,* June 17, 1842

Joseph Smith invented Mormondom. Brigham Young made it work. The Saints called Brigham the "Lion of God" for the blistering zeal he showed leading Joseph's substantial following out of the Sodom of Illinois to create the Zion that became Utah. To do so, he first fought his way to the top of the splintered hierarchy remaining after the slaughter of Joseph and Hyrum. Afterward, he fought the elements and the landscape to bring his followers across half a continent to the banks of America's own Dead Sea, the Great Salt Lake. He masterminded what was hailed as the emigration feat of the age, a hegira to match the forty-year trek of the Jews to their own Promised Land. Finally, ensconced in the hard-won Mormon homeland, Brigham fought the Indians, the bureaucrats in Washington, and, eventually, the United States Army to keep what the Saints called their Great Basin Kingdom of Deseret.

To the amazement of all who looked on, he won every one of those fights. As a result, Brigham Young left behind the Church of Jesus Christ of Latter-day Saints as an established, globe-spanning institution. He left as well a unique state called Utah that even today is a happy home for Saints if a decidedly strange land for Gentiles.

Unlike Joseph, whose image comes to us only in the form of a plaster-of-Paris death mask and a few unremarkable portraits rendered by mediocre artists, Brigham lived in an era of photography. Brigham's clean-shaven face in photos resembles a hand-

51

some 1950s cowboy actor named Joel MacRae. Later, his broad face wore the same fringe beard as Aleksandr Solzhenitsyn and his girth rivaled that of jazzman Al Hirt. It was said he had gained a pound for each of his seventy wives.

Joseph Smith's biography is of immense importance to Mormons because it became nothing less than scripture—the theophany in the sacred tree grove, the opening of Cumorah, the translations of the plates, the baptism with Oliver Cowdery that restored the Aaronic Priesthood. By contrast, Brigham's biography is the Horatio Alger story. In Brigham's case what's important isn't how he got to the top but what he did after he arrived. Brigham Young thus belongs in the company of other great mid-century architects of American Manifest Destiny. What Carnegie was to steel and Mellon to banking, Young was to nineteenth-century American religion.

Brigham was born June 1, 1801, and grew to young manhood in an impoverished frontier family obsessed with religious seeking and swept up in the same revivals of upstate New York that so compelled Lucy Mack Smith. Orphaned at 15, Brigham learned the carpenter's trade in the same New England and New York precincts where the Smith family farmed. When Young first encountered the "Golden Bible" of Joseph Smith in 1830 he owned a sawmill and was making baskets and rough-hewn furniture that he sold door to door. For the next two years, according to Mormon lore, Brigham and his lifelong best friend, Heber Kimball, who boasted eleven days of schooling between them, talked about Joseph's book and made repeated visits to Mormon families in the area who were only too pleased to read the *Book of Mormon* to them. Brigham and Heber were baptized in Young's "own little mill stream" in 1832, and Young immediately gave up carpentry to take up convert seeking for the Mormons, even before his first meeting with Joseph Smith. That encounter between the two strapping young prophets occurred late that same year in Kirtland as Joseph was chopping wood. At that evening's prayers, Brigham burst into an incomprehensible monologue speaking in tongues, and Joseph declared the speech to be "of God" and added the prophecy, "and the time will come when brother Brigham Young will preside over this church."

Putting his carpentry skills to good use, Young earned a stable living helping build Kirtland and he apparently became particularly close to Joseph by doing much of the woodwork for the interior construction of the first Mormon temple there. He also accompanied the young prophet on the ill-fated Zion's Camp excursion into Missouri, and when Smith formed his first Quorum of the Twelve Apostles in 1835, Brigham Young was the second member to be chosen.

In the next few years, as the bank failure wrecked the Kirtland colony and forced the prophet to flee, Brigham remained Joseph's key confidant, aiding him when others like the Whitmers and even Sidney Rigdon became estranged over the financial losses each suffered. By sticking with Joseph when so many others in the Ohio inner circle defected, Brigham's relationship with the prophet became cast in iron. When Joseph ended the turbulent Missouri years in Liberty Jail, he chose Brigham to lead the mass emigration to Illinois and Nauvoo. Once in Nauvoo Brigham led the early missionary initiatives to Great Britain and brought in the thousands of first converts that made the Illinois Zion bloom. When the Saints began to practice polygamy, Brigham openly took wife after wife while Joseph, faced with a "murmuring" Emma and always in the national spotlight, was more discreet. When Joseph died, Brigham was out in the field leading the missionary corps on the domestic campaign to make Joseph Smith the president of the United States.

Rushing back to Nauvoo, Brigham confronted two other leading contenders for the slain prophet's mantle, Rigdon and Joseph's often contrary brother William Smith. It was a power struggle in which Young prevailed largely because while both Rigdon and Smith had made substantial numbers of enemies during periods when they had quarreled with Joseph, Young had never strayed from the prophet's side. The climactic event was Brigham's stirring performance at a church meeting on August 8, just two months after Joseph's martyrdom, when he used his full rhetorical arsenal to tell the Saints that they could name Rigdon or William Smith their new leader but added, "Here is Brigham, have his knees ever faltered? Have his lips ever quivered? Here is Heber and the rest of the Twelve, an independent body, who have the keys of the Priesthood—the keys of the kingdom of God to deliver to all the world: this is true, so help me God."

There was no vote taken that day. But Brigham started to lead. From then he thundered his dictates from the pulpit vacated by Joseph, and the Saints followed. Rigdon and William Smith were first shunned and then driven away.

Next Brigham asked none other than Emma Hale Smith to become one of his wives. Emma, who hated the Principle, rejected Young and married a hard-drinking, non-Mormon businessman named Lewis C. Bidamon. The Bidamons stayed behind when the Saints headed west, and Emma thus proved a source of embarrassment to those who gave their all to the memory of Joseph even as she chose to marry a Gentile.

Whereas Joseph Smith had been an often joyous and playful prophet who had mingled with the masses, wrestled the men, and bedded many of the women, Brigham Young was an angry and outspoken man. His sermons were filled with talk of extracting the death penalty for apostate Mormons and Gentile interlopers alike.

"Thieves," said Brigham, should "have their heads cut off, for that was the Law of God and it should be executed." Counterfeiters? "Their throats should be cut." Backsliders or Jack Mormons? "You will be hewn down."

After divorcing himself from Smith's survivors and Rigdon's sympathizers, Brigham put down several other rebellions even as he faced a stream of legal writs from various governmental bodies in Illinois, Iowa, and Missouri with claims against Mormons. Finally, notes Stanley P. Hirshson in his Brigham Young biography, *The Lion of the Lord,* Brigham established "a police state in Nauvoo . . . he strapped on a pair of six-shooters and vowed he would kill any man who handed him another summons or grabbed hold of him."

Then Brigham single-handedly led his flock of fourteen-thousand Illinois Mormons on the epic hegira across the American plains and deserts. With Young leading the way, the long-persecuted Zion-seeking Mormons carved a permanent home out of what seemed a most unlikely location, the sometimes scorched, sometimes frozen high plains Great Basin desert. He found the

Saints the space they needed in a sanctuary deep in the wilderness protected from the east by the craggy Rocky Mountains and from the west by the High Sierras of California.

The hegira was a miracle of faith, organization, and sheer human fortitude, unmatched anywhere on the western frontier. The Mormon Exodus was accomplished only through the genius of the new prophet. He thought of everything, from having the first wagon trains pause periodically at secret locations to plant crops to feed those who followed in the next wave, to detailing the contents of the sewing kits that each family must bring along to mend their clothing and to sew covers for their wagons, to the canvas that Brigham bought for them in bulk with church funds.

As Brigham Young led his Saints to this unique desert paradise, the parallels to Moses are striking. The prophet, through the sheer force of his personality, led, goaded, threatened, fought, pummeled, cajoled, and otherwise drove the thousands of Mormon men, women, and children through the wilderness to an American Canaan called Utah on the shores of an inland Dead Sea called the Great Salt Lake. Brigham even fell ill just as his flock reached the promised land and had to be carted to the hillside overlooking the new homeland where he rose weakly to proclaim, "This is the right place."

For Brigham and the first party it was an enormously difficult trek blighted by hunger, bad weather, disease, unfriendly Indians, and other trials. They had established winter quarters after fleeing across Iowa from Nauvoo as the snow fell in 1846 and then crossed the rest of the country in the summer of 1847. The advance party led by Brigham included 143 men, three women, and two children in seventy-two covered wagons. They made the trek in less than three months arriving on or near July 20, 1847. While he roared across the countryside like an Old Testament patriarch, unlike Moses, Brigham didn't die on the heathen side of the homeland. He recovered from the bout of Rocky Mountain Spotted-Tick Fever that was ailing him when the Mormons reached Salt Lake and directed the building of the Kingdom.

Brigham's party laid out Salt Lake City, including the Mormon Mecca's famous 132-foot-wide streets and its orderly grid system of addresses radiating outward from the intersection of

Main and South Temple Streets. As in all Mormon town plans, Salt Lake was laid out along its grid in square blocks of ten acres that were divided into eight lots with a house on each. Every other block had four houses on the east side and four on the west side but with none facing north or south. On the alternate blocks, the houses faced north and south but not east or west assuring that houses on opposite sides of the street would never front on one another. Each house was at least twenty feet from the street and 132 feet from its neighbor on either side. Each house had gardens extending 330 feet to the center of the block. Most residents also were issued tracts of farmland outside town which they tilled by day but left for nights in urban surroundings in keeping with the dream of urban organization that Joseph had for the ill-fated Missouri colony.

Years later when Brigham sent missionaries abroad, they loved to tell the story of the Miracle of the Sea Gulls of 1848 when the first crop the beleaguered Mormons planted was attacked by hordes of fat grasshoppers of a species now called Mormon crickets. Desperate attempts to beat the insects back with fire, water, and brooms failed. When starvation appeared all but certain, flocks of gulls from the Salt Lake descended upon the fields and engaged in a feeding orgy in which the crickets were destroyed and the all-important first crop saved. The sea gull would later be named the Utah state bird, and a statue to the avian Godsend was erected in Temple Square itself.

Even as Brigham was leading the first wagon train of Saints fleeing from Nauvoo to Utah, he had dispatched his trusted inner circle, including his friend Heber Kimball, to Europe to seek converts with the skills to build an empire for the American Saints, who unfortunately tended to be people largely with a Midwestern agricultural background and virtually no technical skills. An 1855 listing of Mormon emigrants leaving Liverpool for Utah included 10 boilermakers, 46 engineers, 2 ironmongers, 226 miners, 8 printers, 22 spinners, and 9 weavers.

In that same spirit, Young's workers built most of the Union Pacific's Utah trackway themselves, knowing that while the transcontinental railroad would bring Utah hordes of despised Gentiles, it also would vastly cut the church's staggering costs for bringing European converts across the endless prairies. The new converts often signed all they owned over to church elders and then crossed the Atlantic in church-chartered ships to keep the young religion growing in its frontier years. They came by riverboat, by covered wagon, and even pushing their worldly belongings before them in peddlers' handcarts.

Between 1846 and 1887, European emigration to Utah totaled more than 85,000. Through 1855, when the Mormon empire took on much of the character it exhibits to this day, 21,911 emigrants included 19,535 Britons, 2,000 Scandinavians, and a handful of French, Italians, and Germans. The number of Scandinavians eventually reached more than 30,000 before the end of the nineteenth century.

This gathering of emigrant Saints spread far beyond the confines of Salt Lake. When the Mormons finally arrived in the West they quickly established colonies as far west as San Bernardino in southern California, where Brigham's counselor Amasa Lyman founded a town of fourteen hundred Mormons in 1850. Other outlying colonies were opened in Las Vegas, New Mexico, and in central Idaho at a town near the Salmon River called Lemhi. Other settlements were opened in Carson, Nevada, and ultimately to the north in Canada and to the south in Mexico. In all, Young founded more than 325 Western towns for his Great Basin Kingdom.

Historians note that this network of helpers everywhere from the missionaries working the streets of Wales to the scouts in buckskin pants who rode out from Salt Lake to escort newcomers the last two hundred miles was unique among all the other groups who made treks westward at the time. Furthermore, for a long while the Saints had the territory mostly to themselves simply because they had probed so far into the continent in a single march. Historian Ray West notes in his 1957 work *Kingdom of the Saints* that most settlers tended to simply go forty, fifty, or sixty miles beyond what seemed to be the last settlement and then set up their new homes. The next batch would extend the frontier another few miles, and so on.

These canny LDS pioneers of 1847, however, pushed twelve hundred miles into what was virtually terra incognita and built their new home on the far side of the Rocky Mountains. The Saints thereby rightly earned a reputation as being masters of the wagon train, and that was to lead to an overconfidence that proved fatal for a hapless group of particularly impoverished emigrants, the Handcart Companies.

Typically Brigham would gather his growing flock in a sprawling but crude building just off Temple Square called the Bowery and dictate who was going where. He might call for carpenters and shoemakers in Sanpete County or for millers at Payson or weavers in Bountiful. He would allot farm land, appoint leaders, and then send them off to their new homes with scarcely a murmur of dissent.

As people arrived with special skills—iron workers, for example—he would try new strategies such as when he attempted to open an iron industry in southern Utah near the settlement of Parowan by sending converted Welsh miners and iron workers from Birmingham to colonize there. When missionaries brought in Waldensian converts from Switzerland, he opened dairies and cheese factories in the Cache Valley north of Salt Lake and in the Mormon town of Afton in Wyoming's Star Valley, a short distance from the Grand Teton Mountains.

To hurry along the inflow of needed skills, Brigham sent abroad a crew of expediters with his missionaries, men who arranged deals with ship owners to transport loads of converts. Many of the techniques they employed had been developed by Brigham himself during the 1830s and early 1840s when Joseph had sent him to England and Wales as a missionary. As part of their work, these LDS managers often took title to new converts' property waiting for the most propitious moment to sell it and then returned the sum to the converts—less ten percent tithing and other costs—when the new Saints reached Utah. After 1850, part of this money, along with other church funds, also went into the accounts of the Perpetual Emigration Fund Company under the business-wise Brigham's management. Converts without enough money to get themselves to Utah, particularly if they had a needed skill, could borrow from this fund and Brigham and his overseers then saw to it that the fund was repaid with 12 percent interest from the borrower's first Utah earnings. Between 1853 and 1855 the church spent $200,000 per year from that fund chartering ships, buying food, livestock, farm implements, and wagons and moved nearly eight thousand emigrants to Utah.

Ultimately this Mormon apparatus for moving human cargo across half the globe became so efficient that the company was spending only ten pounds per emigrant for the entire journey. Typically, converts moved from Liverpool to New Orleans and then up the inland river system to what was called Winter Quarters near present-day Council Bluffs, Iowa, on the Missouri River just across from Omaha, Nebraska. From there the trail west stretched across virtually unsettled prairies dotted with bison all the way to the sagebrush of Wyoming then through Indian country, across the Continental Divide and the Uinta Mountains to the Great Salt Lake.

In 1856 Brigham decided that since members of a wagon train typically walked alongside their Conestogas rather than riding them, it was possible to cut costs by piling one's belongings onto the sort of handcarts he had watched porters using in railroad stations in New York and pushing them from Nebraska to Salt Lake. Church recruiters in Britain were amazed at how eagerly people there bought into the strange-sounding challenge. But because the handcart scheme made the trip from Liverpool to Utah far cheaper than it had for earlier converts, droves of poor people signed up. In 1856, nineteen hundred eager immigrants arrived in Iowa City and were equipped with pushcarts built from materials that Brigham had bought in bulk at St. Louis.

The carts had boxes three or four feet long with sides eight inches tall mounted on two wheels and each weighed four or five hundred pounds when fully loaded. They could be pushed by three or four people walking abreast or pulled by five. As a result there was one handcart for every five people and for every twenty carts a wagon and three yokes of oxen to carry as much food and other necessities as possible. The Europeans painted the carts in bright colors and scrawled hopeful slogans on their sides—"Truth Will Prevail," "Blessings Follow Sacrifice," "Merry Mormons," "Going Home to Zion."

They started across the prairies singing a song, "Hurrah for the Handcarts":

> Oh, Our faith goes with the handcarts
> And they have our hearts' best love:
> 'Tis a novel mode of traveling,
> Devised by the gods above.

And Brigham's their executive,
He told us the design:
And the Saints are proudly marching on,
Along the handcart line.

It was one thousand two hundred miles from Iowa City to Salt
Lake City, and the three "companies" of five hundred people
apiece pushing one hundred carts and driving five wagons each
soon were spread out over hundreds of miles. A typical company
covered twenty miles each day. Provisions came from the accompanying wagons rationed as one pound of flour per adult every
other day along with portions of tea or coffee, sugar, and rice.
A few head of beef cattle which were gradually slaughtered en
route to supplement buffalo meat provided the protein. Most of
the first company arrived in Salt Lake in late September. There
was jubilation in Mormondom but it proved short-lived.

Unbeknownst to Brigham, several hundred members of the
later companies had been forced to build their wagons out of
green wood, which made the carts heavier. The green wood
shrank on hot days causing the iron rims to fall off the wheels.
Soon they were moving much more slowly than the first waves,
a slowness that came even as the area was to be hit with one of
the worst winters on record.

The extra weight from the green wood meant that the oxen
couldn't carry as much flour as the earlier companies had toted
and these ill-fated Saints carried a ninety-eight-pound sack of
flour in each of their handcarts, far too little to make it across
the vast expanses but all they could push or pull. Gamely, they
first ate from the handcarts pushed by their weaker and older
members to lighten their loads. To fix the cart wheels, which
cracked repeatedly as the wood dried, they hammered their cooking utensils flat or cut shoes and boots for patches. Lacking
lubricants they sacrificed their soap and precious bacon grease
to keep the green axles turning.

They reached Fort Laramie, Wyoming, in early September,
but the fort had no food to spare and so they pressed on to
Independence Rock on the now-frozen Sweetwater River by late
that month. Snow-drifts and howling winds took a quick toll
because the lightly equipped emigrants hadn't brought proper
clothing or bedding. With food being rationed at a few ounces

for the men who pulled the carts and fewer ounces still for old men, old women, and children, dysentery set in. At first they stopped to bury their dead, but soon there wasn't energy left both to dig the graves and push the carts. A string of abandoned bodies stretched over seventy miles, all the way from Independence Rock to South Pass, the opening through the Rocky Mountains that had welcomed thousands of more fortunate Mormon converts in the past.

One widely quoted journal, written by a man identified only as Chislett, described the last desperate encampments before they were forced to simply lie in the snow and pray for rescue:

> We killed more cattle and issued the meat; but, eating it without bread, did not satisfy hunger, and to those who were suffering from dysentery it did more harm than good. This terrible disease increased rapidly amongst us during these three days, and several died from exhaustion. Before we renewed our journey the camp became so offensive and filthy that our words would fail to describe its condition . . . I visited the sick, the widows whose husbands died in serving them, and the aged who could not help themselves, to know for myself where to dispense the few articles that had been placed in my charge for distribution. Such craving hunger I never saw before, and may God in his mercy spare me the sight again. As I was seen giving these things to the most needy, crowds of famished men and women surrounded me and begged for bread!

In late November the relief wagons from Salt Lake finally broke through the drifting Wyoming snows and reached the miserable final handcart camp. The survivors soon found their way to Zion. The exact toll is not known but at least two in every ten who tried to push handcarts to the promised land died that first year. In one company of five hundred people, sixty-seven succumbed in a single blizzard. The other company lost even more whose bodies were simply left where they fell. Historians like Wallace Stegner and Leroy and Ann Hafen give estimates of handcart dead varying between 197 and 217 of the 1,096 known to have left Iowa City as members of the last two companies of 1856. Such historians frequently quote a particularly moving few paragraphs from the diary and autobiography of survivor Mary Goble now held in LDS church archives:

61

> We arrived in Salt Lake city nine o'clock at night the 11th of December 1856. Three out of four that were living were frozen. My mother was dead in the wagon.
>
> Bishop Hardy had us taken to a home in his ward and the brethren and sisters brought us plenty of food. We had to be careful and not eat too much as it might kill us we were so hungry.
>
> Early next morning Bro. Brigham Young and a doctor came. The doctor's name was Williams. When Bro. Young came in he shook hands with us all. When he saw our condition—our feet frozen and our mother dead—tears rolled down his checks.

One wonders, however, whether they were tears of pity or of rage. There was tremendous anger building against the Gentiles in Utah. As Joseph Smith had dictated in the *Book of Mormon* in the language of the Book of Revelation, there were wars and rumors of war all across the land.

The new prophet had learned that even in religion the hand that wears the ruler's velvet glove must be clenched in a fist of steel. He took that lesson with him to Utah with a vengeance.

Once ensconced in his Salt Lake Mecca, Brigham used many roughshod techniques to hold power, but from today's perspective, the most significant ploy was the often brutal retaliation against Gentiles and apostate Saints called the Mormon Reformation. This amounted to an 1850s LDS version of the Chinese Cultural Revolution of the 1960s during which survival often hinged upon one's ability to convince roving mobs of enforcers of one's ideological solidarity with the cause.

Key to this reformation was Jedediah Grant, an elder who crossed the frontier at Brigham's side in 1847, and who rose to the mayor's job in Salt Lake City from which he convinced Young in 1856 that even as the brave men, women, and children were dying for their faith in the handcart companies, the rank and file of Mormondom were becoming dangerously complacent about their faith and their calling as a people to establish the Biblical City of Zion.

This Jedediah proved an amazing force on the face of Mormondom. While clearly committed to spiritual matters and reform, he displayed a fixation with human waste that was to confuse greatly those who came afterwards and attempted to write a Mormon catechism from such strange material as this message to Saints everywhere from Grant:

> Do you wash your bodies once a week, when circumstances will permit? Do you keep your dwellings, outhouses and door yards clean. The first work of the reformation with some should be to clean away the filth about their premises ... Many houses stink so bad that a clean man could not live in them, nor hardly breathe in them ... I would not attempt to bless anybody in such places.

Grant lived only a short time after this reformation began, but he joined forces with Brigham in an orgy of recrimination and rebaptism among the Salt Lake Saints. Overtones of the reformation still flourish in today's Mormon culture, notably in the form of the questions that church members are required to answer when visited by priests acting as "home teachers," a common program in the various wards and stakes, as Mormons designate their congregations to this day. The questions asked in Jedediah Grant's heyday included:

1. Have you shed innocent blood or assented thereto?
2. Have you committed adultery?
3. Have you betrayed your brother?
4. Have you borne false witness against your neighbor?
5. Do you get drunk?
6. Have you stolen?
7. Have you lied?
8. Have you contracted debts without prospect of paying?
9. Have you labored faithfully for your wages?
10. Have you coveted that which belongs to another man?
11. Have you taken the name of the Lord in vain?
12. Do you preside in your family as a servant of God?
13. Have you paid your tithing in all things?

The key to this reformation was that those who were found lacking by these questions were forced to undergo a rebaptism on the spot and then were subjected to constant scrutiny by their peers, a process that did much to insure the most extreme clannishness and orthodoxy within Mormon circles. The "home teachers" continue today in Mormondom, albeit in a far less thunderous format, and keep many a potential backslider firmly in the fold. Today the home teacher is a fixture of Mormon culture and these difficult questions are asked just as they were a century ago.

Do you tithe?

Do you read only material that is faith promoting?

Do you participate in ward activities?

Do you obey general authorities?

Do you help those less fortunate than yourself through the bishops' welfare programs?

This practice of continual reinforcement through questioning does much to insure Mormon solidarity even as it fosters a yawning gap between practicing Mormons and Gentiles in Utah and any other place where Saints gather. It also quickly separates the backsliders, or Jack Mormons, from the faithful. Mormon tradition thus perpetuates the us-versus-them dynamic today just as it did then when Brigham and other elders enforced their wishes through the action of the Danites.

The Danites came into play here because the most striking feature of the reformation was the revival of the concept of "blood atonement," the principle that there are certain sins, most notably the spilling of innocent blood and heresy against the prophet that can only be forgiven once the sinner's own blood is shed and flows into the ground. In an 1856 sermon Brigham thundered from the pulpit:

> There are sins that men commit for which they cannot receive forgiveness in this world, or in that which is to come, and if they had their eyes open to see their true condition, they would be perfectly willing to have their blood spilt upon the ground, that the smoke thereof might ascend to heaven as an offering

for their sins; and the smoking incense would atone for their sins, whereas, if such is not the case, they will stick to them and remain upon them in the spirit world.

Over the years since that stunning bit of preaching anti-Mormons have alleged that dozens of murders of Gentiles and apostate Saints were blood atonements. Partisan church sympathizers such as historian Ray West acknowledge that even if the church hierarchy itself didn't actively pursue murder as a policy option, numerous zealots in the flock did indeed spill blood in the spirit of atonement.

Two murders of the era's prodigious reign of terror often are cited to explain the phenomenon:

Case 1. In the spring of 1857 a Mormon named William R. Parrish, a deacon in his ward, had lost his faith and decided to leave with his family for California to try their hand at gold mining, something that Brigham absolutely forbade Saints to do out of fear that gold fever would dilute Mormon ranks.

Parrish's apostasy became evident by his answers to questions from two elders on a family home visit. In the next few days a church member posing as a fellow apostate approached Parrish with an offer of helping him to leave the territory.

As the Parrish family rode their wagon south of Provo en route to California, snipers shot Parrish and his seventeen-year-old son to death and inadvertently killed one of their own who was riding in the family's wagon.

Anti-Mormons insisted that this one documented case was similar to many others that happened and were never documented when church insiders tried to leave.

The Parrish case ultimately was cited in debate before the U.S. House of Representatives over anti-Mormon legislation and was roundly denied by church officials. But Parrish's wife gave the allegations substantial credibility when she produced a document from Brigham who tried to console her by saying he "would have stopped it had I known anything about it."

Case 2. Dr. J. King Robinson had moved to Salt Lake in 1857 to open a practice and quickly enmeshed himself in local intrigues by marrying the apostate widow of a top church official. He clashed with the Salt Lake City government over ownership of a hot spring on the city's north side, which he hoped to use as the centerpiece for a health spa.

One night while returning home from his office he was beaten to death by a crowd of men who were said to be "Shenpips," an LDS code name for Danite enforcers.

A widely quoted statement by Young in the October 1, 1856, edition of the church-owned *Deseret News* reads, "I could refer you to plenty of instances where men have been righteously slain, in order to atone for their sins. . . . I have known a great many men who have left this church for whom there is no chance whatever for exaltation; but if their blood had been spilled it would have been better for them."

The strongest link between blood atonement and mainstream Mormondom exists in the simple fact that to this day the states of Utah and Idaho, unlike the other forty-eight, provide a condemned prisoner the option of dying by firing squad rather than by lethal injection in order that his or her blood might mix with the soil and become that "smoking incense" that will "atone for their sins."

The Danites or "Brigham's Avenging Angels," as they came to be called in the popular press of the day, are another of those topics which Mormon establishment scholars tend to deemphasize while less friendly scribes glory in describing and, most likely, exaggerating.

But today, more than a hundred years after the fact, the Danites stand as an answer to perhaps the greatest Mormon conundrum of them all: Why did the Gentiles so hate and attack this essentially Christian religious sect?

At least part of the reason for that persecution was that through their Danite warrior class the Mormons often gave as good as they got from their old settler neighbors. Once transplanted to Utah, these Danites became something of a frontier secret police, a church force that dealt with both apostates within LDS ranks and troublesome Gentiles with cold steel or hot lead.

There are strong indications that the Danite movement vexed the first prophet just as they have troubled his successors. After Joseph allowed his followers to retaliate in Missouri by attacking Gentile houses, he later had difficulty in persuading his Saints to stop depredations against Gentile neighbors.

In his anti-Mormon book, *Mormonism Unveiled,* a self-confessed apostate Gentile killer John Lee quotes Smith as giving a talk at an early church general conference in which he made this plea:

> I wish you all to know that because you were justified in taking property from your enemies while engaged in war in Missouri, which was needed to support you, there is now a different condition of things existing. We are no longer at war, and you must stop stealing. When the right time comes we will go in force and take the whole State of Missouri. It belongs to us as our inheritance; but I want no more petty stealing. A man that will steal petty articles from his enemies, will, when occasion offers, steal from his brethren too. Now I command you that you that have stolen, must steal no more.

Then, to enforce this edict, Joseph set up a police force or palace guard of forty men who also formed the Danite nucleus. This force, led by perhaps the most notorious of all Mormondom's Avenging Angels, Orrin Porter Rockwell, did the work of destroying the printing press of the Nauvoo *Expositor* that ultimately led to Joseph's arrest and fatal imprisonment in the Carthage jail.

Rockwell was the man who historians almost universally conclude shot the Saints' arch enemy, former Missouri Governor Lilburn Boggs, author of the vicious "extermination" order, in the head shortly after the Saints settled Nauvoo. Rockwell later shot to death Frank Worrell, the leader of the Carthage Greys militia that had played a key role in Joseph's assassination.

Throughout Brigham Young's reign, Rockwell stood at his side as body guard, errand runner, and as the prophet's occasional hit man. Various accounts of the time attributed anywhere from fifty to one hundred murders to him, although scholars like Harold Schindler dismiss such high death counts as legend. But, undisputedly, Rockwell killed for his faith—the only question is the number of his victims.

In a famous Salt Lake speech on July 5, 1857, Brigham said, "If men come here and do not behave themselves, they will not only find the Danites, whom they talk so much about, biting the horses' heels, but the scoundrels will find something biting their heels. In my plain remarks, I merely call things by their right names." The allusion was to Genesis 49:17: "Dan shall be a serpent by the way, an adder in the path, that biteth the horse heels, so that his rider shall fall backward."

Today there is scarcely a Mormon child who hasn't heard the sanitized story of "O. P. Rockwell, the Mormon Samson." Shortly after Governor Boggs was shot, Rockwell was arrested and languished for nearly a year in a Missouri jail before winning freedom when a church-affiliated lawyer raised numerous legal technicalities in his behalf, none of which included a denial of the attempted murder.

Once released, Rockwell, barefoot and dressed in rags, made a legendary escape back to Nauvoo at the head of pursuing Missourians. He stumbled into Joseph's Nauvoo ballroom on Christmas Eve and was graced with an instant prophecy, which read, "I prophesy, in the name of the Lord, that you—Orrin Porter Rockwell—so long as ye shall remain loyal and true to thy faith, need fear no enemy. Cut not thy hair and no bullet or blade can harm thee."

Notes Rockwell biographer Schindler, "From this day forward through thirty-five violent years in which Rockwell encountered hostile Indians, desperadoes, and other characters on the Western scene, he managed to avoid a single physical injury at the hands of another man." O. P. Rockwell, Man of God, Son of Thunder, went to his grave with braided hair that reached his well-worn spurs, Samson to Brigham's Moses and Joseph's Jesus.

Rockwell cut his hair only once, in 1855, to provide a wig for the widow of Joseph's younger brother, Don Carlos Smith, who was made bald by a case of typhoid. He claimed for the rest of his life that after he cut those flowing locks he could never again control his swearing and drinking, even after the hair grew back.

For Mormon children, Porter Rockwell stands alongside Davy Crockett and Daniel Boone, even if scarcely a Gentile alive has ever heard of him. In Brigham's Utah, Rockwell became a member of the highest priesthood, that of Melchizedek.

It is doubtful that Brigham could have brought his Saints to the Great Basin Kingdom in the first place without the help of ruthless enforcers like Rockwell, John D. Lee, and Bill Hickman. Nonetheless, there is wide disagreement between Mormons and critics about much of the secret war waged by the Danites against Gentiles and apostates. Historians inside Mormon circles work to paint characters like Rockwell, Hickman, and Lee as mere rustics with rough edges but with hearts of gold, while scholars in less friendly circles paint them as murderous henchmen of a ruthless and sometimes hate-ridden prophet.

The stakes here are quite high. Anti-Mormons quickly suggest that the Danite phenomenon set the tone for the entire religious movement and trot out a long list of alleged Danite atrocities against apostates and Gentiles.

Unhappily, there is one Danite travesty that both sides agree happened, the infamous Mountain Meadows Massacre of 1857 in which more than 120 Gentiles trekking across Utah for California were slaughtered by a band of Saints and Indians who pretended to be escorting the victims to safety and then turned and started shooting.

John Lee, who did some of the shooting that grim day, claimed the massacre and other killings had been directly ordered by Brigham. Young vehemently denied ordering the bloodshed at Mountain Meadows and a raft of both Mormon and non-Mormon historians largely agree that his canny political instincts assured that he never would have allowed the Gentiles the sort of public relations coup that came their way as a result of the heartless massacre.

But while it is doubtful that Young ordered the bloodletting on the Meadows, many Mormon scholars, including the late Juanita Brooks, whose work on the topic is considered the most definitive, note that Brigham did much to whip up anti-Gentile fervor among Utahns even as the ill-fated Fancher party's wagon train entered the state in early August. Brooks, whose suspicions were fueled by the fact that even though her church credentials and scholarship were impeccable, the elders denied her access to key documents, went so far as to call Brigham an "accessory after the fact" in her acclaimed work, *The Mountain Meadows Massacre.*

The massacre needs to be explained in context because it happened while the Mormons were suffering acute anxiety after getting news that an army was marching against them from Washington. Just weeks before the massacre, on Pioneer Day 1857 marking the Saints tenth year in the valley, Orrin Porter Rockwell rode into a picnic being hosted by Brigham with word from Fort Laramie that a column of federal troops was heading to occupy Utah and install a Gentile governor named Alfred Cumming in Young's place.

The prophet responded by sending General George Smith, head of the Nauvoo Legion, Utah's militia, all the way south and west to San Bernardino, California, to urge church members everywhere to refuse to sell any food or other supplies to future Gentile wagon trains. At each stop, Smith made ringing anti-Gentile speeches even as Brigham sermonized in the same vein at Salt Lake services.

On the Sunday before the massacre, Brigham told the congregation, "We have borne enough of their oppression and hellish abuse and we will not bear any more of it; for there is no just law requiring further forbearance on our part. The thread is cut between them and us and we will never gibe again. No, never, world without end." The crowd shouted a hearty "Amen."

In this climate the doomed Fancher party of 137 people including thirty families from Arkansas and roughly a dozen rowdy young men who called themselves "Missouri Wildcats," headed south out of Salt Lake in early August, hoping that by crossing the deserts of Nevada and southern California they would avoid the fate of the Donner party, which had become snowbound in the High Sierras of northern California the year before and was all but wiped out when starved members turned to cannibalism to survive.

These "wildcats" made the suicidal error of boasting—probably falsely—that they had been involved in the murder of Joseph Smith and that they had joined others in Gentile mobs to drive the Saints from their beloved Missouri settlements which Mormon prophecy to this day holds will be the ultimate site of the all-important city of Zion.

Under orders from General Smith not to sell food to any Gentiles, the people south of Salt Lake refused to supply the Fancher wagon train and the young "wildcats" responded with stupid threats and boasts and eventually started breaking into gardens and even stealing food from houses in the southern Utah town of Parowan, named for a *Book of Mormon* warrior.

John D. Lee, who twenty years later was executed blood-atonement style before a firing squad for his role in the subsequent massacre, wrote before he died that the rowdies who were to die at the hands of Danites "had two bulls, which they called one 'Heber' and the other 'Brigham' and whipped 'em thro' every town, yelling and singing, blackguarding and blaspheming oaths that would have made your hair stand on end."

Lee, a Mormon Indian agent at the time, continued, "At Spanish Fork [south of Salt Lake]—it can be proved—one of 'em stood on his wagon-tongue, and swung a pistol, and swore that he helped kill old Joe Smith, and was ready for old Brigham Young, and all sung a blackguard song, 'Oh, we've got the ropes and we'll hang old Brigham before the snow flies,' and such stuff."

These boorish if benighted travelers also paused on their trek to shoot one passing Indian to death, crippled another with gunfire, and poisoned a spring in the area with the result that several Indians died when they ate animals killed by the water. In Cedar City, about a two-day ride from Brigham's winter retreat of St. George, a crowd of more than thirty angry ward elders met and discussed what to do about the intruding party of emigrants. Virtually all sides now agree that the leader of this Danite group was Lee and that he persuaded a number of church elders in Cedar City to join him and a group of Indians in a murderous attack on the "wildcats" and Arkansas travelers.

Church historians dispute outsiders on just how many Mormons joined the slaughter, but both camps generally agree that the Saints involved accompanied a band of Indians that mounted the first attack as the party camped at Mountain Meadows, a small valley in what is now the Dixie National Forest about forty miles north of St. George.

Lee tells how, after the Indians at the urging of their Mormon

71

companions engaged in three days of skirmishes with the party which had circled wagons in the valley, a group of Saints, including himself, rode into their camp under a truce flag and made an agreement with the Gentiles' leader, Captain Charles Fancher, to escort the party out of Utah, through Indian lines. The badly outnumbered wagon train grasped at the offered straw and soon Fancher's crowd left with Mormons accompanying them in each wagon. The emigrant men were marched in front and taking up the rear were wagons filled with women and children. A short distance down the road, however, the first shot rang out and the Saints and Indians slaughtered 120 men, women, and children in a matter of minutes.

The only ones spared were seventeen children aged nine and younger who were placed in a single wagon and later distributed among numerous Mormon foster homes. It generally is agreed that the Mormons and Indians killed all those older than nine because the Saints involved wanted the world to think that the atrocity was the sole work of Indians.

Understandably, much effort since has gone into trying to fathom just how such a nightmare could have sprung from a people so clearly committed to Godly principles. Church insiders, like the late Professor Eugene E. Campbell, dispute the extent of Mormon participation along with the Indians. They also emphasize that the Saints who acted had suffered immense persecutions on the long road from Palmyra to Kirtland to Far West to Nauvoo to Salt Lake and found the "Missouri wildcats" intolerable.

In his acclaimed history, *Establishing Zion,* Campbell of Brigham Young University also suggests that the Saints acted out of panic that the Fancher party would reach California and disclose that Mormons were joining Indians in attacking wagon trains in the West, a revelation which would have been extremely serious with federal troops fast approaching from the East. As it was, Brigham and his allies were able to buy time denying that Mormons had anything to do with the travesty until the truth came out after years of probing. Lee wasn't executed for the murders until 1877, twenty years after the massacre.

Less devoted observers tend to view the tragedy of Mountain

Meadows as the logical consequence of the doctrine of blood atonement that continues as a Mormon principle to this day. Brigham's blood-soaked rhetoric, the Mormon belief that the church has "restored" the world to a renewed period of direct communication with the angry and vengeful Old Testament God the Father, and a history of unremitting conflict with an unfriendly outside Gentile world, all combined to drive Lee and his henchmen to massacre the Fancher party.

A Mormon defector verbalized widespread suspicions when he told the New York *Times* in May of 1858, "Brigham never tells one of the 'angels' to commit a depredation straight forward, but a wink, a nod, or a 'you know, Porter,' or whoever it may be, will settle the matter as easily as a sermon on the subject." That tradition of blood atonement, avenging patriarchs, and conflict with Gentiles often surfaces as bizarre outbreaks of violence in modern Utah just as it did when Brother Brigham led the Saints on the harsh frontier.

For most of the 1850s the Mormons had either ignored or harassed the various government officials sent by Washington to serve in such posts as Indian agent, prosecutor, federal judge, or territorial governor. But even as the troops sent by President James Buchanan headed across Wyoming, Eastern newspapers carried accounts of how many of these officials had been outrageous scoundrels, most notably, Judge William W. Drummond, whose office was sacked by close associates of Brigham in 1856.

Drummond sent word back East that the Mormons were un-American because they did not view themselves as part of the United States and even went so far as to teach the Indians that there were two kinds of whites, Americans (sometimes called "Americrats") and Mormons. Saints explained convincingly that they made the distinction between other whites and themselves simply to survive in an era of Indian hostility. But critics insisted that the Mormons were traitors to the American flag.

In typical Young rhetoric, the prophet gave a talk to his followers in 1845 in which he explained that the exodus to Utah was, indeed, an effort to leave the United States, adding, "We do not owe this country a single Sermon . . . I do not intend to stay in such a hell of a hole . . . They [Americans] are as corrupt as Hell from the president down clean through the priest and the people all are as corrupt as the Devil."

When that godless American government, as Brigham saw it, finally moved against the Utah Saints, the soldiers came not as strangers but as friends. President Buchanan had cited Drummond's complaint about harassment and anti-American Mormon attitudes as the reason for sending troops only to find that the good judge was not a very good man at all. Drummond, it was disclosed, had abandoned a wife and child to take his Utah post and had arrived in Salt Lake with a prostitute whom he flaunted before the moralistic Saints and whom he kept sitting next to him on the bench when he heard cases against Mormons.

With the whore (her name is lost in time) at his side, Drummond frequently made disparaging remarks about LDS sexual morality due to the polygamy Principle. One arrogant letter to Mormon Jules Remy from Drummond boasted, "Money is my God, and you may put that down in your journals if you like."

Never at a loss for words, Young complained that, like Drummond, many of the men back East eager to take government appointments to Utah were lured by sexual intrigue to the land of multiple wives. In a typical anti-Mormon tirade of the time, the New York *Times* printed a letter from a former Salt Lake resident who said that one of Brigham's own daughters once told him, "If Salt Lake City were roofed over, it would be the biggest whore-house in the world."

In that tense atmosphere, Brigham mapped plans to resist President Buchanan's approaching troops by harassing them on their march and then by burning all houses, crops, and orchards in the valley once the soldiers arrived.

True to that effort, a Danite named Lot Smith led a force of two dozen men who succeeded in capturing a large number of the unguarded civilian supply wagons trailing the column of regular army troops. Lot Smith's Danites burned roughly seventy wagons while the outnumbered army drivers watched at gunpoint.

When Brigham finally met with the cavalry commanders on the edge of Utah in February of 1858 he was told that the army had received new orders from Washington and no longer intended to arrest anyone. Furthermore, the prophet was assured, the army had abandoned all plans for occupying the territory and wanted simply to serve as a United States government presence on the frontier by setting up facilities in the Great Basin. They assured Brigham that the military planned to merely pass through Salt Lake City and set up a fort, named after Secretary of War John Floyd, about twenty-five miles from town.

When the troops reached Salt Lake a few days later they crossed a vacant city without incident as promised. Virtually every house not owned by Gentiles had been boarded up and most of the men, all of the women, and all of the children, had taken their family belongings in their wagons and moved into the mountains, leaving behind a force of men who would burn the city if the soldiers stopped.

The troops passed through without incident, however, and within two days had founded Fort Floyd, an immense military outpost for the day with a garrison of three thousand people and boasting a payroll the likes of which the state of Utah/Deseret had never before seen. The occupants of the fort proved to have a voracious appetite for buying the goods and services that the Mormons readily offered once the tension had passed. It later was estimated that the expeditionary force to Utah had cost more than $15 million and that much of that money went to civilian—in Utah that meant Mormon—contractors for supplies and services. Better still for the Saints, less than three years after Fort Floyd was established the Civil War erupted and the army was forced to abandon much of the rolling stock, animals, food, tools, and other supplies that the troopers had lugged all the way to Salt Lake.

The Utah War, which never rose to the level of bloodletting except for the 137 blighted members of the Fancher party at Mountain Meadows, thus turned out to be a major blessing for the new kingdom aborning in the shade of the Wasatch range. It taught the Saints that no matter how fierce the rhetoric might grow among the ranks of their critics and enemies, the Mormons never again would have to flee in the face of Gentile mobs. They had a home in Zion, if not forever, at least until the Second Coming.

Furthermore, Saints in today's America have won their status as important players in a highly complex world by sticking to their own roots despite the worst efforts of outsiders to brush them aside. The Saints wrested this trust and power from their fellow citizens by operating with unmatched devotion and fidelity to a set of principles foreign in the extreme to all that mainstream Judeo-Christian traditions hold sacred. They died, were driven off, ridiculed, and scorned by the majority of their fellow citizens for much of their history, yet they endure, prosper, and continue to believe.

Chapter 4

The Tenets of Zion
A Gentile's View of Mormon Beliefs

They [the Mormons] are Jews in their theocracy, their ideas of angels, their hatred of Gentiles, and their utter separation from their great brotherhood of mankind. They are Christians inasmuch as they base their faith upon the Bible, and hold to the divinity of Christ, the fall of man, the atonement and regeneration. They are Arians inasmuch as they hold Christ to be "the first of God's creatures," a "perfect creature, but still a creature." They are Moslems in their views of the inferior status of womankind, in their polygamy, and in their resurrection of the material body.

—Richard F. Burton in *The City of the Saints*, 1862

- Jesus slept with Mary Magdelene. He has other wives as well and they are bearing him children to this very day.

- One day Joseph Smith will be just as powerful as God. In fact, Joseph, Brigham Young, and other LDS giants will "progress" until they all attain the same stature as the God of the Old Testament.

- Almost nobody is going to go to hell. The lowest rung of the Mormon hereafter is a paradise for Gentiles where their every need is met, a "Telestial Kingdom" of earthly delights where people in perfect bodies live forever. Mormon missionaries usually tell Gentiles on the first visit about how Joseph Smith once said that if outsiders knew just how wonderful the next world would be for them they would commit suicide just to get there as quickly as possible.

- God lives on a planet circling a star called Kolob on which a single day takes a thousand earth years to unfold. He has a physical body and to this very instant is sexually active with our Heavenly Mother and other wives.

Each of these propositions has been pronounced as Mormon dogma either by Joseph and Brigham or by other important elders starting with founding fathers Orson Hyde and Parley Pratt and continuing on to the present. Clearly, when various Mormon tenets are baldly and unsympathetically stated, the beliefs of Zion fly in the face of traditional Judeo-Christian ideals. Indeed, they ring like blasphemy or worse in the minds of rigid Gentiles.

Much of their long history of persecution can be traced to the simple fact that Mormons confront any and all comers with such theological zingers from the outset. They win an amazing number of converts by so doing, but they also make enemies among people whose sense of propriety or whose concept of intellectual integrity is offended by such starkly variant beliefs. It is not uncommon for fundamentalist Protestants to gather at Mormon public functions to pass out literature warning of the church's "blasphemies" and outlining what the protesters find the most bizarre about LDS beliefs.

A 1985 article in *Newsweek* magazine about anti-Mormon groups aptly noted that "Mormon scriptures totally recast Christian doctrine while retaining much of Christianity's traditional terminology." Thus it is that LDS members speak of Our Father in Heaven but, unlike other Christians, they also believe there is a Mother in Heaven. The church espouses the concept of a Holy Trinity but holds that two of the three members are separate individuals of flesh and blood while the third is "pure spirit."

Mormons talk of Adam and Michael the Archangel, but many in LDS circles hold that Adam is, in fact, God, and that his firstborn was Jesus Christ. In Mormon circles volumes of quarreling monographs and sermons have been written about what is usually called the "Adam-God Dilemma."

It should be emphasized that Mormons don't march in ideological lock step in doctrinal matters. There is no LDS College of Canon Law, although much of Mormon orthodoxy is stated fairly inarguably in the compendious volumes of history, discourses, and essays compiled in the faith's unique pursuit of historical authenticity. Despite that somewhat informal written canon, the central LDS principle that the clergy be composed of part-time laymen results in a loose interpretation of doctrine among individual congregations except on matters such as the ban on polygamy or abstention from drinking and smoking directly ordered by one of the church's living prophets through revelation.

After tumultuous decades in which Mormons were castigated over the polygamy issue, the church's prophet of the time in 1890 announced he had received a direct revelation from God ordering a suspension of the Principle. Similarly, in the mid-1970s the LDS hierarchy announced a divine revelation that required a reversal of the church's antiblack policies which had been in effect ever since Joseph announced his own revelations to the effect that people of color were inferior to others.

This Mormon emphasis on direct revelation from God, which can come at any time and greatly alter the church's core practices, introduces an element of chaos into the calculus of religion that is unique to Mormondom. Joseph Smith wrote in his *History of the Church* that "The latter-day Saints have no creed but are ready to believe all true principles that exist, as they are made manifest from time to time."

Thus while church elders in Salt Lake made compassionate pleas for mercy toward AIDS patients, bishops in downstate wards were excommunicating men with the disease for moral turpitude. Similarly, a growing number of Mormon thinkers admit that they are working in the background to move the church's teachings to emphasize tenets that Mormons definitely share with other Christians and to deemphasize the more striking variant beliefs, such as a sexually active God. These more sensationalistic LDS principles are stated in ancillary church literature such as the many volumes called *Journal of Discourses.* They are filled with sermons, letters, and other teachings of the closest associates of Joseph Smith and Brigham Young, who were elevated to the rank of General Authorities, as the church calls the eighty-five elders who make up the hierarchy of Twelve Apostles, the three-member First Presidency, and the Council of the Seventy.

BYU English professor Eugene England noted in an essay published in the periodical *Sunstone,* "Our theology has tended to be quite rough and ready-made, developed piecemeal in response to continuous revelation in complex and changing historical conditions." Those, like Professor England, hoping to tone down some of the more bombastic aspects of LDS doctrine, work to turn emphasis away from the widely quoted Joseph Smith and the rambling Brigham Young and to focus on the *Book of Mormon* and *Doctrines and Covenants* in tandem with the Old and New Testaments shared with Jews and other Christians. The *Book of Mormon,* with its strong parallels to Old and New Testament stories, dictums, and parables, is nowhere near as removed from the Judeo-Christian tradition as are subsequent Mormon theological writings. Those scholars who would move LDS doctrine toward the mainstream shy away from the third volume of Joseph Smith's sacred trilogy, *The Pearl of Great Price,* which contains allusions to the inferiority of blacks and the multiplicity of Gods and has upset church critics. The revisionist movement, usually called "neo-orthodoxy," is hailed by those seeking a solution to the dilemma created by polygamous fundamentalists who claim to be in direct contact with God and whose bloodletting and other disturbing actions have cast the church in an unfavorable light.

The landscape of Mormon theology starts with "progression," the core Mormon tenet that the youngest baby is as old as God and one day that baby may move through the continuum and become a God too. It was a sublime understatement when Elder Neal A. Maxwell, one of the church's ruling Council of the Twelve Apostles, told a hushed crowd of the faithful at the Mormon Tabernacle in 1985, "Premortality is not a relaxing doctrine." He added, "This doctrine brings unarguable identity but also severe accountability to our lives."

Joseph Smith's concept of the universe was that every entity that ever has existed or that ever will exist either already is present in a "spirit world" or has left that plane to move down the continuum from spirit baby to personhood in this world to Godhood or some other "exalted state" in the next life. The Mormon cosmology is not based on a Big Bang, but rather on a seething steady-state eternity of body seekers that always has included a God and all other lesser forms. When Joseph told his flock that he had visited with God, he said that God had arms and legs and was a creature of flesh and bones. In the *Book of Mormon* a prophet named Mahonri Moriancumer, the brother of another prophet named Jared, describes how Christ had a finger and that "it was the finger of a man, like unto flesh and blood" (Ether 3:6).

In his de facto LDS catechism, *Mormon Doctrine,* Elder Bruce McConkie explains, "Animals, fowls, fishes, plants, and all forms of life were first created as distinct spirit entities in pre-existence before coming to this earth; they were spirit animals, spirit birds, and so forth." The challenge to Mormons is to speed along that process of progression from the spirit world to the celestial one.

In terms of this one planet called earth, the culmination of creation—Mormons call it the "Dispensation of the Fulness of Time"—can come only after the entire spirit world has been brought into the terrestrial realm where we all live and work, love and die. Thus it follows that the purpose of human existence is to do all one can to facilitate this great transformation. Working for that goal is the key to much of Mormondom. Human life is a crusade to free all of God's children from their spirit prison and to send as many as possible on to the highest of the three planes of heaven, which the church calls the Celestial Kingdom.

The other two levels of the Mormon hereafter are the Telestial Kingdom, where unrepentant Gentiles wind up, and the Terrestrial Kingdom, which is the final destination for "Jack Mormons," those people whose Mormonism was lukewarm but who had benefited from the blessings that come with various church temple rituals or "endowments." The elite among the masses of the saved, Mormons with "temple recommends," are rewarded with the Celestial Kingdom, the pinnacle of post-mortal existence where each inhabitant is nothing less than a God in waiting. Once ensconced in the celestial realm, the faithful will evolve into gods in their own right and come to rule universes of their own just as the three "personages" known as the Father, the Son, and the Holy Spirit in biblical scriptures rule our universe.

The quest for earthly bodies for the spirit babies so that they can begin the all-important journey to this celestial state drives much Mormon activity. Big families mean that more spirit babies find their earthly start; polygamy meant that even more spirits were freed.

Whether Joseph Smith and Brigham Young were lustful opportunists who used their temporal powers as a force for seduction is debatable, but their logic in instituting the Principle was impeccable. Despite the vast numbers of European immigrants brought in by missionaries, the great growth in Utah came as children were born to the gathering Saints. Researchers at the University of Utah have estimated that there are between one thousand and ten thousand people living in today's Utah who are direct descendants of each of the individual Mormon pioneers.

That phenomenon of big families with deep roots is visible in the demographics of today's Utah. The state's population was youngest of all the United States with an average age of 24.5 compared to 32.1 nationwide in 1987. Utah's birthrate led the nation at twenty-one per thousand in 1988, higher than that of China, even though Utah also slowed down in response to late twentieth-century economic and social pressures. In 1979 the Utah birthrate had been a staggering twenty-nine per thousand, a figure matched only in the Third World. Clearly, a lot of spirit babies find their terrestrial home via the Mormon Mecca's high birthrates.

A pamphlet handed to visitors at the Salt Lake Temple explains, "There is nothing of reincarnation, nothing of Nirvana, nothing of a static heaven, nor a hell of hot flame in Latter-day philosophy. Heaven lies in the growth that comes of improvement and achievement." That achievement comes by doing all one can do to swell the ranks of those exalted in the all-important Celestial Kingdom. Husbands and wives married in the temple are "sealed" together throughout eternity. After death they live an exalted version of earthly affairs along with their offspring and ancestors who also are sealed together by "ordinances" performed in the temples for both the living and the dead. The logic here is simply that the larger one's family becomes in the hereafter, the closer one becomes to reaching God-like stature.

Thus, in addition to the church's massive efforts to draw new-comers into the fold via missionary work and other proselytizing, the Saints spend much time and money inside their jealously guarded temples performing what are called "vicarious ordinances" for unsaved Gentiles whom they can reach in no other way because they are dead. Each proxy baptism of a departed ancestor increases the size of a given Saint's celestial family and moves each closer to Godhood. Therefore family members—husbands, wives, and sons (but not daughters, who must cleave to the line of their husbands in patriarchal Mormondom)—are sealed to one another for eternity. Likewise are dead relatives of the patriarchal line sealed to the family by proxy.

It is the apparatus the Saints have created for this celestial quest that gives the church the external trappings most familiar to outsiders, the string of temples and the extensive genealogical expertise that Mormons so willingly share with all who ask even as they strictly deny outsiders entry to the temples.

Early one sunny afternoon in late 1988, Eve Mortensen, a volunteer guide at the elegant visitors' center alongside the Mormon Temple in Salt Lake, smiled and told a small group of visitors, "These are very sacred buildings. They are not churches. They are open every day of the week from early in the morning until late at night for ordinances."

Like somebody's Mormon grandmother, Mrs. Mortensen spoke happily of how men and women kneel in the temple's opulent Sealing Room and exchange wedding vows that will bind them together throughout eternity. She added, "Other weddings say 'until death do we part' but we believe marriage is an ordinance of God that continues forever—whatsoever is bound on earth is bound in heaven."

She spoke of the absolute need for chastity and fidelity if marriages are to endure forever and emphasized Mormons' love for their children. She spoke of premortality, saying, "We believe the spirit existed in a preexistent state and that we came here and acquired a body. The reuniting of the body with the spirit makes an immortal soul that will never again taste of death . . . We don't believe in hell. We believe that people can make their own hell, however."

Mrs. Mortensen explained that the church has forty-four temples in use all around the world from Manila in the Philippines to Santiago, Chile. "Mormons," she said, "are great builders of temples." Each Mormon temple has a swimming pool–sized baptismal font designed from the biblical descriptions of the giant censers outside Solomon's Temple held up with twelve oxen. A replica of the Utah font is on display in the Salt Lake visitors' center because it is forbidden for non-Mormons to enter the temple proper.

A former Mormon named Latayne Colvett Scott described her experiences as a Brigham Young University student performing vicarious baptisms for the dead in her book, *The Mormon Mirage*:

> One by one we were called by name to descend into the font. A recorder sat on a high stool, not unlike a lifeguard's stand, at one side of the font, and witnesses watched. An elder stood in the font in garments like ours (terry cloth smocks), and beckoned for each participant as his or her turn came. He spoke the baptismal prayer in a hurried, monotonous voice, stopping only to lower a proxy into the water.
>
> I sat on the platform, looking furtively for the angels I had heard often appeared in temples. When my name was called, I went down into the water. The baptizing elder turned me around so that he could see a large screen, something like an electronic football scoreboard, which he looked at over my shoulder. On top of the screen was my name, and below it a name I don't remember, but which I'll say was Elizabeth Anderson.
>
> "Sister Latayne Colvett," he said, looking at the screen, "having been commissioned of Jesus Christ, I baptize you, for and in behalf of Elizabeth Anderson, who is dead, in the name of the Father and of the Son and of the Holy Ghost. Amen." Then he quickly dropped his right arm from the square and lowered me beneath the water. As I was regaining my footing (you learn after the third or fourth time to put one foot slightly behind the other to help you get back out of the water) he had already begun the same prayer, inserting this time the name of another dead woman which had flashed onto the screen behind me. Fifteen consecutive baptisms were performed with me as proxy in a matter of about three minutes. As I left the font, another proxy was preparing to be baptized.

In 1985 alone, such temple workers and volunteers performed 4.9 million ordinances for the living and dead, according to the 1987 LDS *Church Almanac*. The almanac notes that since the first ordinances were performed by Joseph Smith at the doomed Nauvoo Temple, the church has performed baptisms or other temple work for 324 million people, most of them dead. One of Brigham Young's early successors, Wilford Woodruff, is quoted in *Journal of Discourses* describing how in 1898 he performed vicarious ordinances for more than one hundred dead world leaders including most of the American presidents up to then as well as the signers of the Declaration of Independence, Christopher Columbus, John Wesley, a few deceased popes, and others. Some speculate that the elders around Brigham Young went so far as to have themselves sealed in marriage to beauties of the day like the legendary Lillie Langtry in anticipation of connubial bliss in the coming Celestial Kingdom.

The temples and the rituals that occur within their precincts are little understood by outsiders. Mormons refuse to discuss them with any but the most ardent of Saints, who pass the stringent demands of dietary laws, tithing, sexual orthodoxy, and other requirements for a "temple recommend." These recommends are professionally printed forms which when filled out by the bishop result in a hard copy for the church headquarters files, one flimsy copy for the ward's records, and a third for the holder to present at the door of a temple for admission.

Since the church believes that one must be "temple worthy" in order to attain the Celestial Kingdom, having the power to grant or withhold recommends gives the local bishops immense power. Furthermore, in predominantly Mormon areas the lack of a recommend can often mean the loss of a job or being shunned by one's neighbors. These slips of paper are most valuable.

Despite church secrecy, dissident Mormons have given anti-Mormons copies of temple recommends, providing outsiders with a glimpse of the church's inner operations. A temple recommend form from the late 1960s printed by Jerald and Sandra Tanner in *Mormonism—Shadow or Reality?* has boxes for the bishop to fill out the holder's name, ward, stake, sex, marital status, and which of four ordinances that person can perform for himself, herself, or by proxy for the dead. These levels of acceptance range from, "All ordinances for the dead; also witnessing marriages or sealings," down to the most minor of temple roles, "sealing to parents." Accompanying instructions include the list of questions that bishops ask each applicant before filling out the recommend.

Undoubtedly such material gives a distorted view of temple Mormonism, but since elders remain adamant about the requirement of total secrecy, this is the only way an outsider can learn about temple rites short of joining the church.

The temple ceremonies where a Mormon receives the "regulation garment"—the underwear that orthodox members wear in the secular world—are similar to such Catholic and Protestant sacraments as marriage, baptism, confirmation, and holy orders in that they can occur but once in a supplicant's life. A Mormon, however, then spends a lifetime returning to the temple to undergo the rituals time and again on behalf of dead ancestors whose identities are uncovered by the genealogists.

For the endowment, participants are issued special clothing, washed and anointed by members of their own sex, and then taken through a series of rooms in which other temple volunteers, called Veil Workers, conduct allegorical ceremonies retelling the Creation, the Fall of Man, and other scriptural events. Typically many dozens of people will move through the temple at a given time, each carrying the names of many dead persons for whom they are repeating the endowments and ordinances. The church almanac for 1985 notes that 25,000 church members served as "veil workers," and "sealers" who helped church members through endowments and ordinances in which nearly five million dead people were represented.

These temple ordinances are very important to Mormons. As missionaries return with converts, each with his or her own familial line stretching back into time, Mormons must find their ancestors, baptize and confirm them, and even marry them to one another vicariously. Mormons feel pressured to fan out across the globe in search of the identities of Mormon ancestors so they too can be added to the ranks of the hereafter. Joseph Fielding Smith, a successor to Brigham Young as church president, declared in his 1938 *Teachings of the Prophet Joseph*

Smith, "The greatest responsibility in this world that God has laid upon us is to seek after our dead." Thus the drive to genealogy.

The same week in 1985 that the notorious Mormon forger-bomber Mark Hofmann set the devices that killed two people, the church moved its vast genealogical holdings from the twenty-six-floor high-rise headquarters building to a cavernous new Genealogy Library on the other side of Temple Square, indicating the burgeoning growth of this aspect of Mormonism. Here in climate-regulated conditions stretch shelf after shelf of some of the most boring books ever collected under one roof—census listings, baptismal records, parish membership lists, and other material collected from all across the world. The racks are jammed with musty volumes of tax records, real estate transactions, diaries penciled by barely literate mothers, voters' rolls, and other documents selected because they allow a researcher to track the life movements of Mormon "kindred dead."

Always on the leading edge of technology, the church has incorporated sophisticated microfiche and computer technology into their $8.2 million complex, and duplicates of all data are stored in an underground warehouse twenty miles away. The Mormons excavated this bunker in Little Cottonwood Canyon seven hundred feet beneath the Wasatch Mountains in the 1960s to protect the all-important genealogical resources in the event of nuclear war or other calamity. There are six underground rooms, each two hundred feet long, twenty-five feet wide, and fifteen feet high. The complex is protected by three made-to-order bank vault doors weighing roughly ten tons each. The archive bunkers contain microfilm copies of every page of every book in the downtown genealogy library as well as the church's most prized historical documents, membership lists, and records of financial holdings.

Before using these vast archival resources a Mormon adherent typically will question relatives to provide a pedigree as far back as possible and then travel to Salt Lake to flesh things out. To obtain a vicarious baptism for an ancestor one needs a birthday. To have one's parents or other forebears married by proxy for eternity, a wedding date is needed. Such data is relatively easily obtained for the 1800s and early 1900s through U.S. census records stored at the library. But moving back deeper into time is difficult and requires a search of the library's 160,000-volume collection of name lists and other allied material. The church finances several dozen camera crews who go to small churches in Europe, government ministries in Asia, and libraries in Latin America to microfilm everything from baptismal records to telephone listings. Data collected by these crews to date fill more than 1.5 million rolls of microfilm.

Recently the church has linked computers at hundreds of Mormon meeting-houses, stake centers, and other facilities into a single network hoping to speed the work. Mormon technocrats dream of the day they can use a computer and a telephone modem to call up databases, seek out relatives, and incorporate them into "online pedigree files" which can be taken to the nearest temple for needed ordinances and thus hasten the advent of the millennium.

If genealogy is the most tangible manifestation of LDS beliefs for outsiders, the next important point is that the church elders are convinced the Second Coming is imminent.

Mormons and the Millennium

Above all other considerations Mormonism is a millennarian religion. Thus as the years tick off toward A.D. 2000 the LDS church emphasizes survivalism with increasing ardor. These are, after all, the Latter-days, the final dispensation before the events foretold in the biblical Book of Revelation are at hand.

Today a wide spectrum of believers—far more than just the Mormons—are taken up with the concept of approaching End-times.

Key to such thinking is the underlying concept of Biblical Dispensations, a term commonly used by fundamentalists for numerous historical periods marked by God's intervention in human affairs. Each dispensation serves to move events along en route to the final epoch when great wars will rage, when the

Four Horsemen will ride through blood-red skies belching with radioactive smoke and when the Anti-Christ will come forth in Jerusalem to trigger the final war between the two great armies of Gog and Magog, gnashing their teeth and wailing in anguish on a field called Armageddon.

Mormons are "premillennarians" in that they hold that most of the agonies foretold by John the Revelator, Joseph Smith, and his successors, have already started. Since the first visitation and revelation to Joseph, humanity has been in the Dispensation of the Fulness of Times. The church's work is to establish the appropriate set of moral, social, and political conditions necessary before Jesus Christ can return and usher in the final thousand years.

When those conditions are fulfilled, by performing ordinances for the dead, creating a just society on earth, and meeting other ideals, Mormons look to the return to earth of the City of Enoch and the establishment of Zion in Jackson, Missouri, the holy city from which Joseph Smith and the others were expelled a century and a half ago. One of Joseph's most adamant teachings was that the Mormons are to become residents of the city of Zion, described in the Book of Moses, which was taken up into heaven along with its residents shortly before the Dispensation of the Flood. Zion will return to its earthly resting place (Jackson County, Missouri) at the Second Coming.

Joseph Smith and those who followed him were literal in their translation of biblical chronology and the ensuing LDS cosmology divides time into thousand-year segments leading up to the restoration of Adam-ondi-Ahman, or Zion. This literal timetable is another concept that Mormons share with fundamentalists, including many Baptists. Such proponents hold that in Genesis each of the stages of creation were played out over "days" of one thousand years each. To Mormons, that one thousand years is the duration of a day on the planet where Heavenly Father and Heavenly Mother live.

Thus the literalist Mormon timetable counts forward from the first six "days" of Genesis and the seventh day of a thousand years when God rested after Adam and Eve began their time in Eden. In this literalist chronology, four thousand years or Four Kolob days passed between Adam's death at Adam-ondi-Ahman and Christ's death at Golgotha. Now, as the year A.D. 2,000 looms, the sixth day grows short and the seventh day or the millennium will begin. In anticipation of that event, which will be accompanied by rendings of the earth and wars, the LDS church urges every member family to stockpile a year's supply of food, medicines, and other necessities in their homes to tide them over the inevitable turbulence so they can be ready for that Great New Day Coming.

It is axiomatic that those chosen to walk the earth now at the eve of the millennium are special people indeed. This LDS belief was at work at a ceremony in Brigham Young's Lion House in late 1988 when church president Ezra Taft Benson participated in a ceremony marking the start of a special year for young women. Benson rang the bell that Young had used to summon his harem and female progeny to the dinner table the night he created the Young Ladies Retrenchment Society in 1889, an event which established the youth group now known as the Mutual Improvement Association, or simply Mutual. This young adult group provides a support network that allows church members to keep young adults within the fold as they pass through the difficult years of courtship and pair bonding that often alienate non-Mormon children from their parents. Mutual serves to reinforce the Mormon teachings that a woman's primary role is to produce and nurture children in the home rather than to work outside it, a thought very dear to the heart of the politically arch conservative patriarch.

During a 1987 address broadcast on the church's satellite TV network, Benson sent shock waves through the Mormon world when he said,

> Contrary to conventional wisdom, a mother's calling is in the home, not in the marketplace . . . The Lord clearly defined the roles of mothers and fathers in providing and rearing a righteous posterity . . . It was never intended by the Lord that married women should compete with men in employment . . . Too many mothers work away from home to furnish sweaters and music lessons and trips and fun for their children . . ."

These words from the living prophet led to a wave of job resignations by Mormon women in Utah and subsequent fierce debate about womens' issues. Some church elders, such as Brigham Young University President Jeffrey R. Holland, tried to soften the impact of the rigid pronouncement.

A year later, after Benson rang the bell at the Lion House ceremony, a "sister" named Ardeth G. Kapp, one of the church's leading female executives, delivered a short talk in which she brought tears to Benson's eyes by reading one of the living prophet's own past sermons to another roomful of young women in which Benson explained. "You are choice spirits. Many of you have been held in reserve for almost six thousand years to come forth in this day, at this time, when the temptations, responsibilities and opportunities are at their very greatest."

Some of Mormondom's most bitter foes like to quote a monograph published by the famous entertainment Osmond family in Salt Lake on this loaded topic of Mormon specialness. To such opponents the term "choice spirits" is a racially charged code phrase. The Osmonds wrote in their pamphlet, "A Testimonial of the Church of Jesus Christ of Latter-day Saints":

> We, as Mormons, believe that man is an eternal being, an individual of spiritual substance. We believe that we lived before coming to this earth and that in that premortal state we developed many of the attributes or qualities that our spirits now possess . . .
>
> It also seems natural to us that our heavenly parents would want us, their offspring, to become like them. For that purpose, it was necessary for us to obtain physical bodies of flesh and bone and to become mortal as we are now.
>
> Consequently, our coming to earth at a given time or place is no accident. God does indeed control the coming to earth of the spirits born and reared in heaven . . . he selects the most suitable locations for our birth on earth . . .

At its best, this passage encourages young people to take the moral high ground and live good lives. It helps them cope with such external pressures as evolution-teaching professors and cranky anthropologists who expect answers that conflict with LDS teachings. At its worst, however, this sense of Mormon specialness encourages racism.

An anti-Mormon tract titled *Mormonism, Mama, and Me,* distributed by the Moody Bible Institute, quotes the following passage from *Crusade for Righteousness* by Mormon elder Melvin J. Ballard:

> Of all the thousands of children born today, a certain portion of them went to the Hottentots of South Africa: thousands went to Chinese Mothers: thousands to Negro Mothers; thousands to beautiful white Latter-Day Saints Mothers. Now you cannot tell me that all these spirits were just arbitrarily designated, marked, to go where they did . . . I am convinced it is because of some things they did before they came into this life.

In an essay called "The Way to Perfection," Joseph Fielding Smith, tenth church president, wrote:

> Is it not a reasonable belief, that the Lord would select the choice spirits to come through the better grades of nations? Moreover, is it not reasonable to believe that less worthy spirits would come through less favored lineage? Does this not account in very large part, for the various grades of color and degrees of intelligence we find in the earth?

While such sentiments were not remarkable in the 1950s, today they scream of an intolerance that no longer is acceptable. Just as the practice of polygamy alienated Mormons from other Americans throughout the tumultuous decades of Joseph Smith and Brigham Young, lingering Mormon attitudes toward African-Americans and other ethnic groups has widened the rift between Mormondom and Christendom in recent years.

Even more out of synch with changing American values is the Mormon tenet that if people of color (Canaanites and American Indians who Mormons believe are a biblical tribe called Lamanites) will only adhere to the teachings of Joseph Smith they will fade into white skins. This prophecy about nonwhites is in the *Book of Mormon*:

> And then shall they rejoice: for they shall know that it is a blessing unto them from the hand of God; and their scales of darkness shall begin to fall from their eyes; and many generations shall not pass away among them, save they shall be a white and delightsome people.

(2 Nephi 30:6)

A distinguishing aspect of Mormonism is the strong focus on a heavenly combat between Michael the Archangel and Lucifer. In the Mormon cosmos, Jesus, the son of God, was the firstborn of all creatures. The second born was his brother, Lucifer. Shortly afterwards was born another son of God named Michael. Lucifer wanted God to endow all inhabitants of the spirit world with an inability to do wrong. This outraged our Heavenly Father and his son Jesus as well as the Holy Ghost who decreed that mankind must be given "free agency," the right and responsibility to earn salvation through personal deeds. The great conflict between the forces of darkness and of light was waged over the issue of free agency, and that combat involved all those present in the spirit kingdom. It is a spirit's performance in that testing that determines who comes to earth, when and what color his or her "tabernacle," as Mormons often describe their bodies, is to be. Blacks receive their earthly skin color and other "curses" for siding with Lucifer in the great premortal debate over "agency." That "mark" first appeared when Cain killed Abel.

In a 1960s version of his catechism that since has been revised, Elder McConkie wrote in *Mormon Doctrine,* "Those who were less valiant in pre-existence and who thereby had certain spiritual restrictions imposed upon them during mortality are known to us as the Negroes. Such spirits are sent to earth through the lineage of Cain, the mark put upon him for his rebellion against God and his murder of Abel being a black skin."

In *Journal of Discourses* Brigham Young is quoted as saying, "Shall I tell you the law of God in regard to the African Race? If the White man who belongs to the chosen seed mixes his blood with the seed of Cain, the penalty, under the law of God, is death on the spot. This will always be so." The patriarch is quoted elsewhere in the *Journal* as warning, "Cain slew his brother . . . and the Lord put a mark upon him, which is the flat nose and black skin."

Predictably, as American society confronted the Civil Rights Movement and as people came to accept that blacks had endured hatred and discrimination for far too long, Mormon leaders came under the same pressures as did other American institutions. In the 1960s and 1970s a broad spectrum of issues surfaced to pressure the church toward accepting blacks.

- In Brazil, missionaries spent several million dollars of church funds building a temple for Brazilian converts even though the Brazilians in question have black blood in their veins and thus would be unworthy of the very temple they built.

- In Washington, officials of the Internal Revenue Service suggested that Mormonism's racial policies might justify a suspension of tax-exempt status for the entire church.

- Sports-minded Utah came under increasing condemnation from black athletic groups which threatened to boycott future contests with the church-owned Brigham Young University. Stanford University led the way by cancelling all scheduled sports events with BYU.

- Anti-Mormons seized upon the racism issue to urge boycotts of Mormon goods such as record albums of the Mormon Tabernacle Choir. Church foes used the racism issue to discourage travel to Utah where tourism vies with mining and agriculture as the most important economic asset.

- The National Association for the Advancement of Colored People initiated a raft of lawsuits against Mormon Boy Scout troops charging that church policy was foisting racism on minority members.

Then, in 1978, the prophet of the time, Spencer Kimball, declared in a revelation now published in *Doctrine and Covenants* that all "worthy males" in the church should be eligible for the priesthood. Overnight the onerous contempt for nonwhites vanished, and most Mormons changed their attitudes en masse. Elder McConkie told his brethren to simply ignore everything he, Brigham Young, Joseph Smith, Orson Hyde, Parley Pratt, Joseph Fielding Smith, and all the other law givers had ever said about blacks and accept all races as brothers and sisters. The very authoritarian structure that so appalled critics allowed Mormons quickly to disseminate the word that a radical change had been ordered in racial matters.

Although Mormondom's many enemies are loath to dwell on the subject, nowhere in LDS history, with the exception of polygamy, have the Saints backtracked so dramatically and so forcefully as has been the case of the so-called "Negro Dilemma." Like the rejection of polygamy, however, it has been a difficult transformation, and oftentimes the Saints have failed in implementing it. But the current teaching comes across most clearly indeed, and today, it is the racists and not the tolerant who are the sinners. In Mormon circles today, black people are regarded as spiritual equals to white people.

~~~❖~~~

The way that this reversal in attitudes toward blacks was communicated to an essentially intractable and dogmatic membership in the name of divine communication with the living prophet raises the next important aspect of Mormonism: revelation. Saints believe that they receive ongoing direct communications from a God who remains interested in the ins and outs of human existence. Revelation is central to the core Mormon belief that Joseph Smith restored the church to the way it was when Jesus walked the earth. While Christian tradition holds that those days of spiritualism halted with the ascension of Christ, Mormons teach that they have restored such conditions and that as a result divine revelations are common for "worthy males" who once again are conferred with the same priesthood as that given to Aaron in biblical times.

With such an emphasis on revelation comes a world view quite different from what most religions teach. Angels and devils, elves and kindred ghosts flit about the Mormon universe, a world of doppelgängers, gremlins, and assorted otherworldly beings who aid or harass humanity constantly.

The renowned historian of the American West, Wallace Stegner, tells in his book, *Mormon Country,* of the LDS tradition of the Three Nephites, a legend that dramatically illustrates the church's preoccupation with the spirit world even as it gives a flavor of the sorts of traditions in which Mormons are steeped from childhood onward.

In the *Book of Mormon*'s 3 Nephi passages is the story of how immediately after his ascension from the grave, Jesus appeared to members of a lost tribe called the Nephites. In this New World manifestation the Savior raised a man from the dead, healed the ailing multitudes, and even delivered a sermon on a mountain replete with beatitudes similar to, but not identical to, those he offered above the Sea of Galilee.

In his New World appearance, Jesus gathered twelve Nephite disciples together just as he had collected twelve Jews in the Old World. At the end of his stay in the Americas the Savior asked his twelve Nephite apostles to name their desire. Nine of them asked to be with their Lord from then onwards, but three wanted to remain among humankind, to be present as history unfolded and to offer comfort and advice to the living along the way. Although the names of all twelve Nephite disciples are given early in 3 Nephi, later on the angel Mormon, who dictated that book to his son Moroni, declined to name the three who stayed behind. They are simply known as the Three Nephites, and Mormondom abounds with stories of their comings and goings.

Stegner, who did much of his research during World War II when many of those still active in the church could remember back to Brigham Young, tells a typical story in which a grey-haired stranger rode into a farmyard near Manti, Utah, and asked the owner to put him up for the night.

The farmer, a Mormon bishop named Niels Nielson helped the bedraggled stranger unhitch his weary horses and then called on his wife to bring a bar of soap and clean towels for their house guest. While Mrs. Nielson prepared supper, the grey-headed stranger kicked off his tattered and dust-covered boots and described how he had stopped at many houses earlier that day but had been turned away by each.

The simple fare at the Nielsons' was only bread and milk, but the stranger ate with gusto and then leaned back in his chair to talk of all the places he had visited in the world—Vienna, Budapest, Stockholm, London, New York. He had crossed the American continent hundreds of times, he said. Been everywhere. Twice.

At this the Nielsons chaffed. Clearly the old man with the exhausted team was a blowhard. "Ever been in Kansas," asked Mrs. Nielson. "You ever been to Atchison? I came from there."

The stranger passed his test with flying colors. He reeled off the names of Mrs. Nielson's girlhood friends and regaled her with news of their marriages, the men they had wed, and the children they produced. They laughed into the night until suddenly Mrs. Nielson grabbed at her side and bent over with pain from a new complaint that had set in. "They seem to think I have cancer," she said.

The sad-eyed stranger stood up and smiled at her saying, "You will never have pain there any more." She left and went to the outhouse where she passed something that looked like what she imagined a cancer to be.

The next morning the stranger hitched up his team and rode off with a lunch Mrs. Nielson had prepared. A few minutes later a bunch of Nielson relatives came riding down the same road for a visit, but they told her that they had passed nobody for hours.

Old man Nielson rode down the trail but the stranger's wagon tracks stopped right at his gate. Mrs. Nielson's illness disappeared forever. "Oh, my goodness!" said Mrs. Nielson, " He must have been one of them."

Stegner quotes two Mormon scholars who between them had collected dozens of similar stories from church members all with the same elements of a kindly, white-haired man in tattered clothing visiting a spell, bringing great happiness on his host family and then leaving under mysterious circumstances.

In Mormon country such spiritual beings might pop up at any time. Angels come along to help those pure of spirit through life's valleys, even as demons crop up to dangle temptations. In *Mormon Doctrine,* McConkie simply notes of the Three Nephites, "Unbeknownst to the world, they are continuing their assigned ministry at this time." Elsewhere McConkie notes the Mormon credo that one third of all the spirits that clashed in the great preexistent war between Michael and Lucifer now wander the earth tempting humanity and performing other mischief just as was the case in the days of the early church as described in the New Testament Acts of the Apostles.

❦

Another important tenet is that Mormon prophets receive ongoing, direct revelations from God about all sorts of matters, from tithing, abstaining from strong drink and tobacco, to how to set up business organizations. Ordinary men receive direct revelation in this patriarchal church which teaches that "No man can receive the Holy Ghost without receiving revelations. The Holy Ghost is a revelator," as Joseph Smith taught in his *History of the Church.* A father and husband is taught to seek revelations on important family matters, to listen for what Brigham Young called "one's still inner voice," which speaks from heaven to all worthy Mormon males. A father might tell a child he has had a revelation about which college to attend, whether to enroll in the school band or if a planned marriage is "of God."

This tradition of revelation has created some of the most tragic episodes among those on the excommunicated fringes of Mormondom. There polygamists and other fundamentalists have launched bombings, blood feuds, and murder sprees in the name of divine revelation.

Long aware of the pitfalls of revelation, the church in its official statements emphasizes that while men should indeed listen to their inner voices, only the president of the church, the designated prophet, seer, and revelator is infallible in matters of revealed truth. Reinforcing this doctrine are the myriad signs reading "Follow the Leader" that hang on the walls and bulletin boards of LDS facilities. Elder McConkie warns in his *Mormon Doctrine,* "Revelations come to men just as easily from devils as they do from holy sources. By rebellion and wickedness men may commune with evil spirits, whereas by obedience and righteousness they might have seen angels and had the communion of the Holy Spirit."

But much good comes along with the anguish over revelation. Perhaps the single most successful and salubrious revelation in all Mormon history has been that quoted by Joseph in Section 89 of *Doctrine and Covenants,* the vaunted Word of Wisdom. It is a relatively short revelation and worth quoting in full not only to explain the principle at hand but to give a taste of the syntax, style, and flavor of Joseph's revelations recorded in D & C:

A Word of Wisdom, for the benefit of the council of high priests, assembled in Kirtland, and the church, and also the saints in Zion—

2 To be sent greeting; not by commandment or constraint, but by revelation and the word of wisdom, showing forth the order and will of God in the temporal salvation of all saints in the last days—

3 Given for a principle with promise, adapted to the capacity of the weak and the weakest of all saints who are or can be called saints.

4 Behold, verily, thus saith the Lord unto you: In consequence of evils and designs which do and will exist in the hearts of conspiring men in the last days, I have warned you, and forewarn you, by giving unto you this word of wisdom by revelation—

5 That inasmuch as any man drinketh wine or strong drink among you, behold it is not good, neither meet in the sight of your Father, only in assembling yourselves together to offer up your sacraments before him.

6 And, behold, this should be wine, yea pure wine of the grape of the vine, of your own make.

7 And, again, strong drinks are not for the belly, but for the washing of your bodies.

8 And again, tobacco is not for the body, neither for the belly, and is not good for man, but is an herb for bruises and all sick cattle, to be used with judgment and skill,

9 And again, hot drinks are not for the body or belly.

10 And again, verily I say unto you, all wholesome herbs God hath ordained for the constitution, nature, and use of man—

11 Every herb in the season thereof, and every fruit in the season thereof; all these to be used with prudence and thanksgiving.

12 Yea, flesh also of beasts and of the fowls of the air, I, the Lord, have ordained for the use of man with thanksgiving; nevertheless they are to be used sparingly;

13 And it is pleasing unto me that they should not be used, only in times of winter, or of cold, or famine.

14 All grain is ordained for the use of man and of beasts, to be the staff of life, not only for man but for the beasts of the field, and the fowls of heaven, and all wild animals that run or creep on the earth;

15 And these hath God made for the use of man only in times of famine and excess of hunger.

16 All grain is good for the food of man; as also the fruit of the vine; that which yieldeth fruit, whether in the ground or above the ground—

17 Nevertheless, wheat for man, and corn for the ox, and oats for the horse, and rye for the fowls and for swine, and for all beasts of the field, and barley for all useful animals, and for mild drinks, as also other grain.

18 And all saints who remember to keep and do these sayings, walking in obedience to the commandments, shall receive health in their navel and marrow to their bones;

19 And shall find wisdom and great treasures of knowledge, even hidden treasures;

20 And shall run and not be weary, and shall walk and not faint.

21 And I, the Lord, give unto them a promise, that the destroying angel shall pass by them, as the children of Israel, and not slay them. Amen.

In 1842, Joseph's brother, Hyrum, explained that the "hot drinks" in the revelation meant tea and coffee. As scientific awareness grew, Mormon leaders seized upon caffeine as the offending agent and banned cola drinks and other beverages containing the substance. The Saints became as well-known for their Word of Wisdom against smoking and drinking as for their genealogy department. When Mormons receive communion it is in the form of bread and tap water.

It is important to note however, that the significance of the Word of Wisdom isn't that it was revealed or that it is so obviously true, but that millions of Mormons have adopted it without question.

Mormons practice the Word of Wisdom for the same reason they pay 10 percent of all they earn each year in tithing and send their beloved sons on missions around the world. They do so because they are adherents of an authoritarian church whose unique genius is to keep its members firmly in line through a series of practices such as home visits, temple recommends, Family Home Evenings, and the missions that assure that members are occupied with religious practice nearly every waking hour of the week.

An informal survey by historian Leonard Arrington noted that among members of a "composite" LDS family consisting of a mother, father, and at least two or three children, each family member is required to devote about fourteen hours every week to formal church activities. On Sundays men and boys are required to attend an hour-long priesthood meeting followed by Sunday school for men, women, and children. Sunday activities also include a Sacrament meeting when a communion service is accompanied by impromptu sermons and testimonies of faith from individual members.

Young Men and Young Women (Mutual), the two LDS youth groups, meet for at least two hours every week, usually on Tuesday or Wednesday night. The church requires that families spend Monday nights together participating in organized Family Home Evening activities, singing, praying, acting out skits, doing handicrafts, and other activities designed to bring home Christian principles.

Most weeks a two-hour fireside address via TV from Salt Lake or various ward socials—pancake breakfasts, dances, spaghetti dinners—are held at meeting houses. Those who don't show up likely will find themselves visited by "home teachers," priests and women in the church's Ladies Relief Society who are required to make one call per month on all members. It is all but impossible to be just a "Sunday Mormon."

An additional five hours per week are taken up for students who must attend Mormon religion classes at the seminaries that the church maintains in proximity of public schools or, in areas where Mormons are a minority, at similar sessions in the local ward house. Other church activities, such as required fasting from two meals on the last Sunday of each month—with the proceeds donated to a church revolving welfare fund—and volunteer work on farms, handicraft shops, canneries, or other enterprises designed to help the poor, take still more time.

Mormons keep busy at church-ordered activities for the same reasons they follow the Word of Wisdom, tithe, answer the call to missions, and obey other difficult directives. They do it all because if they don't they face being shunned by their brethren, "disfellowshipped," or even excommunicated by their church and perhaps abandoned by their own kin.

Once the process starts, of course, the Word of Wisdom and other church dictates greatly enhance active Mormons' solidarity with one another just as following dietary laws keeps Orthodox Jews firmly within the pale. Being continually thrust into the company of their fellow Saints by the weekly rounds of meetings, dances, home evenings, home teaching, seminaries, and all the rest, allows little opportunity to stray.

The Saints' rewards for hewing to the straight and narrow are every bit as temporal as spiritual. Economically, abstaining from the costly vices banned by the Word of Wisdom enriches LDS families, and it was particularly important in the pioneer days when the Saints were building their society in the face of competition from whiskey-swilling, tobacco-chewing, coffee-drinking neighbors who paid dearly for their habits. First the abstentious Mormons outsaved their Gentile competitors, and then they outlived them.

The Word of Wisdom, quite simply, makes the Mormons among the healthiest people on earth. Once again demographic data tells the story. In 1988 the death rate from heart disease among Americans as a whole was 323 per 100,000 each year. The Mormon rate was 187 per 100,000. Deaths from liver disease, a major consequence of alcoholism, was 11.2 per 100,000 nationwide but only 5.5 in Utah. Deaths from stokes, often attributed to drinking, smoking, and coffee intake were 64 per 100,000 nationwide but only 39 per 100,000 in Utah.

Surveys of Utah high school students found that youngsters there were about half as likely to succumb to substance abuse. While 92.6 percent of all seniors in American high schools had tried alcohol sometime in their lives, only 55.8 percent of Utah seniors had. Similarly during the same study in 1987 the National Institute for Drug Abuse (NIDA) found that only 11.8 percent of Utah high school seniors had tried a cigarette, compared to 29.3 percent of seniors nationwide.

Particularly dramatic in that NIDA study was that the difference between Utah youth and their fellow students in using drugs not directly mentioned in the Word of Wisdom, such as hallucinogens, cocaine, and speed, was extremely small. Among Utah seniors 4.8 percent had tried cocaine compared to 5.8 percent of American seniors at large. In Utah 7.3 percent of seniors had tried amphetamines compared to 8.3 percent of their peers nationwide. The only time that Utah seniors were clearly on the side of the devil rather than the angels was in the area of LSD use. That NIDA survey found that 4 percent of Utah high school seniors had tried acid compared to only 1.5 percent of high school seniors nationwide.

A research project conducted by the National Institutes of Health dramatically illustrates the degree to which authoritarian elders have enforced rules of behavior on the membership. To teach genetic factors in health, researchers in Salt Lake City have prepared a large computer database listing more than a million Mormons whose genealogy was listed on 250,000 church "family pedigree sheets." Also loaded into the database were state death certificates and the entire Utah Cancer Registry, a listing by the Public Health Service of all cancer victims in the state.

Sorting through the data, the researchers at the Howard Hughes Medical Institute at the University of Utah produced one of the most valuable experimental groups ever available, Utah Mormondom. Because of the Mormon principle of the gathering, most of the well-documented people still live in Utah. The church's genealogical work on its faithful made it possible to isolate how the group's parents and other forebears had died. Widespread adherence to the Word of Wisdom served to weed out confusing side issues associated with substance abuse in other control groups. It was a medical researcher's dream come true.

In the late 1980s, researchers had identified individual Mormons whose potential gene-related health problems were flagged by the computer. The medical researchers warned them that they probably were prone to such diseases as colon cancer, diabetes, or heart trouble. The researchers then offered the selected Mormons free examinations as part of the protocol. Researchers will now track those found at risk to study whether such intervention can save lives.

This early detection of potentially life-threatening conditions is yet another reward for Utah's faithful Saints. It also is a dramatic reminder that Mormonism is unique not just in its beliefs, but in the extent to which rank-and-file members rigorously follow those beliefs, preserved and propagated by the Mormon gerontocracy, those elderly white males who rule a global religious kingdom of seven million Saints whose growth shows no sign of slowing.

Chapter 5

One Temple Square

That the senior Apostle of God has outlived all the other Apostles is a clear indication of the Lord's choice in the matter.

—Official LDS church explanation of succession to church presidency, *Teachings of the Living Prophets*, 1982.

E very Thursday morning the twelve men gather in a corporate board room on the fourth floor of the Mormon Temple in downtown Salt Lake City. Each man dons the soft moccasins, the white robe, the Mason's apron, and shapeless white cap required for the church's most sacred ceremonies. For a few minutes the patriarchs pray for divine guidance in their shared roles of prophets, seers, and revelators as they set about the business of governing what has become one of the world's largest corporate entities. The Church of Jesus Christ of Latter-day Saints is an empire of electronic media properties, movie studios, commercial real estate, agribusiness, computer technology, defense contracting, insurance, and even light manufacturing.

The Thursday meetings follow a day of fasting and while the spry participants kneel, others stand, often leaning on canes, while a few of the oldest sit in high-backed chairs. There are twelve oaken chairs arranged in a crescent before an upholstered altar where the church's all-powerful president and his two counselors sometimes sit facing their brethren, the twelve Mormon apostles. After the prayers, each man removes the temple garments and dons a suit and tie for the business part of the weekly meeting.

On the first Thursday of every month this meeting of the fifteen men who make up the First Presidency and the Quorum of the Twelve Apostles is followed by a session of the First Quorum of the Seventy, and the three-member presiding Bishopric, the slightly younger body of top managers who administer Mor-

105

mondom's day-to-day operations both as a spiritual movement and as a financial and political empire.

Mormons have modeled their organizational structure on the book of Isaiah (54:2) which likened Zion to a tent and its people to the stakes that hold up the tent. "Strengthen thy stakes," urged the prophet Isaiah. A stake is like a diocese in the Catholic or Anglican organization with a membership of around 3,500, although it can be larger. As of the late 1980s there were roughly 1,600 stakes scattered around the world.

At the local church level in other religions is the Mormon ward house or meeting house. Oftentimes there will be several congregations called branches sharing any one ward meeting house by staggering meeting and ceremony hours. There are about 13,000 wards and branches today.

While every "worthy male" is a priest, there is a higher lay clergy, and moving up the order translates itself into making the sort of business contacts and professional allies that allows a man to flourish in the secular sphere and to perhaps seize power in the church later in life. It's an "old boy network" with some very old boys indeed.

The top jobs at the ward level are filled by a bishop and two counselors, patterned after the First Presidency in Salt Lake. A similar trinity composed of a president and two counselors preside over each of the 1,600 stakes, where they control several wards.

These elders or high priests who run the stakes are organized into numerous groups called Seventies, taken from the Gospel of Luke (Chapter 10) in which Christ sent missionaries out in groups of seventy "two and two before his face into every city and place whither he himself would come."

The various Seventies each send a representative to one of several quorums of Seventies which, in turn, send their selected leaders to make up the First Quorum of the Seventy. It is this elite of LDS manhood who run the day-to-day activities of a church that is estimated to have a net worth well in excess of 8 billion dollars.

The ambitious elders of the Seventies Quorum make the decisions while the aging prophets on the Quorum of the Twelve and the First Presidency attend to ceremonial requirements such as dedicating temples, addressing conferences, and debating excommunication orders.

In Mormon parlance the First President holds the full "keys to the kingdom" while his two counselors and the Twelve Apostles hold the same keys in suspension. As a man rises in this patriarchal hierarchy, he is said to acquire additional keys. A boy entering the Aaronic priesthood has the keys to baptism and a few other powers. The next step up, the Melchizedek priesthood, has more keys; a bishop still more; a stake president more, and so on.

This orderly progression underscores what probably is the single most distinctive quality of Mormonism, its authoritarianism. The church is authoritarian by definition due to the fact that much of LDS dogma focuses on revelation from an infallible living prophet, seer, and revelator starting with Joseph Smith and continuing down to the present. Much of the church's appeal in a precarious world is that it boasts a firm leadership with hard and fast answers for the complex questions that divide and confuse the hierarchies of other religions.

Mormondom is a patriarchy ruled with an iron hand by a gerontocracy. These elders admonish followers that they must not criticize those in authority even if the leaders are clearly in the wrong, even if they are senile and seem to be most certainly out of step with the times.

To understand the Mormon gerontocracy, it helps to consider a typical transition such as the one in November of 1985 when the elderly arch-conservative Benson, then 86, assumed the "keys to the kingdom" following the death of 90-year-old Spencer Kimball, one of the plethora of grandchildren of Brigham Young's best friend, Heber Kimball, who had forty-five wives. Benson is the great-grandson of another of Young's friends, also named Ezra Taft Benson.

In keeping with what then was a 141-year-old tradition, as the oldest member, and therefore president of the Quorum of the Twelve Apostles, Benson became the new living prophet without a single dissenting voice. Elder Bruce McConkie, the often-consulted expert on LDS doctrine, explained that members believe that with the last beat of Kimball's dying heart, the "keys to the kingdom" passed along to Benson at the next beat of his heart.

One reason the elders sustain the living, if failing, prophet is that they too are elderly. When Kimball's heart beat its last and Benson's took up the prophet's mantle with the next throb, the average age of the First Presidency was 73 and, as noted, Benson himself was 86. The average age on the Quorum of the Twelve Apostles was 67.8 and the average age of the First Quorum of the Seventy was a ripe 61.5. The youngest General Authority was George P. Lee, 43, the oldest was Joseph Anderson, 96.

Rule by longevity gives Mormon culture its unique stamp. It is a world in which doctrine is handed out to young and old alike with stern warnings about raising questioning voices. Books, films, TV shows, records, and other products of secular culture are either accepted as being somehow "faith promoting" or banned for being "non–faith promoting," the kiss of death in LDS critical circles.

Lawrence Welk is faith promoting. So are Donny and Marie Osmond, Jimmy Stewart, and the Lennon Sisters. The Beatles, Mick Jagger, Kiss, and INXS are non–faith promoting. *Jonathan Livingston Seagull* is faith promoting and sold in the Deseret Bookstore on Temple Square. John Steinbeck or William Faulkner are non–faith promoting because they deal so graphically with human frailty and fly in the face of the Word of Wisdom. Elders have made it clear that they seek a world that asks no questions, voices no doubts, but instead prayerfully follows their "restored" Church of Jesus Christ.

Those who raise questions about the church's startling theology either in public or among their brethren at the meeting house, stake house, or temple, are told to stop doubting under pain of disfellowshipment. Members who are disfellowshipped can no longer receive communion or attend sessions of the priesthood or Ladies Relief until they repent. If questioning Saints don't repent, and soon, they face excommunication. Those who fail to follow the dictates of the Word of Wisdom banning coffee, tea, tobacco, alcohol, and other pleasures also face shunning and sanctions. Such authoritarianism permeates Mormondom.

At the family level, the husband is in charge of obedient children and a submissive wife. The family head, in turn, must bend to the will of his ward's bishop. That bishop gives total obedience to the stake president who likely sits on one of several quorums of Seventies. The lesser quorums of Seventy, in turn, are overseen by the First Quorum of the Seventy which must obey the Quorum of the Twelve. The Twelve Apostles in their Quorum bend their knees to the Prophet and his two counselors on the First Presidency. The First President bends his knee only to God. When he speaks, God speaks. Just as this rigid system brings the church much criticism from within its own ranks and from outsiders, it also brings Mormondom the strength and singleness of purpose that has made it a world force today.

These rigid, right-wing, often intolerant old men seem to be moved by a deep spirituality quite out of keeping with the pragmatic and materialistic personae they present while ruling roughshod over the church's temporal empire and cracking the whip of authority over potentially apostate rank-and-file men and women in the pews. The overwhelming impression is that at least the prophets, seers, and revelators in Mormondom are convinced that they really are in direct and continuing contact with God.

In Mormon parlance, church members are required to "sustain" these prophets everywhere from the church president down to individual stake presidents and bishops. The faithful are taught that only the hierarchy holds the power to appoint leaders and that the congregation at large then is called to "elect" or "sustain" the choices by raising their right hands when called upon at the church's two annual conferences. Other than keeping one's hand down, there is no mechanism for debate.

❦

Mormonism is a right-to-work shop of a religion with a clearly defined temporal agenda and a startling cosmology. Mormons know exactly where they stand on the Equal Rights Amendment, the MX missile, civil rights, abortion, pornography, labor unions, civil defense, taxes, and even whether one should play cards (certainly not!). They learn it from the unbending prophets. And just as Brother Brigham, the original Ezra Taft Benson,

109

and the other Utah pioneers taught them, they make savvy and excellent use of modern technology to draw those inside Mormon circles together as a unified people.

Communicating the words of the living prophets throughout Zion, always a special church goal, never has been as easy as it is today thanks to the efforts of the LDS media conglomerate, Bonneville International Inc., which owns and operates a string of television stations, radio stations, newspapers, magazines, book publishing houses, and other communications facilities worth at least $500 million.

In recent years one of the major tools of Mormon solidarity has been the satellite television dishes that can be seen on the lawns outside stake houses as well as in front of growing numbers of meeting houses and other LDS facilities worldwide. In 1981 Bonneville Satellite began installing broadcast-quality television dishes at church properties to connect all the stakes of the tent called Zion to the mother church via uplinks. By the end of 1988 more than a thousand of the dishes were operational, and in many quadrants far-flung church outposts were able to beam data to Salt Lake as well as to receive it.

The uplink breakthrough was announced dramatically at the church's 1980 general conference in Salt Lake when a gigantic TV set was suspended from the rafters in front of the pulpit where the First Presidency usually sits. The day before, frail and failing Spencer Kimball had flown to Fayette, New York, to make a live broadcast from the farmhouse once owned by Joseph Smith's friend Peter Whitmer, where the LDS church was founded on April 6, 1830. Accompanying Kimball was the prophet's First Counselor, Gordon Hinckley, who noted that they had taken only six hours to cross the territory that it took the Saints thirty-seven years to pass through en route to Salt Lake. Just as the corporate jet made that trip back in history possible, said Hinckley, the TV satellite network would propel the Saints into the future.

The resulting LDS satellite network is by far the largest private closed-circuit TV system in the world with the exception of the telephone companies and news media institutions like Associated Press and Cable Network News. The church buys expensive broadcast time via satellites like Westar to beam speeches by General Authorities, gospel lessons, instructions for tithing settlement sessions, clarifications of doctrinal questions, and other purposes throughout its worldly kingdom. On November 13, 1988, for example, the entire 1989 plan for preaching gospel doctrine was beamed to the far corners of the globe as a Sunday "fireside" session that recipients in outlying stakes videotaped for later use. The movie, in which the teaching plan was presented by Elder Hugh Pinnock of the Seventies, had been produced in the church's sophisticated movie studios in Provo by fifty cast and crew members. For several years communications experts have predicted that the church probably will launch its own satellite sometime in the early 1990s because its heavy use of leased systems approaches the cost of putting up a Mormon-owned one.

Church spokesmen like to boast that the big move into linking Mormondom by satellite dishes is nothing more than the logical extension of Brigham Young's work in the 1870s to wire the State of Deseret with telegraph lines, a network so effective in linking LDS outposts everywhere from Idaho to Arizona that the church later sold it to Western Union. The Mormon telegraph system proved particularly effective in warning polygamists, including church presidents Lorenzo Snow and Joseph F. Smith, to flee when federal authorities approached Salt Lake with warrants for their arrest.

Mormon visionaries anticipate having new ways to pass genealogical data and requests for pedigree information back and forth via the satellite network. By the late 1980s church general conferences were being beamed to at least thirty countries and translated into more than twenty languages via the hookup.

The church values its ability to communicate instantly with its global membership, not only for promoting the faith, but for its potential value when the long-predicted turmoil of the Endtimes arrives. It is estimated that the church has spent upwards of $75 million on the satellite network. The uplink chain, however, amounts to only a small part of the LDS communications bureaucracy, a public relations machine that has reached virtually every American with its TV spots about Mormon family values. This package of ads, which the church calls its "Homefront Series," doesn't explain why the church dwells so on familial values—the drive for fecundity to release the last remaining spirits trapped in preexistence and usher in the millennium—but they provide an excellent door opener for the domestic missionaries whose daunting challenge is to get past the front doors of sales-resistant Americans. The spots serve a general Mormon goal to bring decency into the Gentile world in hopes that a higher moral climate will make potential converts more receptive to their word about the restored Church of Jesus Christ.

Mormon filmmakers also produce feature-length movies that are never seen outside of Saintly circles. These are film versions of the super-secret temple rituals that are recorded in church-owned studios and used in many of the more modern temples in lieu of live actors who have traditionally performed the rites in which they take the roles of God, Adam, Lucifer, Jesus, and others. They lead the faithful through ceremonies of initiation, sealing, and consecration. Before movies were used in the ceremonies, at least four different rooms were needed to provide the required settings. With filmed rituals, however, the audience sits in only one room, which greatly speeds up the rate at which the faithful can perform the vicarious ordinances for the dead. Thus when the church opened its temple outside Washington, D.C., the filmed rituals allowed temple managers to provide ceremonies simultaneously for six separate groups of more than one hundred persons each.

The church also owns two major television stations in the West, KSL-TV in Salt Lake City and KIRO-TV in Seattle, which are operated strictly as businesses in keeping with Federal Communications Commission regulations, which puts a damper on using the properties as church organs. Nevertheless, KSL is a substantial media force in the western United States, with a network of 121 translator stations to beam its signal all across the original State of Deseret, from Idaho to Arizona. The FCC noted in a 1974 renewal of KSL's license that this network gave the station the largest "Area of Dominant Influence" in the United States. By contrast, church-owned KBYU-TV, an educational station at Brigham Young University, carries a variety of church programs including daily sermons from members of the General Authorities. This programming, in turn, often is

Joseph Smith as a young man (Brigham Young University Archives, Provo, Utah)

Brigham Young pictured with the fringe beard he wore in Salt Lake City (Brigham Young University Archives, Provo, Utah)

Left to right: Gordon B. Hinckley, Ezra Taft Benson, and Thomas S. Monson

One Temple Square in Salt Lake City

The interior of the Mormon Tabernacle during a General Conference

The Missionary Training Center in Provo, Utah. The flags indicate which languages are being taught that day at the center.

Mark Hofmann examining his Salamander Letter forgery while in court (*Deseret News* Photo)

Ross LeBaron, the oldest brother of Ervil LeBaron. Ross now lives in Salt Lake in fear that the roving hit squad of his nephews and nieces may seek him out.

Dan Lafferty being led out of the Utah County courthouse during his trial in January of 1985

Ron Lafferty leaving the courthouse during his trial for murder in
April of 1985

The polygamist family of Vickie Singer and Addam Swapp in January of 1988. Addam Swapp is seated on the couch between Heidi Singer-Swapp and Charlotte Singer-Swapp. Vickie Singer is seated to the right of her daughter Charlotte.

Police at Singer-Swapp standoff in Utah

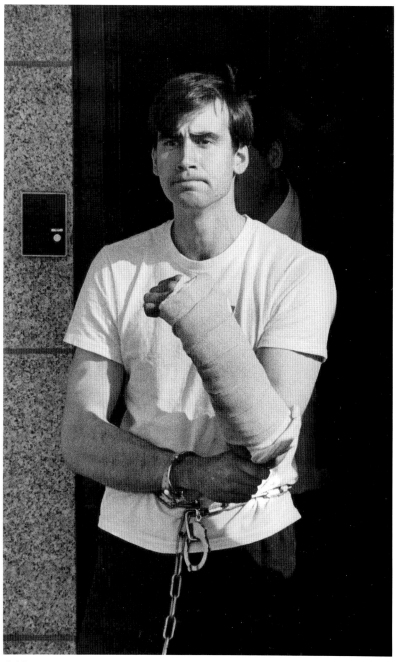

Addam Swapp, who proclaimed himself the One Mighty and Strong, is pictured walking out of the courthouse in Salt Lake still bandaged from the wounds he suffered in the gunfight that took Fred House's life. (*Deseret News* Photo)

Left to right: Vickie Singer, Charlotte Singer-Swapp, and Heidi Singer-Swapp in belly chains a few hours after being arrested in the January 28, 1988 shootout at their armed compound in Kamas, Utah (Tim Kelly Photo)

Jerald and Sandra Tanner outside their house and bookstore on the edge of downtown Salt Lake, where they eagerly hand out copies of the secret temple ritual to any who ask

The Mormon temple at Manti, Utah, which is busy around the clock with baptisms and other temple rituals beamed via the satellite uplinks to meeting houses around the globe.

KSL's roots date back to the dawn of the television age when editors at the church-owned newspaper, *Deseret News,* installed a radio shack on the roof and beamed programs so that Mormon Boy Scouts could use them to test the crystal radios they made as projects for their merit badges. Not long afterwards, a young engineer at the University of Utah, Philo T. Farnsworth, invented the electronic switching device that made television possible. By the time the TV station was operational, the church's investment managers decided to stay in electronics as much for the profits as for the converts. Although the Mormon media portfolio changed with time, throughout the 1970s and 1980s the church owned seven highly profitable radio stations:

KSL-AM in Salt Lake

KIRO-AM/KSEA-FM in Seattle

WRFM-FM in New York City

KMBZ-AM/KMBR-FM in Kansas City

KBIG-FM in Los Angeles

WCLR-FM in Chicago

KAAM-AM/KAFM-FM in Dallas

KOIT-AM/KOIT-FM in San Francisco.

In the 1920s the church obtained a valuable block of Times-Mirror stock by trading a church-owned paper mill in Oregon to Los Angeles newspaper baron Otis Chandler. Today, the Times Mirror Corporation is the owner of the Los Angeles *Times,* the Baltimore *Sun,* New York *Newsday,* and several other publications as well as a string of radio and television stations. Church ownership of this publicly traded stock does not appear to have influenced the Times-Mirror Company's newspapers in Mormondom's favor. One of the most critical newspaper series ever printed about the church ran in 1983 in the Denver *Post,* owned at the time by Times-Mirror. Furthermore, the Los Angeles *Times* itself has run major articles highly critical of the church on such topics as polygamy and blacks in the priesthood.

Nicholas Johnson, the onetime chief of the FCC known for his direct speaking and opposition to concentrated ownership of media outlets, called the church "a media baron of substantial proportions" and in a 1969 Commission Report advised against allowing the purchase of the two Los Angeles radio stations in "a city in which it already has a $20 million interest in the prestigious and dominant Los Angeles *Times.*" Since then the value of that stock has more than tripled.

The church has overcome objections to its electronic empire at almost every turn, as its lawyers and other experts have prevailed and made some very lucrative investments. For example, when the Mormon church bought WRFM-FM in New York in 1966 for only $850,000, FCC Commissioner Robert Bartley objected because a church would become owner of a station with the largest potential listening audience in the United States. He was overruled and today that property is estimated to be worth nearly $20 million. In a 1985 study of Mormon corporate power, John Heinerman and Anson Shupe estimated church media assets at $547 million, including $134 million for the seven radio stations, $178 million for the three television stations and $59 million for the church-owned *Deseret News,* which shares production and distribution facilities with the non-Mormon Salt Lake *Tribune.* That study estimated the value of various movie studios and other film facilities at nearly $30 million and described a publishing operation for church tracts and other literature valued at nearly $15 million.

The church's media empire isn't quite as large as the giants that own stations and publish newspapers like the Chicago *Tribune,* the Washington *Post,* or the Los Angeles *Times,* but its holdings do make it a "media baron" of some significance. Unlike traditional media companies however, the church has the potential to expand simply by raising more money from its tithe-paying membership and snapping up additional newspapers and stations.

The Take from Tithing

Perhaps the most closely held of all the church's business secrets and the most difficult to estimate with confidence is the income pouring in from rank-and-file members and from the global missions. The hierarchy continually presses the faithful to follow the law of tithing by donating one tenth of their gross income to the church. This tithing is still the primary source of Mormon wealth despite the church's many income-producing properties. The tithing ethic underscores yet another unique quality of Mormonism, the LDS strain of materialism.

A widely quoted sermon on tithing by Elder Stephen L. Richards, a former counselor to the First Presidency, observes, "You can tell the sincerity of a man's interest in anything by the way he puts his money into it. Indeed it has been said that the measure of a man's Christianity may be determined by the way he gets and spends his money. It is said that Jesus had more to say about money and property, strange as it may seem, than about any other subject. In sixteen of thirty-eight of His parables money and property are made his theme." Richards added this uniquely LDS homily, "Someone has said, 'God never gives a quit-claim deed, he only grants a leasehold estate, and he who receives the lease must ever return the rental.' " Yet LDS elders refuse to say just how much this "rental" on the quit-claim of Jesus brings them each fiscal year.

Perhaps the best way to estimate income from tithing in the absence of church guidance is to examine some key demographic points and perform some simple multiplication. To isolate tithe payers one must first know what percentage of the church's membership is active and likely to follow to the letter the words of the living prophets. In 1985 Professor James L. Clayton, Dean of the University of Utah Graduate School, estimated that while 68 percent of Utah's 1.5 million residents was Mormon, only between 40 and 45 percent of those Mormons were "active," while between 23 and 28 percent were "inactive," i.e., Jack Mormons. Clayton said that church records on attendance, tithe paying, temple worship, abstinence from stimulants, and other "obvious indicators of Mormon religiousness," indicate that about two-thirds of the active members can be considered "Orthodox Mormons" while about 30 percent of the church members are not only "orthodox" but "authoritarian" adherents, a ratio of zealotry that would bring envy to the Vatican and Billy Graham alike.

Making the risky assumption that Utah Mormondom reflects

the church elsewhere in the United States, it is possible to conclude that about one-third of the nearly two million U.S. Mormon families are at least orthodox if not authoritarian Mormons and therefore likely to pay tithes. If one then makes the barebones assumption that the average LDS tithing family makes at least $15,000 a year, then 660,000 (one-third of two million) tithing families would bring the church an annual income of $990 million or nearly $1 billion. A more conservative assumption of only a quarter of LDS families actually paying tithes would net the church tax-free income of at least $750 million per year. Because median U.S. family income in the late 1980s hovered around $28,000 rather than $15,000, an estimate of between $750 million and $1 billion is conservative enough to serve as a credible minimum for estimating this key income source for the LDS kingdom.

In 1975, a team of Associated Press reporters investigating Mormon business interests in publishing, electronic media, agriculture, real estate, and merchandising estimated that *daily* revenues were around $3 million, with the church's annual return on investments in excess of $1 billion. While these estimates are rough, they make clear that the church receives more than $2 billion per year, a performance that would place it in the top half of the Fortune 500. By the year 2000, church membership will reach twelve to fourteen million, with eighty-four completed temples, 16,000 chapels and 2,600 stakes. At that point, of course, the LDS portfolio will be substantially fatter than it is today.

Rounding out the picture of church wealth are the vast holdings in real estate, both temporal and ecclesiastical. Foremost are the thousands of church stake houses, meeting houses, chapels, and temples with some of the priciest addresses on earth, from downtown Tokyo to Manhattan. These buildings are the responsibility of the Physical Facilities Department, whose team of architects, interior designers, purchasing agents, and other experts oversees the construction of every building throughout Mormondom.

The real estate division of the church conducts brisk dealings in land. Zion's Security Corporation, the church's commercial real estate arm, controls numerous office buildings in Salt Lake including regional headquarters for Kennecott Copper Company, J. C. Penney, Prudential Federal Savings and Loan, and many church facilities. It also owns the sprawling ZCMI (Zion's Cooperative Mercantile Institution) Mall in downtown Salt Lake as well as a controlling interest in the ZCMI store chain. Since 1977 a sister corporation, Beneficial Development Corporation, has taken over development work for the church, and has established several industrial parks in association with private developers in Florida, Arizona, Los Angeles, Hawaii, and Utah.

The known LDS agricultural lands consist of at least 928,000 acres including the 300,000-acre Deseret Ranch near the Disney complex in central Florida and 95,000 acres near Cardston, Alberta, Canada. All together the holdings are larger than the famous King Ranch empire of Texas, which holds 825,000 acres.

Other sources of Mormon wealth are the insurance companies, retail stores, office buildings, and other business properties in Utah and elsewhere. The Beneficial Life Insurance company, founded to provide life insurance to church members, has expanded into a major subsidiary with holdings in the Deseret Mutual Benefit Association, Continental Western Life Insurance Company, the Pacific Heritage Assurance Life Insurance Company, and the Western American Life Insurance Company, which, according to Utah state government records, have a combined value of $94 million.

Mormon historian Leonard Arrington observes in his book *The Mormon Experience,* "In recent years the management of these 'church companies' have been enhanced by the addition of well-trained young Latter-day Saints who have graduated from such business schools as Harvard and Stanford."

The first thing these money managers with their Masters of Business Administration degrees did was to teach the elders the need for concentrating their authority, prompting a move which recent church historians and the LDS faithful call "correlation." While a correlation movement had been underway since the early 1960s to streamline the teaching of the gospels, in the early 1970s the elders converted it into a draconian restructuring of the entire church organization. This new correlation drive was designed to concentrate the church's middle management power in the all-male priesthood whose role had been diminished by various other groups such as Young Women's Mutual Improvement Association and the Ladies Relief Society, who had assumed many of the responsibilities once handled by priests. The new wave of LDS MBAs noted that there was substantial overlapping by groups that didn't want to relinquish whatever responsibilities each had gleaned over years of evolution. For example, both priesthood quorums and Ladies Relief groups published lesson manuals for Primary, as the church calls its Sunday school for the very young. Both groups had developed offices to handle the same tasks and neither was willing to abandon its prerogatives. More importantly, both groups took their annual budgets to the General Authorities, essentially doubling their work in this one area of responsibility. With this pattern repeating itself day in and day out in an ever-growing church bureaucracy, the top Mormon managers were bogged down in minutiae when they should have been dealing with the bigger issues that required their attention.

A series of correlation committees working in the 1970s recast Mormondom into the form it holds today. This restructuring led to profound changes in how the church's vast wealth was managed, invested, and distributed. Correlation also brought sweeping changes to the most visible of church practices.

Correlation leaders took advantage of a nationwide energy crisis brought on by the Arab oil embargo of 1974 to announce that the Mormons would save money by changing their meeting schedules to be more energy efficient and more family oriented at the same time. Henceforth, instead of driving to the meeting house several nights a week for various groups and quorums, church members would devote Sundays to three-hour "block" sessions where the activities once spread over the week would be held all at once.

To continue energy savings and to further foster emphasis on the family, and therefore male primacy, church members were instructed to schedule a Family Home Evening every Monday in which mother, father, and children would gather for two hours of prescribed prayer and family activities. These evenings are laid out in an annual book passed along to the faithful as part of another correlation project to standardize the church year so that the same readings from biblical sources and the Mormon canon are taken up on the same day churchwide.

This strategy has allowed the church to guide its membership through a reading of the complete Mormon canon—The *Book of Mormon, Doctrine and Covenants, Pearl of Great Price* and the King James Bible—at three "age levels," children, youth, and adults. Until then the scripture readings had been left to local discretion. Now each fall elders in Utah lay out the coming year's lesson plans and beam them across the face of worldwide Mormondom by closed-circuit satellite broadcast.

The other large change in daily church life brought about by correlation was the institutionalization of the home teaching visits that are made to every LDS household once each month by representatives of the priesthood quorum and by women from Ladies Relief. The visiting teacher policy has helped keep church members from straying because now when a Saint's faith starts to slip a brother or sister appears at the door to bolster his or her ardor. Some of the church's foes view this reenforcement of members by members as a practice that qualifies the church as a religious cult. Whatever the merit of the charges of cultism by the church's enemies, the Home Teaching does produce a more stable membership and a more robust tithing by all concerned.

In the 1970s, the church experienced phenomenal growth as a result of the streamlining and reorganization brought about by the professional managers hired to run the church's business interests. The concomitant correlation movement restructured not just everyday Mormon practices, but actually played a role in reversing the church's position on "worthy" blacks. Mormons have reversed themselves twice on matters of long-held dogma in the wake of Gentile pressures. The first time, Wilford Woodruff's 1890 revelation banning polygamy, is known among Mormons as the "Great Accommodation," Spencer Kimball's reaching out to blacks in 1978 likewise is called the "Second Great Accommodation."

Clearly, the way to bring about change in Mormon inner circles is to convince the ruling Saints that they have too much to lose from the world outside unless they act. For all their insularity and for all they have suffered in persecution from those outside Mormondom, the Saints want very much to be part of the world that surrounds them.

To that end of seeking acceptance in Gentile circles Mormons work mightily in the political arena to ensure that the United States becomes a country that shares their views about matters of morality and policy and thus will be less likely to discriminate and persecute Mormondom. They do this largely through sending their best and brightest out into the outside world to look after Mormon interests while working alongside their Gentile brethren. These secular Saints often move into key government jobs, top corporate posts and other influential positions. They commonly move into the Gentile world in groups rather than alone, and they often later bring in more fellow Saints to help once they get established. Sometimes these expatriated patriarchs speak of themselves with irony as The Sisterhood.

Chapter 6

The Sisterhood

*The church, its teachings, Mormon culture and tradition—
all that was at the core of my existence and around which
my life revolved. That I was Mormon was my first and
most significant identification. Mormon first, human being
second. American, wife, mother—everything else sprang
from that firm center.*

—Excommunicated suburban Washington, D.C.,
Equal Rights Amendment advocate Sonia Johnson
in *From Housewife to Heretic*, 1983

The proud page-one headline in the church's own daily newspaper, the *Deseret News,* on the eve of George Bush's inau-
guration as the forty-first president of the United States marked
one of the finest hours for Mormondom in American history:

Utahns a vital part of Bush team
Will advise him on foreign
U.S. policy, polish image

Even before taking the oath of office, Bush had named Brent
Scowcroft, Roger Porter, and Steve Studdert, all Mormons, to
top White House posts in foreign affairs, domestic policy, and
political scheduling. The "Sisterhood" was overjoyed. Never before had a president chosen Saints for so many key posts on his
executive staff.

Bush's selection meant much to those in LDS circles who long
had striven to win acceptance for Mormons as members of just
another religious body and not a cult with plural wives, wild-
eyed patriarchs, and tithe-obsessed zealots. Part of the patriarchs' strategy for gaining acceptance has been for the church
to send its best men out into the Gentile world to seek positions

of leadership. Mormon elders know that as their members become leaders of society, the church gains greater acceptance.

Scowcroft, Porter, and Studdert were not the first Mormons ever to win top government jobs or even cabinet posts. The 1983 edition of the church *Almanac* devoted a special section to members with top federal careers and noted that among still-living church members were seven former cabinet officers, four sub-cabinet officers, and four ambassadors.

Ezra Taft Benson had been President Eisenhower's agriculture secretary and David Kennedy, a Mormon and a Chicago banker, had been Richard Nixon's treasury secretary before going on to serve as the church's roving ambassador pressing for Mormon needs with leaders all across the globe. Terrell Bell, Utah's state education superintendent, served four controversial years as Ronald Reagan's education secretary where he supported Mormon family values by diminishing the federal role in schools and pressing for parents' rights to censor schoolbooks.

While Scowcroft, Porter, and Studdert were the most visible Mormons running the government as the Bush administration began, they were only three among hundreds, perhaps thousands, of D.C. Saints with influential positions in the federal government. Furthermore, similar Mormon "knots" thrive at the state, county, and local levels throughout the country. The same claim could be made for groups of Catholics, Baptists, or even Buddhists with government jobs, but among Saints there is a difference. With their tradition of gathering together, of dedicating much private time to church activities and of socializing only with other Mormons, Saints in civil service seem more powerful among their co-workers than their numbers might indicate.

Mormons with government posts are part of a growing LDS establishment that extends from the ward house to the White House. In and around the nation's capital with its eleven stakes and a cavernous Mormon Temple dominating the suburban Maryland skyline, the LDS population has enjoyed substantial growth since the temple was consecrated and set aside from Gentile visits in 1974. At the end of the 1980s, the church announced that 200,000 members from throughout the eastern United States were being served by the Washington Temple, with roughly 50,000 Saints concentrated in the Washington area. The resulting power elite—a tightly knit, almost exclusively white male assemblage of jurists, journalists, FBI agents, CIA executives, Interior Department managers, Pentagon brass, corporation chiefs, and other Mormons of stature, labors for respectability and acceptance while looking out for LDS interests in the top councils of government.

In his church-sanctioned biography, *Marriott,* J. Willard Marriott, Sr., the hotel and fast food tycoon and likely the richest Mormon in history, recalled how he moved to Washington and opened his first Hot Shoppe restaurant under the sponsorship of Senator Reed Smoot, who had been admitted grudgingly to the World's Most Exclusive Club and went on to serve as chairman of the Senate Finance Committee and to become a trusted friend of Presidents Calvin Coolidge and Herbert Hoover. Marriott told his biographer that Smoot had brought a "knot" of Mormons to Washington and "most of them had minor government jobs . . . were putting themselves through George Washington Law School."

By sticking together, lending one another money, providing moral support, and helping lobby for changes in the rules and regulations of government, this early knot of Mormons prospered then as it does today. In Marriott's case, he fondly recalled, fellow Saints not only lent him money to build the first of his thousands of restaurants, but other churchmen got certain zoning laws changed so he could open the nation's first drive-in restaurants with curbside service. Senator Smoot, Marriott recalled, happened to be chairman of the Senate Committee on Public Buildings in the District of Columbia.

Larry Bush, an official at the Agriculture Department and an estranged member of this "Mormon Mafia," explained in a 1981 interview that today's Washington Saints refer to themselves, among themselves, as a "Sisterhood." It's a term with roots at the CIA where the church is particularly well represented. CIA agents also refer to one another as "sisters." When a reporter for *Harper's* magazine in 1980 asked Wendell Ashton, the church's chief spokesman at the time, why so many Mormons were "attracted to the CIA," Ashton responded cryptically, "The question is 'Are our young men attracted to the CIA or is the CIA attracted to them?' "

George Bush learned to appreciate the Mormon sisterhood within the larger CIA sisterhood in 1974 when he served as director of Central Intelligence. At that time he worked closely with Scowcroft at the Ford White House, and the two men became friends. For Scowcroft the Bush cabinet-level appointment capped a long career serving those at the seat of power from Richard Nixon to Gerald Ford and Ronald Reagan.

Scowcroft had proven to be of pivotal value to LDS interests during the Reagan administration when he headed a blue-ribbon White House panel that persuaded the U.S. government to scrap a church-opposed Pentagon plan to base the new generation of MX long-range nuclear missiles in Utah. The church had taken a rare public stance in opposition to a defense project when the MX scheme was surfaced because the underlying philosophy was to locate hundreds of the missiles scattered throughout Utah and Nevada in such a way that would have forced the Soviets to drench the two states with warheads in order to nullify the U.S. threat.

The plan had been to keep a few hundred MX missiles continually moving about the complex of thousands of possible launch sites so that the Soviets would have to expend much of their arsenal to destroy all possible launch sites. Virtually all of Utah's nonmountainous terrain would have been taken up by the project. At one point Guy Hecker, the air force general in charge of explaining the MX project to people in Utah and Nevada, acknowledged that the Pentagon envisioned the two sparsely populated states serving as a "nuclear sponge" by drawing Soviet missiles that might otherwise rain down on the rest of America.

With its teaching that the cataclysmic Endtimes may be approaching as rapidly as the turn of the twentieth century, Mormondom was even less willing than was the rest of America to play decoy to the Soviet nuclear arsenal. An irradiated Zion would hardly be a suitable city of Enoch as the church long has dreamed Utah will become when the current dispensation draws to a close.

The Scowcroft Commission found a ready solution that recommended basing the MX missiles in existing Minuteman guided missile launch silos at Warren Air Force Base outside Cheyenne,

Wyoming. Thus the Pentagon got a missile force of 100 modern missiles, and One Temple Square was spared becoming the site of the new American ground zero. Brother Scowcroft had served both the Pentagon and Zion well and might easily be permitted an occasional glass of wine or a manly jolt of java from time to time, two small vices he often acknowledged.

One floor above Scowcroft's cramped office in the White House basement, Roger Blaine Porter occupied the office of the President's Assistant for Domestic and Economic Policy. Porter, a graduate of Oxford and Harvard as well as BYU, found his way into the national policy elite as a protégé of non-Mormon William Seidman, who served as head of the Federal Deposit Insurance Corporation, the nation's chief banking regulator, when the savings and loan scandal struck early in the Bush administration. Seidman, in turn, had gained access to the centers of power in the mid-1960s when he served as financial adviser to Michigan's Governor George Romney, a life-long Mormon who lost the 1968 Republican presidential nomination to Richard Nixon. Other notable Seidman protégés include Secretary of State James Baker and Paul Volcker, the former Federal Reserve Chairman.

The third top Mormon as Bush took office, Studdert, a former law officer and public relations expert, won the president's confidence while serving as an "advance man" in the Ford White House arranging presidential trips to maximize the political impact of each visit. As the campaign aid in charge of the Bush "image" during the 1988 election season, Studdert was credited with such major themes as the famous call for a "kinder, gentler nation," a slogan that Mormon scholars were quick to attribute to Joseph Smith. *Utah Holiday* magazine noted in its April 1989 issue that *Doctrine and Covenants* Section 121 includes Joseph Smith's teaching that leaders should gain power "only by persuasion, by long-suffering, by GENTLENESS and meekness, and by love unfeigned; by KINDNESS and pure knowledge which shall greatly enlarge the soul without hypocrisy and without guile." The passage is frequently quoted at priesthood quorums when questions are raised about how elected Mormons should act while in office.

As the Bush administration got under way the church announced the results of its annual worldwide census showing 6,650,000 people on the membership rolls with nearly four million of them in the United States. Thus as listed in the 1988 *Yearbook of American and Canadian Churches,* the Church of Jesus Christ of Latter-day Saints greatly outnumbered the 2.8 million members in Bush's own Episcopalian church not to mention the Presbyterians (3 million), all Pentecostal sects combined (3.3 million), the American Lutheran Church (2.3 million), Missouri Synod Lutheran Church (2.6 million), and all Jewish congregations in the United States (3.5 million combined).

On the other hand, while there never has been a Mormon president or a Mormon vice president, no fewer than twelve American presidents have claimed membership in Bush's Episcopalian church, a statistic that one should keep in mind as a ready antidote for overestimating either the political clout of Mormondom or the importance of religion in political life.

While the inaugural edition of the *Church News,* a weekly supplement to the *Deseret News* distributed throughout English-speaking Mormondom, proudly noted that no fewer than 11 church members had been elected to Congress, it also reported that 139 Catholics had been elected, 76 Methodists, 63 Episcopalians, 55 Baptists, 51 Presbyterians, and 26 Lutherans.

Nonetheless, with just eleven members of Congress, Mormons have succeeded far beyond many other constituencies in bringing federal contracts their way whether in Utah or elsewhere. Over the past four decades, Utah lawmakers succeeded in bringing intense military activity to the Valley of the Great Salt Lake. In 1987, nearly $2 billion in Pentagon money was spent in Utah and more than four hundred of the state's companies, owned largely by Mormons, had Pentagon contracts. The state of fewer than three million people ranked fourth among all states in defense spending per $1,000 of personal income. But, as always, such successes came not because Mormons were voted into power but because a sophisticated network of "old boys" exerted influence on national affairs far beyond their numbers.

This will change, of course, as LDS membership grows and Mormons gain wider political acceptance, but meanwhile the disparity between church membership and offices held by members will motivate the Sisterhood to find back-channel means to foster LDS interests, as have other minorities whose political power does not reflect their strength in numbers.

❦

Whether Scowcroft was acting as a Saint or patriot, his role in the MX decision marked a case of Mormon interests being served by the secular activities of one of the faithful. There have been other times, however, when the Sisterhood flexed its muscles to far less acclaim. Here the best example of Mormon clout changing the face of America is the case of Sonia Johnson and the ERA.

For Sister Johnson, a tiny woman with laughing eyes and a love of playing hymns on the organ at the meeting house, the wrath of the patriarchs began raining down in 1977 when she timidly showed up at the Sterling, Virginia, ward of the McLean stake with a pin reading "Another MORMON for ERA."

Her memoir, *From Heretic to Housewife,* has been criticized by Mormon elders for making inaccurate and emotional charges about how the church worked to keep the U.S. from ratifying the controversial amendment. The elders openly opposed the ERA to the point that the Quorum of the Twelve Apostles ordered all LDS members serving in Congress to vote against the measure. Mormon defenders say that any church has the right to fight against public policy it judges immoral, be it Catholic bishops crusading against abortion or Jews railing against a president's decision to visit a Nazi cemetery.

While elders can challenge Johnson's interpretation of their motives and the propriety of their actions, nobody can question her personal anguish as she lost her husband of twenty years, was forcibly expelled from a church she revered, and was alienated from friends, children, and family for refusing to obey the words of the living prophet from One Temple Square. In retrospect her rapid descent from faithful housewife and Women's Relief leader to apostate enemy is clearly understandable. For Mormons, the Equal Rights Amendment debate aims at the heart not only of a century and a half of stern patriarchal rule

127

but at the recent restructuring of the church which established today's organization and power structure by revitalizing the all-male priesthood.

Toward that end, the Council of the Twelve Apostles decided early on that the ERA was contrary to the church's teachings about marriage and the family. The council ordered its legal experts to map a strategy to defeat the amendment. Leading the LDS lawyers in this project was another powerful "Sister," BYU law professor Rex E. Lee, who after Johnson's excommunication went on to become Solicitor General of the United States during the Reagan administration.

Not only was Johnson's cause threatening to LDS circles, but she waged her angry campaign for equal rights with a zeal and cunning gusto that flabbergasted the hierarchy and quickly forced their hand. Less than eighteen months after she first walked into the Mormon service with her ERA pin, Johnson stood in Temple Square during a general conference of the entire church. She looked on as horrified elders watched a hired plane fly overhead with the scalding banner that perhaps only a Mormon can fully grasp which read "Mother in Heaven Loves Mormons for ERA."

Among the more startling aspects of LDS dogma is the concept of a sexually active godhead, a Heavenly Father married to a Heavenly Mother. Calling attention to the less orthodox of Mormon tenets helped Johnson win favor among Gentiles, but it enraged church elders.

In the course of the ensuing fight over women's rights in the Mormon church, much was revealed about how the Sisterhood operates and how ordinary Mormons struggle with such contemporary issues as feminism while surrounded by unsympathetic Gentiles quick both to idolize a Sonia Johnson for her obvious courage and to condemn the patriarchs. A predictably vicious cycle is set into motion. Knowing it cannot win public acceptance, the LDS hierarchy operates in secret and cracks the whip hard when rank-and-file members like Johnson stray. The unforgiving stance reinforces Gentile suspicions and the church becomes even more authoritarian in its dealings. The Sonia Johnsons of the Mormon world often are ground up in the process.

Johnson recalls that she made her decision to oppose the

church on ERA in April of 1977 when Mormon elder James Fletcher, later to become head of the National Aeronautics and Space Administration (NASA), visited the Sterling ward house to read the letter from the Twelve Apostles ordering Saints to oppose the amendment. That letter was sent to Mormon lawmakers on Capital Hill, Saints on the White House staff, at CIA headquarters, in the FBI, and throughout the federal bureaucracy. It led to an expertly organized LDS effort in a half dozen states from Florida to Illinois. The support it marshalled against the ERA ultimately killed its chances for ratification.

Much of Johnson's work against the church focused news media attention on the often hidden role of Mormon elders in setting up anti-Era demonstrations and in working through the Sisterhood to oppose the amendment. When it appeared that a pro-ERA measure extending the time allotted for ratification might actually clear a U.S. Senate committee and reach the floor for a vote, LDS Senator Orrin Hatch (R., Utah) vowed to stage a filibuster to head off the Senate vote on extension. Sonia Johnson called a press conference and pledged to fast as long as Hatch filibustered. If he didn't stop stalling, she promised, the church would have to confront the specter of a Mormon housewife starving to death on the Senate steps.

The bill failed to clear the subcommittee, however, and the Hatch-Johnson confrontation was averted, but the stage was set for her excommunication. She had used her grasp of church traditions to threaten a fast, which is a common practice among the LDS faithful seeking divine guidance. When George Romney decided to run for the presidency, for example, he had abstained from food and drink for three days.

Johnson then devoted the next few months to publicizing documents written by the church's political arm, the Special Affairs Committee in Salt Lake, organizing such anti-ERA events as visits of busloads of Mormon women to walk the statehouse halls buttonholing lawmakers and urging them to reject the amendment. At one point Johnson disclosed that the de facto leader of the church, Gordon Hinckley, chief counselor to badly ailing President Spencer Kimball, had made a secret trip to Washington to coordinate anti-ERA work both on Capitol Hill and in neighboring Virginia.

Mormon state and ward organizations along with the various Women's Relief groups in several states organized anti-Era fundraising drives and conducted phone operations using church facilities to call voters in Florida and Nevada. A so-called "phone tree" system run by the Women's Relief Society for communicating in emergencies was used to fight the ERA in many areas. The Mormons have created an impressive apparatus for home visits, emergency preparedness mobilizations, TV dish hook-ups, and other resources that make political organizing a snap.

Money solicited by phone from Mormons in California financed the fight in Florida. As the ERA crusade gained steam, pro-amendment forces won ratification in thirty-five of the thirty-eight needed states and seemed on the verge of victory, prompting even greater LDS activity, which came quickly and effectively. Church officials viewed the amendment as a test of their ability to play a role in public debate. Their opponents countered with charges that the church had made donations to sympathizers in excess of legal limits and had concealed the fact that many of the "local housewives" lobbying various state legislatures actually were Mormon women bussed in from outside.

In response to Johnson's headline-grabbing charges, the news media asked the church for comment and was referred to her bishop, Jeffrey Willis, the longtime CIA personnel director. While no stranger to public controversy, Willis was forced by the Johnson case to face the cameras personally rather than relying on CIA public relations staff. His comments revealed that many other CIA men were ward members, and that he had sought public relations advice from an old friend, newspaper columnist Jack Anderson, himself a member of the Silver Spring, Maryland, ward.

The November day in 1979 when Johnson was summoned to the Sterling ward house to hear the charges filed against her for excommunication, a crowd of roughly one hundred ERA supporters gathered in the parking lot under a banner which carried the entire text of the amendment causing all the fuss:

Equality of rights under the law shall not be denied or abridged by the United States or by any state on account of sex.

Reporters from the major TV networks and a number of daily newspapers also were on hand as Johnson entered the building to hear and debate charges against her.

LaMar Petersen, a member of the advisory board of editors for the Mormon History Association, noted in a 1978 essay in *The Humanist* that,

> In an age when many churches have abandoned the ancient practice of excommunicating its dissidents, the Mormon Church is still using the purgatorial system of church courts to determine the guilt or innocence of some of its members . . . The court is presided over by a Presidency of three men, plus a High Council of twelve, all fifteen being High Priests . . . Six are appointed to defend the accused against insult of injury, six to sit as jurors in concert with the entire court, and one to act as attorney for the defense, presumably without prejudice. The court opens and closes with a prayer. Witnesses may appear singly and speak briefly for or against the accused; each must leave the court immediately upon completing his testimony. Throughout the trial the defendant may not have at his side his own attorney, secretary, tape recorder, supporting relative, or friend, nor is he permitted to have a transcript of the trial for his own files at the conclusion. At the onset of the trial he is not provided with a bill of particulars beyond the general charge . . ."

Johnson's trial was held in the church's Oakton Stake Center in the Washington suburbs. The building's windows were covered with black paper to prevent TV crews from filming snatches of what went on inside as witnesses filed in and out. A building guard, a retired FBI agent whom Johnson called the Avenging Angel, prevented media representatives from entering the building. To this day there is little agreement about what actually happened inside.

Johnson said that she asked for mercy and emphasized her lifelong affiliation and faith. She later recalled telling her bishop and the CIA's recruiting chief:

> Jeff, I pay a full tithing and have all my life. I'm the ward organist and spend many extra hours practicing alone and with the choir. I teach the cultural refinement lesson in Relief Society, I am a visiting teacher, I attend church, we hold family

home evenings, I attend the temple. If you're going to excommunicate everybody in the ward who is doing this much or less, you won't have anybody left in the congregation when you're through.

Even though she tithed, visited other Saints as a home teacher, and kept a two-year supply of food and other necessities in the basement in keeping with church survivalism practices, Johnson wasn't like most other ward members. She was a feminist in a decidedly antifeminist world. She later joked that Mormons for ERA was as oxymoronic as Astronauts for a Flat Earth. When she taught lessons, such as one lecture inspired by the Chinese practice of binding the feet of baby girls, at the Relief Society "cultural refinement" lesson, her fellow women complained to Bishop Willis that such talks were non–faith promoting and he asked Johnson to find other topics. Mormon women largely proved every bit as antifeminist as their men. By her own account, Johnson was able to enlist fewer than a dozen women in the entire McLean stake despite the enormous favorable publicity she received.

Even as her painful case served to flush out rare glimpses of how the LDS network operates in Gentile circles, it also underscored that the Saints, men and women alike, do indeed stick together when confronted with an unfriendly outside world. In a gripping lament in her memoir, Johnson predicted that Mormon male dominance will prevail far into the future because it is the very essence of the faith:

> In our patriarchal world, we are all taught—whether we like to think we are or not—that God, being male, values maleness much more than he values femaleness, that God and men are in an Old Boys' Club together, with God as president, where they have special understandings, figurative secret handshakes, passwords. God will stand behind the men, he will uphold them in all they do because he and they, being men and having frequent, very male, very important business dealings, know what they know, a large part of which is that women must be made to understand that females are forever outside their charmed circle, forever consigned to the fringes of opportunity and power. Forever second-best, and a poor second at that. I had been taught as we all have, not in so many words

but nonetheless forcefully, that in order to propitiate God, women must propitiate men. After all, God won't like us if we don't please those nearest his heart, if we don't treat his cronies well.

And thus is stated, perhaps as bitterly as it possibly can be stated by a heartbroken Mormon woman, the essential operating principle of the Sisterhood: men rule Mormondom and they rule as a tightly knit unit (an "Old Boys' Club") that is the Saints' last line of defense against an unfriendly world today just as much as it was a century ago.

Johnson's bold actions did more to reinforce public condemnation of the church proper than it did to promote the amendment she so diligently sought. When she was tried for heresy, Johnson's three male Mormon judges in the impeachment court weren't concerned just about stopping ERA, they wanted to remove a source of embarrassment from their ranks who was endangering their status quo in the national capital area. "Every Sunday is Father's Day in this world," Johnson told the Sterling ward during one 1979 sacrament meeting shortly before being excommunicated for "evil speaking of the Lord's anointed," and for violating a temple oath (the "law of consecration") to devote her life to supporting the church.

In the subsequent letter of excommunication Willis wrote, "You testified that you believe and have publicly stated that our society, specifically including church leaders, has a savage misogyny when, in fact, it is church doctrine that exaltation can be gained only through the love that results in the eternal bonding of man and woman."

A member making such charges against her own elders, he noted, harms the church and undermines efforts to operate according to the longtime teachings of Mormondom by shaking the resolve of the faithful and making it ever more difficult to evangelize Gentiles who are alienated from Mormonism by the debate over ERA. The bishop told Johnson that her attacks against the elders had "damaged such church programs as temple work, the welfare program, family home evening, genealogy and family preparedness (food storage)," recalled Johnson's longtime associate and Mormon reporter/author Linda Sillitoe in a 1980 *Utah Holiday* magazine article about the closed trial.

133

While most of the charges raised in that closed session apparently were as nebulous as those cited by Sillitoe, the strongest condemnation against Johnson proved to be a charge that she had attacked what is perhaps the most important asset that Mormons have in their quest to spread the Sisterhood across the globe—the Missionaries.

In a videotaped speech to a National Organization of Women meeting in Kalispell, Montana, Johnson had said,

> The leaders of the Mormon church are somewhat isolated in Utah. Those who are directing this anti-ERA activity need a taste of the consequences of their behavior, and one of the things everyone can do is write and call church headquarters and say, "I am outraged that the Mormons are working against my equal rights, and if your missionaries ever come to my door, I wouldn't consider letting them in."

At that moment, Johnson, the woman who had survived after flying her "Mother in Heaven" banner above Temple Square and after challenging fellow Mormon Senator Hatch to a fasting contest on the grounds of the U.S. Capitol itself, had gone too far. She had threatened the long arm of Mormondom, those 35,000 young men and a few young women whose strength and resolve are the hope of the future and the glue that binds the Sisterhood together in the present.

Chapter 7

Missionary Mormons

After these things the Lord appointed other seventy also, and sent them two and two before his face into every city and place whither he himself would come. Therefore said he unto them, the harvest truly is great, but the laborers are few . . . I send you forth as lambs among wolves. Carry neither purse, nor scrip, nor shoes and salute no man by the way

—Luke (10:1–4)

Elder Stark and his "senior companion," Elder Jesperson, both were 19 years old in late 1988 when they rang my doorbell in the Denver suburbs on a mission from God. They wore black wingtip shoes, white short-sleeved shirts, narrow dark ties and dress slacks. Each had a black nametag pinned on the starched white shirt over his heart reading "Church of Jesus Christ of Latter-day Saints."

Such young people are perhaps the best-known manifestation to much of the world of the Mormon church. Dressed in their distinctive garb, LDS missionaries likely have knocked on every door in America at least once. What is less well-known, however, is that these guileless youngsters are executing the most successful door-to-door sales campaign in world history. It is a campaign in which every move is thought out, preplanned, and rehearsed from first knock at the door to first tithing payment. It is a sales pitch refined for more than a century and executed by a sales force trained for years before they hit the field, an army of committed sellers flush with energy and the promise of youth, having the time of their lives going "two by two" in a way that Luke's gospel hardly anticipated. They may get in few doors, and when they do, they may make few sales, but each sale means another tithe-paying convert joins the ranks.

Fresh from weeks of sales training and indoctrination at the church's Mission Training Center in Provo, Elder Jesperson carried a zippered leather "scripture bundle" of the LDS cannon (*Book of Mormon, Doctrine and Covenants, Pearl of Great Price* and King James Bible). Young Stark grasped a similar black leather binder that he had filled a few weeks earlier, during his MTC indoctrination classes, with drawings and lessons about the dispensations, eternal progression, spirit babies, celestial marriage, and the rest of the LDS basics. One set of painstakingly rendered drawings traced the dispensations from Adam and the Jewish lawgivers ("Dispensation of the Law") through Jesus (the "Dispensation of the Meridian of Times") to Joseph Smith (the "Dispensation of the Fulness of Times") and beyond to the "Dispensation of the Millennium" and the rest of the LDS Armageddon scenario. He had rendered other sketches showing the realm of spirit babies yearning for bodies, and yet others outlining the sundry LDS levels of the hereafter, the celestial, the terrestrial and the telestial realms.

One of the first things the two missionaries assured me was that even the least of these three Mormon hereafters, the telestial, was so much better than life on earth that a Gentile who could see "through the veil" might opt for suicide just to get there posthaste. Devout Mormons, of course, have every reason to stay on earth and work toward "exaltation" in the Celestial Kingdom where they will be Gods in their own right or, at the very least, they can work on earth toward the magnificent realm called the terrestrial in the special Mormon meaning of the term where joyous physical, sexual, sensual life goes on and on without end.

They asked me to imagine that the word of God is a large mirror hanging on the wall reflecting the true church as created by the original twelve apostles. About the time of the second Pope of Rome that mirror fell to the floor and shattered into many pieces. Each piece reflects a bit of the true word of God, but not all of it. Nineteen centuries later, however, God came to Joseph Smith and restored that mirror in all its splendor, they said. The church Joseph created, then, is just as true and good as was the one that Jesus established. As Joseph Smith put it, the *Book of Mormon* is "the most correct of any book on earth, and the keystone of our religion, and a man would get nearer to God by abiding by its precepts than by any other book" (*History of the Church,* 4:461).

My two "elders" came calling with these canned speeches because during a visit to Temple Square the month before I had agreed to a home session with "church representatives" in exchange for a free copy of the *Book of Mormon.* I simply jotted down my address on a card, went home, and awaited the inevitable.

For an irrepressibly evangelical people such an invitation as I offered is a salesman's dream come true. Mormon missionaries make almost all their calls "cold" simply knocking on each door as it presents itself, a dismal pursuit called "tracting" because of the *Book of Mormon* copies that they leave behind whenever possible hoping that they'll be admitted to talk about it the next time through the neighborhood. Produced in great quantities at the church's printing plants, these hardcover copies of the central scripture either are purchased for the missionaries by their parents, or more commonly supplied by the wards and stakes in the area where the missionaries are working. Old mission hands note that simply giving away the costly looking hardback book with its title embossed in gold on a blue cover sometimes opens the door long enough to get inside and make a pitch.

On the title page of my complimentary *Book of Mormon,* Stark had jotted down his phone number and also listed four passages for me to read including the all-time missionary favorite, Moroni 10:3–5 which promises that if "ye would ask God, the Eternal Father, in the name of Christ, if these things are not true; and if ye shall ask with a sincere heart, with a real intent, having faith in Christ, he will manifest the truth of it unto you, by the power of the Holy Ghost." That Mormon "magic bullet," as missionaries call it, is fired every time an investigator opens the door.

The idea that no outsider can resist the LDS message if he or she will only pray as Moroni urged is central to the missionary ethic. One can debate whether Moroni 10:3–5 really works, but one can hardly deny that it keeps many a missionary going in the face of daunting odds.

Veterans of missionary tours debate among themselves the

difficulty of getting inside the door in the sales-resistant American heartland, a territory most certainly "burned over" by generations of Fuller Brush sellers and encyclopedia hawkers, versus seeking converts among inhabitants of a foreign country with strange customs, a difficult language, and indigenous strains of Roman Catholicism and anti-Americanism. In response to such difficulties, Mormons have developed their own traditions which assure that inexperienced missionaries benefit from the wisdom gained by those who have gone before them. In that spirit of nurturing traditions to ensure their own solidarity, my two Saints dropped by riding bicycles, the usual mode of transport dating back to when Mormon families couldn't afford to buy gasoline. The bikes symbolize how, for much of LDS history, the cost of sending children on two-year missions has been one of the major financial obligations of membership in a church which demands large families and where tithing, fast offerings, special building assessments, and other money demands from the elders take a continual toll on the family budget.

Recent estimates place the cost to the family of keeping a young missionary in the field at $350 per month or $8400 for a typical two-year mission. Additionally, missionaries need about $1,000 in cash to buy clothes, obtain needed medical and dental exams, passports and visas, and to pay a share of their travel costs. Mindful that they are making one of the best investments possible, church leaders pay all but the first $50 a trainee spends traveling from anywhere in the U.S. to Provo for training, and they pay all but the first $100 in travel costs to get the missionary to the field. Such costs are recouped once the converts start tithing and making other contributions.

While they are in the field, the young "elders" and "sisters" are watched over by a system of mission presidents, usually an older man accompanied by his wife, who are "called" by Salt Lake and sent on foreign tours as a reward for faithful service.

In 1990 the church was operating 221 missions in 97 countries, almost all of them presided over by a married couple. This system assures parents that their offspring aren't entirely on their own in a hostile world even as the supervision helps ensure that the missionaries will conduct their quests in a businesslike fashion. A mother and father can always ask their ward's bishop to check with the mission president on their children's welfare and progress and thus keep family tabs while obeying an all-but-ironclad rule that communication between missionary and parents be kept at a minimum for the two-year tour.

The missionary president system serves to protect traditions that have evolved among missionary Mormons. The mission presidents enforce a strict code of conduct that sets a clothing code, bans all entertainment, and forbids males to engage in contact sports, which could cause injuries and thus impede the mission.

❦

Mike Stark and Brent Jesperson endured an almost monastic lifestyle that kept them in one another's company day and night, week in and week out, sharing long days of praying, knocking on doors, attending church meetings, and making home visits. They had only a few free hours set aside each Thursday for doing the laundry, shopping for groceries, or writing a letter home. In longstanding missionary tradition they were allowed no phone calls home except for one on Christmas, and as befits blossoming patriarchs, they were allowed another call home on either Mother's Day or on their mother's birthday.

The missionary experience is as important for the missionaries as it is for the converts. No matter how they perform in the quest for conversions Mormons return from their missions more committed to their religion than they were when they left. Barbara Christensen, wife of a one-time head of the church's Mission Training Center in Provo, noted in a March, 1989, article in the church magazine *Ensign* that the experience of training for a mission and then performing it greatly reinforces each participant's faith. "My husband and I often said that we had in Provo the mission with the greatest number of missionaries and fewest baptisms, but still many, many conversions."

There are approximately 35,000 missionaries working two-year tours at any one time. The shared bond that missionary service provides for so many who later will be called to lead in LDS circles is at least as important as are the quantum leaps in church membership that the teams of young men "two and two" bring. The missionary experience is the glue that binds Mormon men together in a tightly knit lifetime circle of high priests, lay teachers, bishops, and kindred patriarchs. Friendships and contacts made in the missions carry a Saint through a lifetime just as membership in a fraternity forges lifelong alliances among a Gentile elite. Historian Leonard Arrington calls returned missionaries the "shock troops of Mormonism" because they are destined to fill the positions of leadership in wards, branches, and stakes throughout their lives.

In Saintly circles the missions beckon from the start. They are the essential fabric of LDS life. As part of a churchwide ethic of frugality and self-denial in the name of future rewards, families are urged to start saving for missions even when the future elders are yet in diapers. Saving for a mission is one of many ways that young Mormons prepare for their seminal two years. Young Saints first study their catechism at "primary," as the church calls its classes for the very young. Later they learn Mormonism at "Sunday school" which all LDS members, regardless of age, attend during the church "block" of events. Doctrinal study continues through high school at seminaries located near public schools and at LDS institutes located near most major college campuses.

Much of ordinary church life serves to imbue mission skills. Nascent proselytizers learn public speaking as nine-year-old boys addressing primary classes on Sunday. They hone those skills as fourteen-year-old priests conducting communion services dispensing bread and water LDS style to the entire congregation. They learn to stand before a crowd at the meeting hall and unabashedly bear witness to their faith in God. They do these things at the beck of patriarchs; those who do well emerge as patriarchs in their own right.

Once in my living room young Mike Stark and Brent Jesperson insisted on being called "Elder Stark" and "Elder Jesperson" even though they were, indeed, boys. They also were newly ordained members of the authoritarian Melchizedek priesthood, holders of the "keys" to baptize, lay on hands, heal the sick, speak in tongues, to ordain others as priests, and to perform marriages. They also were typical nineteen-year-olds away from home for the first time and on the verge of sensory deprivation living the spartan life of a true believer *sans* TV, *sans* magazines, and *sans* movies.

The 1990 *Church Almanac* published by the *Deseret News* lists 33,376 missionaries in the field of whom 27,050 were single men ("elders") and 6,317 were single women ("sisters"). Since they cannot baptize converts or exercise any other priestly "keys," female missionaries usually are assigned administrative tasks for the mission presidents. Another 1,215 married couples also were serving post-retirement missionary tours bringing the world total at the start of the last decade of the millennium (at least the millennium with a small *m*) to 35,806. It was anticipated that these missionaries would convert 125,000 Gentiles each year. That figure, coupled with about 175,000 children born into church ranks each year and another 100,000 who join through the recruiting efforts of nonmissionary members, places annual church growth at around 400,000 per year or 6 percent of overall membership, a rate of growth unmatched by any other Western religion.

Statistics also show just how dramatically the missionary experience influences Mormons in general. Of the 6.7 million church members on the rolls in 1990, no fewer than 826,000 of them had served two years as missionaries sometime since 1960, the *Church Almanac* noted. The Mormon church has produced a cadre of almost one million people indelibly marked by the two years invested working for their church at levels of commitment virtually unheard of throughout the rest of Christendom.

A particularly telling statistic is quoted by Richard O. Cowan in his book, *The Church in the Twentieth Century,* where a bar chart dramatically illustrates that between 1976 and 1980 the average missionary was bringing in seven recruits in the course of a two-year tour. Cowan's charts show that by 1986 the best missions were in Latin America where each missionary brought in more than seventeen converts, followed by the West Coast of the U.S. with an average conversion rate of almost nine per missionary. In Europe the Saints were bringing in converts at a rate of slightly below three per missionary.

While it may seem haphazard to send untutored youths abroad seeking converts, in fact much behind-the-scenes work has been done by LDS scholars to prepare the way. Close attention is paid to each young proselytizer's performance in the field be it in Dover or Denver.

In the United States, missionaries like Stark and Jesperson

learn their stuff at what may be the most efficient sales boot camp on earth, the Mission Training Center on the campus of Brigham Young University in Provo, Utah, known throughout Mormondom as the MTC. Other training centers operate in Mexico, Japan, Chile, Brazil, New Zealand, England, Korea, Guatemala, Argentina, Peru, and the Philippines, but these prepare Mormon youth to seek converts in country while the MTC trains those who must carry the word to foreign countries.

Each week, usually on a Wednesday or a Thursday, a new class of about 600 "greenies" arrives at the MTC, each with a suitcase packed full of white shirts, a zip-closed leather "scripture bundle," two pairs of black shoes and a couple of new off-the-rack suits with neckties to almost match.

The first order of business is a trip to the MTC barber for that most universal of all boot camp rites of passage, the shortest haircut possible. Then the indoctrination begins in earnest. "You are so bad," goes a typical taunt at recruits, "that you have spoiled the Spanish language. After hearing you, nobody will ever again speak it."

"Maggots," goes another. "You have spoiled religion for many who are yet unborn!"

Here is a typical daily schedule at the MTC:

6:00–6:30	Arise, shower, dress, personal prayer
6:45–7:20	Breakfast
7:45–8:00	District meeting (session with all those assigned to the same country)
8:00–10:00	Memorization drills
10:00–11:00	Scripture study
11:00–12:00	Memorization drills
12:00–1:00	Lunch
1:00–4:00	Language class
4:00–5:00	P.E./cultural lectures
5:00–5:45	Dinner
5:45–6:00	District meeting
6:00–7:00	Language laboratory
7:00–10:00	Group study
10:00–10:30	Group prayer and lights out

James B. Allen and John B. Harris, two members of the BYU faculty, described the mood of the place in an article in *Sunstone Magazine* (April–May, 1981):

> Imagine the feelings of a nineteen-year-old Mormon boy, a lover of sports, full of energy and mischief, relatively unrestricted in his choice of activities and conversation topics, proud of his appearance and clothing, possibly involved romantically with an attractive young female. Take this young man, shear him of his proud locks, dress him in a dark, conservative suit, white shirt and tie, separate him from his family and friends, give him the title 'Elder,' and then propel him into an intensive language training program. There he will be forced to speak primarily in the language he is trying to learn; he will be assigned a 'companion' who will accompany him for the most part of his waking hours; he will have his schedule completely outlined for him . . . He will be allowed no dates, no visits or calls from home, no outside reading, no movies or TV, no leaving the hall without his assigned companion, and only one day off in which to do his laundry, write letters, shop for necessities, mend clothes or complete all the tasks which have piled up during the week.

Since 1978, when the MTC was opened at BYU, all Americans called to missions have been trained in Provo. To emphasize obedience and the role of divine intervention, Mormon culture doesn't allow young people any say in where they will be sent for their two years. Instead, local bishops, relying on prayer and advice from Provo about where recruits may be needed, write each inductee an Uncle Sam–style "greetings" letter with news of where he or she is being "called" to go.

It is not uncommon for young Hispanics who speak fluent Spanish to be sent to London, while youngsters from the white suburbs of Los Angeles get the call to Bolivia. All train extensively in the languages and cultures they will encounter. Those missionaries with domestic assignments spend only two or three weeks at the MTC, while those headed for missions in foreign countries undergo two months of training in the "live your language," total saturation method.

A faculty of language experts that rivals the linguistic training staff of the CIA instructs the new recruits in tongues as diverse as Korean, Tagalog, Swedish, Portuguese, Japanese, and even Native American Navajo, as well as the more universal French and Spanish. By 1990 the church was operating missions in ninety-seven countries and had rendered the *Book of Mormon* into eighty languages.

In addition to the full-time faculty, the center draws upon between 600 to 800 returned missionaries to drop by as volunteers and assist during training sessions. Likewise, more than thirty-one church branches (or parishes) in and around Provo allow the mission trainees to visit their meetings in order to gain practice at public speaking. Their personal testimonies about Joseph Smith's restored gospel are given before strangers, a method they are trained to use on assignment whenever possible in which the proselytizer gives an impassioned description of his or her personal conversion.

Trainees are taught that when they encounter an investigator with probing questions or objections that the missionary can't handle, it often is best to simply say something like, "Yes, I'm sure there are many questions that professors and scholars can ask that I can't answer, but let me tell you what it feels like in your own heart to accept Jesus Christ and the restored gospel. I'm only nineteen, but Jesus has filled my heart just as He filled Joseph Smith's heart when he was only fourteen and just like He'll fill your heart."

But while they learn this emotional and effective fall-back position, the missionaries also devote hours each day during their MTC cram session gleaning the basics of Mormon doctrines and teachings and undergoing intense reviews not just of LDS scriptures but of King James verses. One can argue that the experience of passing through MTC and then a mission itself does much to mark a Saint for life and reinforce the sense of separation from those in Gentile circles. Certainly, whatever other purpose the missionary mindset serves, it is an essential part of a formula that has made the LDS church one of the most spectacular evangelizing movements in recent world history.

Church leaders themselves have marvelled at the successes from the missions. A common LDS saying goes, "If the church weren't true, the missionaries would have destroyed it a long time ago." For much of the twentieth century the missionaries went abroad after two months of language training but with little or no education in the unique culture of the targeted country, its traditions, taboos, or other distinctive traits. Thus did avid young missionaries preach in pidgin Japanese to housewives about the evils of tea, not even knowing that the Japanese variety contains none of the caffeine banned by Joseph Smith's celebrated Word of Wisdom. They stepped off the plane at Osaka and surveyed the crowds of Japanese only to remark about how many foreigners were present. They went to working-class neighborhoods in Liverpool and put on Fourth of July celebrations. In the South Pacific they cajoled Samoans into celebrating Columbus Day and even Utah Pioneer Days. By the mid-1980s, however, the church had implemented reforms in mission training emphasizing the cultures missionaries would visit. The rote lessons were replaced with more measured presentations, but the basics remain the same.

At Provo all missionaries work around a plan which focuses on seven principles, and in ideal circumstances, the LDS sales force tries to make seven different presentations to any Gentile who opens the door for a first visit. Missionaries are taught that they must evaluate each potential convert and that their relationship with any given investigator should determine which of the principles they raise first.

These seven core lessons have been refined over decades of successful selling:

1. Restoration. The story of the mirrors. How the Catholic church distorted the true words of God and how Joseph restored the gospel by reading his golden plates with his sacred Urim and Thummim.

2. Progression. Every plant, animal, and human that ever will live always has lived. The purpose of human existence is to bring as many as possible across from the spirit kingdom to temporal existence where each can work for exaltation. Here lies the great unifying theme that keeps Mormons striving always to meet concrete and understandable goals no matter how taunting and unfriendly Gentiles view their zealotry.

3. Revelation. That God talks to his chosen people today just as He did in scriptural times. That all worthy males should listen for that "one still voice" that speaks the will of God. Here is the great excitement for practicing Mormons, the utter conviction that each man—and even some women—will hear directly from God when life's most vexing questions arise.

4. Ordinances. That baptism by immersion and induction for all "worthy males" into the Aaronic and Melchizedek priesthoods are the keys to salvation. That apostates starting with the Whore of Babylon (Catholic church) have corrupted these ordinances by calling them sacraments and otherwise diluting God's true message.

5. Patriarchy. By obeying the words of the Living Prophet and following the direction of other elders, one finds peace and happiness because the Mormons have restored religion to the perfect state of those gloriously patriarchal years when Jesus personally walked the earth accompanied by his disciples.

6. Jesus Christ. Each Mormon has a personal relationship with Jesus. It was Jesus' atonement for mankind's sins that ensures all living creatures will enjoy resurrection, and only Mormons understand the true message offered when God's own Son walked the earth and taught humans how they too could become Gods.

7. Heavens. How baptism assures that all will enjoy an eternal life and how it is up to each person while living on earth to work for the highest possible exaltation, which is to say, to strive for the Celestial Kingdom where each occupant stands to become a God over a new universe just as the God of the Old Testament reigns over the earth. The more one does at a Mormon temple and on a mission to bring dead ancestors and spirit babies through the veil separating the temporal from the eternal, the higher one's station will be in the hereafter.

Even in today's enlightened climate, missionaries still spend much of their time simply learning by rote speeches in various languages describing these seven principles, which are known as the Uniform System for Teaching Families and which lie at the heart of each missionary's game plan hammered home at the MTC.

It is estimated that with each missionary bringing in seven

converts in two years of labor, they are getting into only one door for every hundred they approach. Behind that statistic, however, lies the secret to LDS conversion successes. The largest source of converts appears to be not foreigners won over by teen-aged missionaries from Provo, but people brought into Saintly circles by the handful of people the missionaries do win over. These newly minted Mormons start preaching the creed to their friends and neighbors the moment the young missionaries move on.

Campaigns waged by new converts are known as home missions. They too are the product of years of trial and error and they are more effective than are the missionaries themselves. Writing in the *American Journal of Sociology* (May 1980), Rodney Stark and William Sims Bainbridge traced how LDS literature instructs church members in how to use personal friendships and other contacts with Gentiles to proselytize as home missionaries. The authors outline how leaders teach the Mormon rank and file—including new converts in foreign countries—to use their everyday encounters with Gentile neighbors to encourage conversions.

This plan starts with simple neighborliness, doing such favors as babysitting, running errands, lending tools. With each gesture, Saints are taught to reveal a new bit of the Mormon lifestyle and faith. When a Gentile praises a Mormon girl's performance as a babysitter, her parents reply that the church's tight family bonds make members good with children. A loaned tool comes with a brief sermon about being self-sufficient and prepared for any eventuality. Appreciation for running an errand is met with an explanation that Mormons stick together and see to one another's needs in good times and bad.

Gradually the talk moves toward doctrinal matters such as how the gospels in most Christian churches are mere fragments of a truth shattered by early church schisms and now have been restored by Joseph Smith. Stark and Bainbridge in their study, "Networks of Faith: Interpersonal Bonds to Cults and Sects," observed as well that the instructions urge Mormons to shy away from discussing religion directly but rather to ease their targets toward such consideration by incrementally exposing them to LDS beliefs and practices.

It amounts to nothing more than making friends with the neighbors by doing truly friendly things and then eventually offering the new friends a chance to visit their church. The Stark and Bainbridge study compared LDS church figures from a single year (1976–77) in the state of Washington and found that even though door-to-door missionaries were winning only one convert for every *thousand families* they approached, the home mission method was working in a startling 50 percent of the cases.

Ordinary Mormons operate under an informal quota requiring that they bring one person per year into the church through the home missionary work. The key here isn't that every Mormon brings in a new believer each year, but that families work for many years, chipping away at their Gentile neighbors until eventually they win them over. It may take years of insinuating church ideas into a relationship based largely on talks about what to feed the children and how to fight crabgrass, but finally the targeted Gentiles come over. If it takes six years to convert a Gentile family of six, then the proselytizing Mormon family has met its quota, and the growth continues.

Thus the eager young missionaries are really the first foot in the door for a sales program that has evolved to make Mormonism an amazingly robust movement in ways that few of its critics suspect. Indeed, a similar strain of opportunism pervades missionary training itself. Much time is spent, for example, on the all-important question of what to say when somebody opens the door you have just knocked on.

"Hello, have you ever heard of the Mormons?"

"Hi, we were just wondering who grew these wonderful flowers in your yard. They remind me of my mother's flowers back home in Utah."

"We see you have a gun rack in the back of your pickup truck, sir. Are you a hunter? My dad and I hunt all the time."

"Selling? No ma'am, we're not selling, we're giving. Here's a free book for you, it's the most perfect book ever written."

Significant here is that growing up Mormon is growing up immersed in lore about how to get inside that reluctant Gentile door to make the first pitch. A rule of thumb long has been that a good sales person gets into about three living rooms for every

125 doorbells rung, and that one out of every three prospects given the full pitch will buy a set of books, a vacuum cleaner, or whatever is being sold. Encyclopedia salespeople and other hustlers tend to do much better once in that living room than do LDS missionaries, who perhaps make a convert in only one of every thousand living rooms entered. The Mormons do succeed occasionally in those awkward living room sessions, and in so doing they plant a seed that blooms in ways purveyors of the *Encyclopaedia Britannica* can't hope to match. Few buyers of encyclopedias will assume the daunting task of selling more books to their friends and neighbors, but that's exactly what newly converted Mormons often do.

In that sense Mormondom is a pyramid sales scheme like few the world has ever seen. Many of the techniques that work for other sales organizations are used by Mormons. It is not uncommon for the church's advertising network to flood an area with family-oriented LDS "Homefront" TV commercials just before missionaries hit there, a gambit that allows them to say something like, "Hi, we're Mormons. Perhaps you've seen our commercials on TV this week. May we leave this book with you?"

It is relevant to note that the church sells itself in far more ways than just by sending out its best young people on the missions. Particular attention is paid to projects such as movies and media ownership that allows the church to produce programming in support of uplifting sales pitches elders want to make.

Mormons win considerable goodwill simply by opening the doors of their holy sites and historical shrines to Gentile tourists. In 1989, for example, more than four million tourists visited Temple Square in Salt Lake City, while only 2.1 million people visited Yellowstone National Park, 200 miles to the north. Another site operated for curious tourists is the LDS visitor center in upstate New York in the shade of the Hill Cumorah. Each year an audience of more than 100,000 views the annual Hill Cumorah Pageant called "America's Witness for Christ," a show along the lines of a passion play but without a crucifixion in which various scenes from the *Book of Mormon* are acted out on three large stages.

The church has established thirty-eight historical centers around the world, and openly uses them as recruitment sites.

Mormons are encouraged to bring their non-LDS friends with them on visits to the Liberty jail where Joseph was imprisoned in Missouri or to the Knight family cabin in upstate New York where the church held its first meeting in 1830.

In a 1989 press release, Sherman M. Crump, a managing director of the Missionary Department in Salt Lake said, "The role of the visitors' center is, first, to preach the message of the Savior. The second is to give the opportunity for members to bring their non-member friends for an introduction to the gospel." He adds that guides are waiting to take a member's non-LDS friends aside and give them an expert proselytizing pitch, but Crump emphasized of these professionals, "they do not use pressure."

In 1989 the *Church News* reported that six million visitors had stopped at one of these centers, which, it added, was a 29 percent increase over the year before and yet another indicator of the brisk missionary activity underway in fashions few Gentiles realize.

Each center uses a different hook to draw in crowds. For example, the site at Kirtland, Ohio, features a masterful restoration of the general store operated in 1827 by Newel K. Whitney when Joseph established the first communal bishop's storehouse there. The caliber of restoration work rivals that at Colonial Williamsburg in Virginia. It draws thousands of non-Mormons who get a sales pitch along with a view of authentic period furniture, machines, and other artifacts. An annual Heritage Days celebration that allows members to bring their Gentile friends for a weekend of historical events now draws 15,000 to the Kirtland LDS visitors' center, according to the *Church News*.

A quite different hook is used at the LDS visitors' center in downtown Mexico City where Mormon artisans have produced a beautiful nativity scene to take advantage of Mexican Catholics' special veneration of the Christmas season. Throughout the Christmas holidays, four-thousand people visit the creche each night, most of them, at least when they enter the grounds, staunch Catholics.

A common criticism leveled at the Mormon missionary program is that it lacks the altruistic qualities common to other Christian missions. There is virtually no effort to feed the hungry, clothe the poor, care for the sick, or adopt the orphaned. Instead resources are channeled into an inexorable quest for converts.

In retrospect, the reason for this Mormon style is clear. Above all, Latter-day Saints are millennarians. They are driven by a firm belief that we all are living on the very cusp between the end of the world as we know it and the start of a thousand-year period in which Jesus Christ will again walk the earth and when all those who have joined Mormon ranks will have a chance to refine themselves to the point that they can enter the Celestial Kingdom and achieve Godhood. But before that millennial epoch of self-improvement can start, the word must be taken to everyone who ever lived in the spirit Kingdom. In these last days, of the Dispensation of the Fulness of Times, much work must be done to bring the relatively few remaining "choice spirits" through the veil.

The sense of a looming Armageddon and an accompanying literalism in much of Mormon teaching on such questions as evolution and divine revelation has saddled the church's mainstream with a fringe of ultra-fundamentalist believers whose actions at times have undermined the labors of the missionaries in a church where, as the late President David O. McKay put it, "Every member is a missionary." When they hold police at bay in blood-drenched shootouts over polygamy or blaze across the headlines of America while conducting bizarre blood feuds, or conduct one-man crime waves that appear as sensationalistic TV docudramas, these fringe Mormons are missionaries too. And thus they also have much to teach about Mormonism, even though they may be rogues and mavericks, abhorred by mainstream Saints.

Chapter 8

Fundamentalists and Survivalists

Revelations come to men just as easily from devils as they do from holy sources.

—Bruce R. McConkie in *Mormon Doctrine*

The Lafferty Brothers

While other American boys were being brought up with the promise that they might grow up to be president of the United States, a pair of Norman Rockwell-perfect Mormon kids named Ronald and Daniel Lafferty were taught that one day they might become Gods, supreme beings in their own right ruling over a gigantic and magnificent universe. Tragically, like a dangerous minority on the fringe of Mormondom, the Lafferty brothers grew up and decided that they already were in direct communication with fellow Gods.

The Laffertys' revelations came in language and style much like those given to the beloved Joseph himself, full of "thus sayeth the Lord's," "so be it's" and "Even so, Amen's." In that sense these divine communications weren't all that different from many of the revelations that ordinary Saints report receiving. A key LDS tenet is that Joseph Smith restored the same sort of ongoing dialogue between living humanity and God that existed when Jesus Christ walked the earth. Such personal revelations are an accepted and central part of Mormon tradition. In fact many Mormons believe that receiving revelations is essential for worthy males who expect to find exaltation in the next life.

For work-a-day Mormons, however, the personal revelations deal with such important but home-bound questions as whether a son should attend a given college or a daughter accept an offered job, whether a child should venture off to summer camp or even whether a wife should buy a new microwave oven. In ordinary Mormon circles, these revelations are not unlike receiving plain-spoken advice from God in the role of a "Dutch uncle." But for the Laffertys and other fringe fundamentalists, the word of God echoing in their heads sounded more like the ravings of a psychopath than the advice of a Dutch uncle.

In March of 1984 Ronald Watson Lafferty used a blue ball-point pen and a lawyer's legal tablet to record the most chilling of all the revelations these two brothers claimed they received directly from God:

Thus sayeth the Lord unto my
servants the prophets. It is my will
and commandment that ye remove the
following individuals in order that
my work might go forward, for they
have truly become obstacles in my
path and I will not allow my work to
be stopped.

First thy brother's wife, Brenda,
and her baby, then Chloe Low, and
then Richard Stowe. And it is my
will that they be removed in rapid
succession and that an example be
made of them in order that others
might see the fate of those who
fight against the true saints of
God.

And it is my will that this matter
be taken care of as soon as possible
and I will prepare a way for my
instrument to be delivered and
instruction be given unto my servant
Todd.

And it is my will that he show
great care in his duties for I have
raised him up and prepared him for
this important work and is he not
like unto my servant, Porter
Rockwell? And blessings await him if
he will do my will, for I am the
Lord thy God and have control over
all things. Be still and know that I
am with thee. Even so, Amen.

No tabloid can overstate the horror of mainstream Mormondom when this revelation in ballpoint was carried out. The Lafferty brothers failed to find the man named Todd whom the revelation said was to serve as their Porter Rockwell, so they did the Avenging Angel's work themselves.

On Pioneer Day, June 24, 1984, while their neighbors were in Salt Lake attending the annual parade marking the anniversary of Brigham Young's arrival in the valley, Ron Lafferty, 42, and his younger brother, Dan, then 36, brought the "slaughter instrument," a ten-inch Chicago Cutlery boning knife into Brenda Lafferty's modest apartment in American Fork. Brenda, 24, was the wife of another Lafferty brother, Allen, and she had spoken against the more extreme varieties of Fundamentalism at Lafferty family councils made up of the six Lafferty brothers, their wives and children.

According to testimony in subsequent trials, the two brothers Dan and Ron speedily carried out God's will. Ron cut a segment from the electrical cord on Brenda's vacuum cleaner and wrapped it around his sister-in-law's throat to expose her jugular. Then Dan grabbed the attractive woman's blond hair and yanked her head backwards while Ron slashed her exposed throat. She died almost instantly. Then Dan went into the apartment's single bedroom and slashed the throat of his niece, fifteen-month-old Erica Lafferty. A star prosecution witness testified that he later asked Dan what it felt like to murder an innocent child and that Lafferty had replied, "No problem, it was easy."

Allen Lafferty came home that horrible Pioneer Day to find the carnage and summoned police, but his reaction to the tragedy was not what one would expect. He later testified in trials for both Dan and Ron that he would have done the same thing they did if he had been given a revelation commanding it. He also admitted that he didn't warn Brenda even after his two brothers had told him "that a revelation had been received. It said my wife's life and my daughter's life were required by the Lord."

In piecing together the complex motives the Lafferty prosecution team documented nothing less than the descent of two outwardly normal Utah Saints into madness after they tripped over their own revelations. The Lafferty saga unfolded in a series of neighboring towns south of Salt Lake City and Provo along the Wasatch Mountains, a suburban corridor alongside Interstate Highway 15 that is the epicenter not only of mainstream Mormondom but of Fundamentalism as well. The six Lafferty brothers all lived close together in and around the town of American Fork about midway on the forty-one-mile drive between Salt Lake and Provo.

Ron Lafferty completed an assignment as an LDS missionary in Florida before returning to Utah and getting married in the temple. Later he served on the city council in the town of Alpine, Utah, in the mountains just outside of American Fork. He devoted many years as a counselor to the American Fork LDS stake president as well. Dan spent his two-year mission in Scotland before returning and also marrying in the temple and settling down at Provo where he opened a practice as a chiropractor.

In the early 1980s, the two brothers met a Fundamentalist named Robert Crossfield, a self-styled prophet who had grown up in a Mormon settlement in Canada. Crossfield moved to the town of Genola, Utah, where he established a sect he called the School of Prophets, patterned after the group Joseph Smith had founded in Kirtland. Crossfield's teachings focus on training worthy males to seek direct revelations from God and to prepare for the imminent arrival of the millennium, a strain of survivalism that, like revelation, is part of mainstream LDS traditions as well as a major Fundamentalist tenet.

Crossfield's method includes prayer, fasting, and practicing just sitting quietly to listen for what Brigham Young called that "still small voice, which whispereth through and pierceth all things, and often times it maketh my bones to quake." Crossfield located his commune at the mouth of the John Koyle Relief Mine in Salem, Utah, a deep shaft sunk in the 1890s by a zealot who was supported for a few years by One Temple Square. Crossfield rigged the mine shaft as a fallout shelter for initiates to ride out the Endtimes. Dan Lafferty later claimed in an article in the September 23, 1984, *Central Utah Journal* that they had hoped to establish a "city of refuge" on the mine grounds. They planned to restore the United Order and to reinstitute the Council of Fifty, an underground body of church and civic leaders through which Brigham Young had wielded much of his secular power in Utah after Washington took away his powers as governor and seized control of the state legislature.

The most striking teaching of the Crossfield School of Prophets, was that men needed to learn the proper way to seek revelations because every man needs these direct words from God to find his eternally designated primary wife. The teaching here is that in the pre-mortal existence of the spirit world, every female spirit is wedded to a male spirit, and it is the destiny of each to find one another and become reunited while living on earth. But in the great war between Satan and Michael the Archangel, one third of all the male spirits were dashed forever into perdition, leaving their female soulmates without male counterparts. Thus each living man must first find the female with whom he is linked for all eternity and then marry other women after establishing through revelation that they are among the sisterhood whose own mates were lost in the spirit war.

Dan Lafferty wrote in a journal produced by prosecutors for his trial, "While the duty of every man in this world is to live as good a life as possible, to become sanctified, the primary goal of every woman is to find the man to whom she was assigned in the pre-existence." Those who find that their men are condemned to hell must then become sister wives.

Both Dan and Ron Lafferty had great trouble selling this tenet to their respective wives. Brenda Lafferty, a one-time on-air host for a TV newsmagazine aired throughout Utah on the public broadcasting station KBYU-TV, was an articulate woman. She repeatedly talked her sisters-in-law out of accepting proposals from the various Lafferty men to bring in secondary wives. She also kept Allen from joining the School of Prophets, making him the only one of the six brothers who didn't belong. And she helped Ron's wife when she filed for divorce and even enlisted the help of Chloe Low, the LDS relief society president in American Fork, who also was targeted for "removal" in the legal pad revelation.

After fasting and praying for weeks, in the early months of 1984, the two brothers, each wearing foot-long patriarchal beards and long-flowing hair, visited the School of Prophets and at a prayer meeting asked fellow members to consecrate the "instrument" for its divine purpose, a request that Crossfield later testified the group rejected in horror. The Lafferty brothers were expelled from the School of Prophets, but they left armed with what they considered the secrets of obtaining direct revelations from Crossfield's Saints.

They then went on a cross-country trip with a pair of drifters, Charles "Chip" Carnes, 23, and Ricky Knapp, 24, who later described how when the brothers wanted to smoke marijuana, they simply had a revelation and then a joint; how another revelation commanded them to buy the services of a prostitute in Las Vegas, and finally how after murdering Brenda and her daughter, they received a revelation to win enough money on the gaming tables in Reno to finance a new church. They were arrested standing in line for a casino's low-cost buffet dinner. They led police to a green van filled with written revelations, journals, and other material outlining their strange set of beliefs.

One of the revelations that Ron recorded claimed that the six Lafferty brothers were nothing less than the "mighty and strong [who] proceeded into battle and cast down Lucifer and his host." In many ways the driving force among Fundamentalists is Section 85 of D & C where Joseph predicts the "One Mighty and Strong" (OMS) will appear in the last days when the millennium is at hand.

In an effort to avoid capital punishment, lawyers for the Laffertys brought in expert witnesses to show that the basic idea of blood atonement that drove the brothers to murder might also drive the Mormons on the jury to vote the death penalty so that a firing squad could mix the Laffertys' blood with the earth to atone for the brutal murders of Brenda and her infant. These witnesses explained most emphatically to the Mormon jurors that their church's current teaching bans blood atonement even though it was once an LDS frontier tradition.

Dr. Jess Groesbeck, a Provo psychiatrist who has studied Mormon beliefs, testified in behalf of Ron Lafferty that he has found in dozens of interviews with church members a prevailing belief that the doctrine of blood atonement stands today just as it did when Brigham Young tamed an unforgiving salt valley. He noted that the common misperception was that the church proper teaches that those who commit murder must atone for the act by having their blood spilled on the ground, preferably from a head wound or a slit throat. Groesbeck testified that in his experience, "most rank and file Mormons believe this."

Dan Lafferty was found guilty of murder and sentenced to life in prison. Ron, however, was sentenced to death by his jury, and Judge Boyd Park of the Utah District Court in Provo subsequently ordered that execution be by firing squad.

The Leaping Longos

While the brothers Lafferty wrote their revelations out in long-hand on paper, another fringe Mormon etched his revelations on the steel blades of knives his followers made for him in Manti, Utah. The tragedy that revelations brought the family of this zealot, a 300-pound giant with pigtails and the assumed name of Immanuel David, was even worse than that which befell the Lafferty clan.

Bruce Longo, who then weighed around 250 pounds and stood at six foot six, was converted to Mormonism in the early 1960s by missionaries who knocked on his mother's door in upstate New York. His mother, Lousanne Longo, and his brother, Dean, later told reporters that he became obsessed with his new religion and would speak of little else. It occupied "150 percent" of Bruce's attention, Dean said.

Soon after his conversion Bruce moved to Provo where he earned a bachelor's degree in Spanish at Brigham Young University and began dating a wealthy Danish girl, Margit Ericsson, who had been drawn to BYU by the fact that many of her ancestors had been converted and had emigrated to Utah. Longo interrupted the courtship to enroll for missionary training and went off on a two-year stint in Uruguay while Margit waited for him in Provo in the typical LDS courtship pattern.

One of his missionary companions later recalled how Longo would knock on a door and, when the prospect opened it, he would drop to the ground and grind out as many as a hundred rapid "snap" push-ups. Then, scarcely winded, Longo would jump to his feet and launch into his carefully memorized mission

talks. His mission was cut short, apparently after he encountered a siege of dysentery, and Longo returned to teach Spanish
at the Mission Training School that was then located in Salt
Lake City. He married Margit Ericsson, and they settled in
Provo briefly before the revelations started.

Unlike the Lafferty brothers, Longo didn't leave his revelations around in writing to be found only after the fact, instead,
he sent them as fast as he recorded them to the general authorities at One Temple Square. Sometimes Elder Longo's letters
to the hierarchy claimed that he was the "father of God," and
sometimes he was just God or the Holy Ghost. He informed the
First Presidency that he had received a revelation stating that
he, Bruce Longo, should receive all the tithes paid by Mormons
worldwide because he was the OMS.

By 1965 he had been excommunicated and had gone through
the required legal processes to change his name to Immanuel
David and that of his wife to Rachal David to signify that he
was the descendant of King David and also the son of God,
"Immanuel." Rachel (or Rachal, as they chose to spell it) was
the favorite wife of Jacob and mother of Joseph whose descendants God called his Chosen People, holders of the coveted
"birthright" to salvation.

Immanuel and Rachal David settled in at a commune just
outside Manti, a town virtually in the center of the state. There
they gathered a score of followers about them and produced a
family of seven sons and daughters.

Details are sketchy about how this strange little cult made
money there in Manti, but it is clear that they made a lot of it
and that they gave most of it to Immanuel. One of David's followers, a man named Mathias David, was convicted of wire fraud
in a case in which the FBI had tapped his phones while he called
Mormons around the country seeking donations for hard luck
cases such as one in which he described a nine-year-old girl who
had been paralyzed in an auto crash in Nevada and needed just
a small sum of money for surgery that would spare her from
carrying deep facial scars for life.

Federal prosecutors built a case in which David/Longo gathered a small number of followers in Manti and convinced them

to make fraudulent phone calls and commit burglaries, turning over the money to him. He likewise pressed his wife's well-to-do Danish relatives to send money to help her and the children.

Growing wealthy on the larceny of his cult, Immanuel David, who had gained substantial weight, decided to move Rachal and the children to Salt Lake. They settled into the Alta Suite in the International Dunes Hotel, just two blocks away from Temple Square. The family lived like transient rock stars on the money sent them by Rachal's parents and by David's followers. He often would walk the two blocks to Temple Square to tell visitors that they should be paying their tithes not to the church but to him. Church security kept a close eye on him, but he never gave them cause for alarm as he seemed a strange but gentle giant of a man.

In 1978 in Salt Lake City, the daily rent for the Alta Suite was $90 per day, a stiff tariff for the place and the time. Immanuel paid each day's rent with a crisp $100 bill and then had gourmet meals delivered to his brood in the penthouse. In less than a year, he peeled no less than $38,000 off the fat wad of bills he kept in his denim coveralls. He told people that he didn't believe in credit and he didn't believe in sending children to Godless state-licensed schools. The David children, who followed mom and dad down Salt Lake's streets like ducklings, received their schooling in hotel suites from their mother and a series of nannies.

Immanuel peppered One Temple Square with letters claiming that his revelations had named him the true prophet, seer, and revelator. He told the elders that he had taken possession of the golden tablets that Joseph had used to translate the *Book of Mormon*. He demanded to be named to head the First Presidency.

As time passed the gourmet restaurant meals took their toll and Immanuel's girth expanded until he was a corpulent figure with long flowing hair whose wardrobe consisted only of the oversized farmer's coveralls that he could find at local stores. On July 31, 1987, Immanuel David drove a borrowed pickup truck up Emigration Canyon, the site of so much Salt Lake Valley history, and committed suicide by rigging a garden hose to the tail pipe. Officials later speculated that he killed himself because he knew the FBI was about to seek his indictment on wire fraud charges. Immanuel David, née Bruce Longo, was 39 years old when he died. So was Rachal.

Three days later the tragedy took on unthinkable dimensions. On Aug. 3, 1978, Rachal led her seven children to the balcony outside their eleventh floor suite in the International Dunes Hotel and helped each child over the brass rail for a tragic jump into eternity.

Most of these children simply climbed on a chair their mother had leaned up against the railing and jumped without hesitation. Rachal jumped last.

Papers left in the suite indicated that they expected to immediately join "Daddy" in the next world and that when they got there, "Daddy" was going to "destroy California." A single Longo child, Elizabeth, 16, survived, but her injuries were profound and she later said she had absolutely no memory of the horror on the balcony, or, for that matter, of her own childhood.

The tragedy was absolutely numbing. With characteristic gallows humor, Salt Lake newspeople called the blighted Fundamentalist family "the leaping Longos," a bit of irreverence that somehow made the tragedy bearable by reducing it to a sick joke. By contrast to the gallows humor about Leaping Longos, when Ervil LeBaron and his followers struck, even sick jokes couldn't deflate the horror.

The LeBarons

Thundering words are typical of the tone taken by Fundamentalists when talk turns toward revelation. God doesn't speak to these people of love, toleration, and charity. He hollers from on high for bloodshed, for retribution. To this day He speaks to those of Ervil LeBaron's biological and spiritual heirs who have spent more than two decades waging an underground murder campaign against those they perceive to be their enemies. They kill often, and they do so in the name of revelation.

To understand the LeBarons is to understand that Mormon Fundamentalism has its own history, its own patriarchs and traditions just as does the LDS church itself. And the best way

161

to examine that sometimes murderous tradition is to start with the LeBarons' most infamous blood atonement, Ervil LeBaron's attack on Dr. Rulon C. Allred.

The afternoon that death came in the form of two LeBaron female avenging angels, Allred was finishing up another hectic, patient-filled day at his clinic in the Salt Lake suburb of Murray, Utah. Chagrined police later were to acknowledge that they were aware that Dr. Allred, a non-M.D. naturopath, was leader of what was by far the largest polygamy sect in the Salt Lake Valley proper. His busy practice focused almost exclusively on members of that church, a group that experts have estimated anywhere from 2,000 to 5,000 followers in the Salt Lake Valley. A few hundred other Allred followers live in communes in Idaho and in Pinesdale, a settlement in Montana's Bitterroot Mountains.

Around Salt Lake Allred's followers operated polygamy schools in Murray and another suburb, Bluffdale, where his brother, Owen, oversaw things at a complex of buildings surrounding a large central meeting hall called the Apostolic United Brethren Center. The largest of all Utah's polygamy schools still gathers at the AUB center to provide offspring with education that they cannot get under their proper family names in the Utah public system.

As patriarch of an empire of tithing believers who own land, mines, auto dealerships, hotels, motels, and other businesses, Rulon Allred was an important business figure despite the fact that his Fundamentalist status kept him shunned from valley LDS circles except financial ones. One of the key witnesses to his murder was Richard Bunker, a millionaire land owner and investor, who was waiting along with Allred's final patients to discuss a land deal after the doctor's clinic closed.

Bunker told Detective Paul Forbes of the Murray police department that when the two young women walked into the waiting room just before five he thought one was quite attractive and that the other one was more than just a little dumpy-looking.

The good-looking one, whom prosecutors charged was Ramona Marston, the young plural wife of Ervil LeBaron's second in command, a zealot named Daniel Ben Jordan, sat next to Bunker on the waiting room couch. The other woman walked past Melba

Allred, one of the patriarch/naturopath's eleven wives and also his receptionist. This second female visitor, Rena Chynoweth (pronounced *Sha-noth*), one of Ervil's thirteen wives and a leader in a commando group the LeBarons called United Women of Zion (UWZ), confronted the doomed patriarch as he was testing a blood sample in the clinic's small lab.

She promptly emptied the six-shot magazine of a .25 caliber automatic pistol into Allred as he begged, "Oh, my God. My God," according to Melba and Bunker's later testimony in various court proceedings.

With Allred mortally wounded on the floor the women fled the office and Bunker haplessly decided to give chase in hopes of getting their license plate number. But as he pushed through the clinic door, the two women pushed their way back inside, where they scuffled. Bunker got one of the duo—probably Marston—in a wrestler's head lock but let go and ran for his life into a restroom when the other placed a gun to his head.

Melba recalled kneeling beside her husband watching his blood spurt from scattered chest wounds as the shooter returned and placed a .38 caliber revolver to the fallen man's head and fired a final shot, the unique coup de grace required in blood atonement matters.

The tragedy of Rulon Allred remains riddled with doubts. Ramona Marston swore that she and Rena Chynoweth had done the killing but then jumped bail and was never tried in the case. Rena, who in 1990 published a book admitting she shot Allred, was acquitted in a Utah trial in which she was nearly nine months pregnant, a sympathetic figure to jurors. Her defense team successfully noted that the major witnesses cited by prosecutors were either fugitives like Marston or dead. Lloyd Sullivan, a LeBaron follower whose brother, Don, allegedly accompanied the Allred hit team, died of a heart attack before the trial.

Further complicating the legally sanctioned version of the shooting is the fact that although Ramona and Rena were never convicted of doing the shooting, Ervil himself was convicted by another Utah jury in 1981 of ordering Rena and Ramona to kill Allred.

At that trial a total of forty-three prosecution witnesses traced allegations that Ervil LeBaron's Mexico-based fundamentalist cult, The Lambs of God, had sent a hit team to the valley to kill both Allred and Ervil's brother Verlan, who had spurned the Lambs after claiming to have received a revelation that Ervil was a "false prophet."

Ervil LeBaron died in August 1981 in his prison cell, but the blood bath against those he considered his enemies and enemies of his many polygamous families has continued to this day. This strange prophet left behind a "Book of New Covenants," in which he is believed to have issued a hit list starting with some of his own children and ranging up to members of the First Presidency. Since Ervil's death, nearly a dozen enemies of the clan have died in classical blood atonement fashion.

Counting the people Ervil is known to have killed personally or to have ordered killed over the years, law officers like Utah's Dick and Paul Forbes identify twenty to thirty murders, both before and after the Allred murder, as directly attributable to the strange cult. The victims run a gamut from Ervil's brother Joel, who briefly offered competition for the prophet's mantle, to some of Ervil's own hired guns like Dean Vest, a seven-foot-tall giant prone to wearing black frock coats and elevator shoes, who died of a fatal shot to the head administered while he was fixing a washing machine for Vonda White, one of the original Allred hit crew. Ervil even ordered his own teenaged daughter killed blood-atonement style when he decided she was mentally unbalanced and had committed treason.

The latest round of blood atoning began in October of 1987 when Daniel Ben Jordan was gunned down with a ritualistic head shot while on a deer hunting trip in a Utah national forest campground with three of his eight wives and twenty-two children from his brood of forty-six. The murder spree continued on June 17, 1988—almost exactly 144 years to the hour from the deaths of Joseph and Hyrum Smith in Carthage Jail. One of Ervil's closest allies, Eddie Marston, was gunned down in a Dallas suburb at almost the same moment Mark Chynoweth and his eight-year-old daughter Jennifer were murdered three hundred miles away in Houston.

Ultimately police in Phoenix and in Chicago arrested a dozen young people with ties to the LeBarons on charges ranging from auto theft to bank robbery and suspicion in the Jordan murder as well as the blood atonements in Dallas and Houston. By late 1990, however, authorities were still sorting out the various conflicting stories of the accused detainees.

The lesson to be gleaned from all this transcends the merits of issues such as who specifically the Utah prosecutors think did the actual killing. What really matters as one tries to plumb the psyche of Mormon Fundamentalism is the thinking that drives them today just as it drove LeBaron, Lafferty, Longo, and so many others. The Fundamentalists' history and creed are as complex as that of the mainstream church. The bloodshed, however, makes them a danger to the public safety as well as a tremendous source of irritation and embarrassment for the church as it struggles to win acceptance as a mainstream religious body.

Indeed, it is not improper to ask whether there is something unique about Mormonism that creates a deadly fringe element along with a main body of admirable family-loving, civic-minded church-goers. Is revelation something that, like alcohol, most people can handle without trouble, but which can drive certain vulnerable souls to wretched and dangerous excess? Church leaders have long acknowledged that the teaching on revelation is spiritual dynamite. Apostle Bruce McConkie both advised that it is impossible for a worthy male to find exaltation without revelation and warned that revelations can come from hell as well as heaven. "Indeed," wrote McConkie, "the receipt of revelation may lead to damnation as well as to salvation." Nevertheless, McConkie concludes, "With reference to their own personal affairs, the Saints are expected (because they have the gift of the Holy Ghost) to gain personal revelation and guidance rather than to run to the First Presidency or some other church leaders to be told what to do."

Thus driven to their own revelations by the mainstream church that they reject, Fundamentalists simply incorporate their own claimed sessions with the supernatural into the body of Mormon teachings. As a result of this synergy, Fundamentalists exist today with a body of ritual, tradition, and dogma as comprehensive as anything the LDS church, or, for that matter, any other religion, offers. But while rank-and-file Saints strive to live a rational spiritual life along neo-orthodox lines, the Fundamentalists become more rabid. As One Temple Square moves away from the more startling words of Brigham and the other patriarchs, the Fundamentalists move closer to a world filled with latter-day Danites, raging blood atonement, harems, patriarchal power struggles, apostasy, and mayhem. In Mormon circles different fruits spring from the same roots.

The Survivalists

Yet another strain of Mormons are those mainstream Saints who are anticipating the fast approach of the Millennium and preparing for the worst. Along with the teachings about the restored priesthood, tithing, and Heavenly Father, LDS children learn the principle of preparedness. While Gentiles may take similar steps out of nuclear age anxiety, Mormons are driven by a different set of beliefs. Indeed, survivalism is a major concern of just about everybody in Mormon circles.

Saints are taught from earliest childhood that they need to be ready for the political, economic, and natural upheavals that will usher in the Millennium. In ways that few Gentiles understand, this core Mormon doctrine does much to shape the Mormon character. The church's arch-conservative politics spring from survivalist roots just as does the Saints' penchant for joining forces and pulling together in times of adversity. Survivalism is a major component of Mormon clannishness in the midst of Gentile neighbors.

Saints also learn that when the Endtimes arrive, they will take care of their own first and, if necessary, let their unprepared infidel neighbors perish. As early as 1856 Brigham Young's best friend Heber Kimball told the Saints, "We must lay up grain against the famines that will prevail upon the earth. ... Shall we lay it up to feed the wicked? No, we shall lay it up to feed

the Saints who gather here from all the nations of the earth.
. . ."

Drawing on the Old Testament prophecies of Isaiah, Jeremiah, and Ezekiel, as well as the New Testament Book of Revelation and the Mormon holy trilogy, the Saints have developed a complex scenario for the Millennium that revolves around the idea of an immense gathering in the Salt Lake Valley of true believers from throughout the planet. The prophet George A. Smith predicted in an 1856 sermon printed in *Journal of Discourses* describing the last days, "Then it becomes the Saints to store up food of themselves, and for the hosts who will come here for sustenance and protection, for as the Lord lives they will flow here by the thousands and millions and seek bread and protection at the hands of this people."

Mormon teachings on preparedness include not only civil defense–style stockpiling but thrift and cooperation. A first principle is to shun consumer credit and stay in the black financially so that when hard times hit resources are available for survival. Avoiding debt and saving money is clearly as much a legacy of the stressed economic times when the Mormons were wresting a livelihood out of the unforgiving Salt Lake Valley as it is a consequence of a theology about Endtimes.

Mormons are taught the principles of sharing and cooperation with one's fellow Saints in times of need. That unique Mormon cooperation was displayed in 1988 when dozens of Saints sped to the aid of Mormon ranchers and business owners on the edges of Yellowstone National Park after half the park's forests were burned. These Mormon rescuers threw up lines of irrigation sprinklers around motels owned by fellow church members in the tourist hamlet of West Yellowstone, Montana, letting neighboring Gentile motel owners fend for themselves as a wall of flames bore down. Likewise, in 1983, when unprecedented rains flooded the streets of Salt Lake, thousands of Mormons took time off from work to fill and stack sandbags to protect their Mormon neighbors' yards and houses. Nevertheless, it is the survivalism that stands out as the hallmark of LDS preparedness.

Under Ezra Taft Benson, Mormon survivalism has extended far beyond the principle of preparedness to the propagation of

right-wing teachings. To understand this Mormon ultraconser-
vativism, it's necessary to look first at what Mormons call their
"seventy-two-hour kits" and then work one's way along to what
Mormons call "secret combinations" and what scholars like Richard Hofstadter call "the Hidden Hand" theory.

A primary principle of civil defense is that the key to surviving catastrophe isn't just laying in supplies to tide one over the
period during which the irradiated landscape cools down, but
rather taking steps to withstand the rigors and dangers of the
first three days. It is those initial seventy-two hours of upheaval
and rioting as the unprepared struggle to take away the supplies
of their more prudent neighbors that pose the greatest threat to
long-term survival.

Today many Mormon congregations devote meetings of Wom-
en's Relief, Young Adults, and sometimes even Primary to putting together homemade 72-hour kits. In the meantime, commercial operations have sprung up to make and sell the kits to more
prosperous Saints. Emergency Essentials, Inc., offers a "basic"
72-hour kit that an ad describes as

> the perfect way to get started . . . Each kit contains: 18 MRE
> (Meal Ready to Eat) entrees, 6 MRE side dishes, 6 MRE beans,
> 6 MRE desserts, 12 freeze dried fruit, 2 survival candy rations,
> 1–8' tube tent, 1 stove & fuel bar, 1 box extra fuel, 2 stainless
> steel sierra cups, 1 basic first aid kit, 1 5 gallon water con-
> tainer/portable toilet, 2 20-hour disposable hand/body warmers,
> 1 box waterproof matches, 6 tub candles & 2 metalized emer-
> gency blankets. MRE food is full moisture, fully cooked, and
> stores 6 years at room temperature and tastes great.

This kit is designed for two persons and retails for $49.95, plus
$8 shipping and handling.

A briskly selling booklet available at Desert Books, "Emergency Evacuation" by Barbara Salsbury, outlines how to put
together a homemade 72-hour kit and provides insights into how
survivalism becomes yet another unifying theme for those who
live Mormonism. Recalling how she made her first family survival kit in a large wooden footlocker, Salsbury describes how,
from time to time, "I would lift the lid and gaze at the contents,

enjoying the feeling of security it gave me." But, when the Salsbury family gave their survival kit a dry run on an impromptu camping trip, it was so heavy it couldn't be lifted. The survival expert recommends, therefore, that Saints use six-gallon polyethylene buckets—one for each family member—as kit containers. The buckets can be used to carry water, as washbasins, and as toilets.

Foods inside the buckets should be things like granola bars, "trail mix" of nuts, seeds, and dried fruits, jerked (or smoked) meat, dried fruits, and, if the pocketbook allows, the expensive freeze-dried rations sold by sporting goods stores. To serve and prepare the rations, a kit should include a small pot, spoons and forks, a knife, a tin "sierra" cup, paper towels, a can opener, a portable camp stove, and matches. Rounding out the kits are some sort of shelter such as a small "tube" type tent for each adult, blankets, and a flashlight, candles, or a backpacking lantern. Special family health and hygiene needs, such as contact lenses or diabetes medicine should be included in the kit along with a first-aid kit of Band-aids, tweezers, aspirin, needles, scissors, and safety pins. Another "must have" is a small battery-operated radio.

Barry G. Crockett and Lynette B. Crockett, in their booklet, "72-Hour Family Emergency Preparedness Checklist," urge that families apply for a special VISA or MasterCard and keep it unused in the 72-hour kit along with a check book and a Ziploc bag containing one hundred one dollar bills and a quantity of postage stamps. They also recommend Saints take along a scripture bundle, insurance policies, stocks and bonds, deeds, wills, immunization records, and various LDS documents such as journals, genealogy lists, family history charts, patriarchal blessings, lines of priesthood authority, and pedigrees.

Families are urged to team up with neighboring families in a "Care-in-a-Crisis Program" by which the two units meet together and plan how to share various duties when calamity strikes. Frequently Mormon women use Relief Society meetings to lay these plans and to put together the 72-hour kits, a shared activity that reinforces both ties to the church and a continued awareness of the tenuous nature of survival in these latter days.

Thus the kits become another icon of Mormonism along with the garments, the genealogy sheets, and the scripture bundles.

Seventy-two-hour kits are just a small part of a longstanding church program that requires the faithful to take numerous steps to survive Armageddon. The best-known of these tenets is the requirement that each family keep at least a year's food supply stockpiled in the home. Basements in Mormon country often are stacked with cases of canned goods. Behind this intensive teaching about preparedness is a rich body of LDS prophecy that emphasizes the core Mormon belief that the end is at hand and holds dearly to a conspiracy view of world affairs. A number of ultraconservatives, including Benson and his close friend, W. Cleon Skousen, devoted long public lives to preaching doomsday and warning about global conspiracies out to destroy true Christians. In that sense many of the old men who lead Mormondom hold views that are shared by the John Birch Society and even less palatable groups such as the Posse Comitatus.

Skousen, a longtime aide to the late FBI director J. Edgar Hoover, a onetime professor of religion at BYU, former chief of police in Salt Lake City, and a founder of Utah's Birch Society, has laid out the Mormon scenario for the Endtimes in a short work called *Prophecy and Modern Times* that features a preface by Benson praising Skousen for his "uncompromising and forthright manner" in describing the Mormon view of Armageddon.

Skousen recounts a biblical history not known to many Americans. Human life began not in the Old World but in America. Adam lived in what is now Missouri. Not far away God established the mysterious City of Enoch which was taken into the heavens intact during the time of Genesis and which soon will return to help usher in the Fulness of Times. Methuselah lived 969 years in America, and it was in America that his grandson, Noah, built the Ark. And thus it continues like a fractured fairy tale up to the point when the Millennium arrives and it is prophesized that the anointed will converge on Salt Lake, a valley filled with food-storing Saints ready with sufficient supplies to hold God's chosen people for a final journey, a triumphant march back to Jackson County, Missouri, and Adam-ondi-Ahman where the central "stake" will be driven to hold up the tent of Zion.

Before that march, however, there will be great earthquakes, tidal waves, and other disruptions that will return the globe to its pristine state with neither impossibly deep seas nor high craggy mountains, but rather a sublime landscape of gentle hills and bright rolling waters. It is this part of the LDS prophetic scenario that makes it particularly difficult for the Saints to accept such essentials of modern science as Darwinian evolution and the geological timetables that measure changes in land forms in hundreds of millions of years rather than hours. In *Mormon Doctrine* Bruce McConkie utterly rejects the geological timescale teaching: "We are now nearing the end of the sixth thousand years of this earth's 'continuance, or its temporal existence,' and the millennial era will commence 'in the beginning of the seventh thousand years. (D & C 77)"

During the holocaust just before the seventh thousand years, Missouri will be wiped clean of the Gentile descendants of those who so horribly persecuted the Saints. The earth will return to its telestial state in which the world's land masses will be joined together and leveled, where the countryside is filled with shade trees and sweet grasses, and all thistles, thorns, briars, and weeds are no more. But much turmoil first must be endured as the seventh Millennium arrives.

Skousen quotes from the *Book of Mormon* to explain that in today's world many "signs of the times" point to the Endtimes, with particular emphasis on how the Gentiles would produce "secret combinations." These cabals of conspirators, Skousen writes, will "become a nation of liars, hypocrites and murderers, addicted to all manner of licentiousness and practicing fraud upon one another through secret combinations." The term "secret combinations" is peppered throughout the *Book of Mormon,* where the Jaredites and then the Nephites destroyed themselves by entering into secret alliances of conspiracy and sedition.

Many Mormons ranging across time from Brigham Young to Ezra Taft Benson have predicted that these secret combinations will focus their venom in an attack on the Constitution of the

United States, which Joseph Smith was told in a revelation was a divinely inspired document given to humanity by God complete with the first ten Amendments, the Bill of Rights.

Skousen and Benson are among many Mormon leaders who teach that these long-feared secret combinations set out to destroy the God-given Constitution by subsequent amendments that abolished slavery, provided for a federal income tax, allowed central banking through the Federal Reserve System, and gave women the right to vote. This same view, of course, has been a hallmark of the anti-Semitic ultra-right since at least the early part of the twentieth century.

The Mormon ultra-right, however, preaches against anti-Semitism even as its leaders tout the same conspiracy arguments Hitler employed. Like other fundamentalist Christians driven by the Book of Revelation, Mormon rightists see a major role for Jews in the unfolding of the Millennium, and devote substantial efforts toward converting Israel to Mormondom in the final days. Furthermore, even as they rail against how hidden forces have diluted the divine words of the Constitution by amendments, Mormon right-wingers stop far short of advocating a return to slavery or a disenfranchisement of women. Nevertheless, both Benson and Skousen have spoken and written adamantly against income taxes, federal reserve banking, social security, and the need to return to the gold standard. Their drive to "restore" the Constitution to its unamended purity would, of course, leave women without the vote and slavery a legal option.

Mormons often speak of a prophecy by Smith that the "Constitution will hang by a thread" in the latter days and only the church's membership will be able to save it. Although the exact phrase "hang by a thread" doesn't appear in Smith's own writings, Brigham Young first attributed the prediction to the founding prophet, and today it has become a popular slogan among the survivalist wing of Mormondom. Young's most quoted words on the topic are: "Will the Constitution be destroyed? No; it will be held inviolate by this people; and, as Joseph Smith said, 'The time will come when the destiny of the nation will hang upon a single thread. At that critical juncture this people will step forth and save it from the threatened destruction.' It will be so."

An oft-delivered Skousen talk about "Prophecy and the Constitution," begins by invoking the preparedness doctrine:

> The Saints need to be aware of what's going to happen in order that they can prepare for what the prophet said they should prepare for. Our brethren have warned us about storing our food, getting out of debt, keeping things in pretty close control, sending our sons and daughters on missions where they're called, paying our tithes and offerings, doing the best we can to get our homes paid for, become as independent as we can, be very frugal as we can about our investments, play them close, don't get too far extended.
>
> All this kind of counsel has been given to us and it's appropriate to remind ourselves that in this immediate future that's just out in front of us we probably will have a test of those teachings and we'll be very grateful to the Lord and his prophets if we listened and did what we were asked to do and probably filled with considerable regret if we find that like the foolish virgin we waited too long to put the oil in our lamps.

The parable of the ten virgins and the lamps is often invoked by Mormon leaders to underscore both the need for preparation and the attendant requirement that the prepared not waste their stores by sharing with the profligate Gentiles. In Matthew 25 Jesus tells the story of the ten virgins who were sent to escort a bridegroom to his wedding and how five were foolish and took no lamp oil with them while the other five took ample oil to fill their lamps throughout the night. When the groom arrived at midnight, the five with oil were ready to light their lamps and guide the way to the nuptials, while the five without oil begged their sisters for enough to tide them over. "But the wise answered, saying, Not So; lest there be not enough for us and you." The parable ends with the well-known injunction "Watch therefore, for ye know neither the day nor the hour wherein the Son of man cometh."

Like Benson, Skousen invokes a strong claim of spirituality to preach his warnings about survivalism and secret combinations, and he has thus provided many Mormon preachers with a template for a mix of ideology and religion that has enjoyed a substantial boost with the ascendancy of Benson to the highest post in Mormondom.

The Skousen/Benson style did something else beside bolster survivalism and fundamentalism in mainstream Mormon circles. It also played quite well to tens of thousands of LDS excommunicants, the men and women who defiantly remain the most fundamental of all LDS fundamentalists, those who live the Principle in these latter days insisting that it is One Temple Square and not themselves who have strayed from the restored gospel of Jesus Christ.

Chapter 9

Polygamists

"I don't see why we can't get along just as well with a polygamist who doesn't polyg as we do with a lot of monogamists who don't monog."

—Sen. Boies Penrose urging his colleagues to seat Mormon Apostle
Reed Smoot in the United States Senate in 1907.

Nothing has caused such anguish in Mormondom as has the prophet Joseph's core teaching that worthy males should cleave to as many women as feasible in this final dispensation when it is so urgent that human bodies be provided to carry the last remaining spirit babies through the veil. Much of the church's early rituals and dogmas were built around the practice because of this sense of Latter-day urgency. Much of the hatred that the Saints have endured springs from Gentile outrage at Mormon plural marriage, but nothing has defined the Saints more than has the Principle.

Polygamy sustained the pioneer Mormon elite as a tightly knit society in Ohio and during the virulent persecutions on the Missouri frontier. It kept the Saints going after they made the long trek to Utah and then set out to populate the harsh landscape of salt and sagebrush. The Principle set the tenor for many of the hymns, family values, and patriarchal traditions that flourish today, concepts that range from Celestial Marriage to the widely revered tradition of Heavenly Mother, often perceived as the primary wife of a polygamous Creator.

Above all, polygamy brought global attention to what otherwise would have been merely another gathering of communitarian Christian fundamentalists out to build a new Eden in late nineteenth-century America. Such communes as the thriving colonies of Shakers in Pennsylvania, the Oneida Communities of New York and New England, the Amana settlements of Iowa, New Harmony in Indiana, and others were common a century ago. Many of these communes were strange by mainstream American church standards, and often as not the fly in the ointment was sex.

The Shakers, led by Ann Lee, a woman who gave birth to four children only to see all die as infants, formed a commune based on total abstinence from sex and devotion to principles of simple living. The Society of the Public Universal Friend, led by Jemima Wilkinson, revered her as the reincarnation of Jesus and taught matriarchy, that the Godhead was exclusively feminine. The Oneida Community practiced open marriage with both women and men taking multiple partners under the belief that each adult was wed to every other adult. Rappites, whose members ultimately opened settlements in Missouri and Oregon, preached that procreation and marriage were sinful.

It was the Mormons, however, who got the bulk of the attention. Brigham Young and his storied harem became a major political concern everywhere from the White House of Abraham Lincoln to the pages of Arthur Conan Doyle's tales, wherein the theme of polygamy and Mormon blood atonement was the subject of "A Study in Scarlet," the first Sherlock Holmes story ever published.

Horace Greeley and William Gordon Bennett, American media giants of their day, traveled, as did Mark Twain, to the Great Salt Lake to write with a grudging admiration about the courage the Saints showed in sticking to their terrible Principle in the face of public condemnation. P. T. Barnum tried unsuccessfully to take Brigham Young on one of his lucrative world tours like those that made the great showman millions with the midget Tom Thumb. Brother Brigham, however, was richer by far than Barnum and an unlikely candidate for anybody's freak show.

Polygamy helped make the Mormon elite prosperous as well as notorious. Recent demographic material shows that taking plural wives vastly increased the number of children each Mormon man produced and thus added greatly to his wealth. A study by Brigham Young University's Jessie L. Embry estimated that 72 percent of Mormon men living in frontier polygamy had broods of between eleven and thirty offspring. In a harsh desert agrarian society like late nineteenth-century Utah, producing large numbers of children to work the land was key not only to wealth and the fulfillment of religious beliefs, but to survival itself. Revered patriarchs including Young, John Taylor, Orson Pratt, Parley Pratt, and Wilford Woodruff urged their people to follow the Principle as the will of God.

In Brigham's Salt Lake a man was judged more by his progeny than by his piety. A man with five wives likely would own five houses, each set on a small farm plot and tended by the children he produced with that wife. Thus while each wife and her children were simply another modest Mormon farm family, their patriarch was a holder of substantial lands and enriched by the product of many farms.

LDS scholars like to point out that polygamy was practiced widely by the church for only a few decades in the last century. Even then only a small number of high-ranking Saints took extra wives. The church always taught that no man should take extra wives until his stature and income were such that he could afford to care for them. It is estimated that in remote LDS strongholds of southern Utah, southwestern Wyoming, Arizona, and in the northern states of Mexico, 30 to 60 percent of the men took multiple wives between 1852, when Apostle Orson Pratt publicly acknowledged that the church practiced polygamy, and 1890, when church President Wilford Woodruff called for an end to marriages that conflict with secular laws.

Historian Leonard Arrington, however, estimates that only 5 percent of all Mormon men and 12 percent of LDS women practiced the Principle. The very fact that one has to estimate the extent of polygamy on the Mormon frontier is itself an indicator of just how sensitive this topic remains in Mormon circles. The highly regarded Mormon historian D. Michael Quinn noted that scholars like Arrington and Embry are forced to extrapolate such estimates from sketchy public records because the church has declined to make public its own temple sealing records which are believed to have recorded every polygamous marriage ever performed under church auspices. Instead, charged Quinn, in its zeal to deemphasize polygamy, the LDS Historical Department withholds these records even from the church's own Genealogical Department. Today, the Principle is anathema to the mainstream church, and any member found participating in plural wedlock faces instant excommunication. However, a dangerous minority rages against this antipolygamy stance by One Temple Square as blasphemous opportunism. To Fundamentalists, church elders clearly abandoned Joseph's sacred prophecy in the face of threats from Gentiles to deny Utah's application for statehood, to revoke the voting rights of all Mormons, to arrest all church leaders and to confiscate all church-owned assets.

Indeed, today few quarrel with the Fundamentalists' premise that the church was forced to cave in over the polygamy issue or face extinction. Even a cursory review of church history shows that these threats were made by the U.S. Congress and the U.S. Supreme Court just before the official prophet, seer, and revelator Woodruff issued a revelation in 1890 called The Manifesto, in which he claimed to be directed by God to abandon the Principle.

The polygamy debate provoked howls of outrage in Victorian America. Starting in 1862 with the Morrill Act which prohibited plural marriage in the territories, Congress pressured the church's leadership with more restrictive laws. The Morrill Act made bigamy a felony and forced the church to abandon its Perpetual Emigration Fund that had been so important to keeping the flow of converts arriving in Utah.

In 1879 the Supreme Court ruled in the case of *Reynolds* v. *U.S.* that it was constitutional for the Congress to deprive Mormons of civil liberties or property for practicing polygamy because plural marriage was against the law and thus not protected by the First Amendment guarantees of religious liberty. A key sentence in the decision advised, "Laws are made for the government of actions, and while they cannot interfere with mere religious belief and opinion, they may with practices." The court said, in effect, that it was okay for Mormons to advocate polygamy in the next world but illegal to practice it in this one. This ruling, known as the "action/belief" doctrine, set a precedent for hundreds of cases in which the practices of a religious minority conflict with the law. Justices likened the practice of polygamy to the Hindu tradition of "suttee" in which a widow is expected to throw herself upon her husband's funeral pyre. This "belief/action dichotomy" has become a cornerstone of U.S. law and has been applied when members of the Jamaican Rastafarian religion demanded the right to use contraband marijuana as a sacrament or when Fundamentalists insisted that they have a right to keep their children from fulfilling public education requirements because their religion bars public school attendance.

All told, the U.S. Supreme Court heard a total of twelve polygamy cases within fifteen years during the late nineteenth century and ruled against the Mormons in all but three of them. The message was clear, Congress could enact virtually any anti-Mormon legislation it wished with impunity.

Ultimately teams of U.S. marshals sent to Utah to round up polygs or "cohabs" (for cohabitation) drove many church leaders "underground." They became fugitives from Gentile law officers in the very heart of their own Zion.

The deciding action Washington took against the Saints over the Principle hit in the pocketbook rather than in the scriptures. The Edmunds–Tucker Act, passed in 1887, proved to be the ultimate force that the church couldn't resist. It provided for the legal dismemberment of the LDS church by ordering the sale of all church-owned property valued at more than $50,000 and making membership a crime. On May 19, 1890, the Supreme Court ruled in a five to four decision (*Late Corporation of the Church of Jesus Christ of Latter-day Saints* v. *United States*) that such seizure and redistribution of the church's property would be legal.

Woodruff was faced with nothing less than having U.S. marshals enter and dismantle the Salt Lake Temple. On September 25, 1890, Woodruff announced his Manifesto:

> Inasmuch as laws have been enacted by Congress forbidding plural marriages, which laws have been pronounced constitutional by the court of last resort, I hereby declare my intention to submit to those laws, and to use my influence with the members of the Church over which I preside to have them do likewise.

In the final pages of *Doctrine and Covenants* are printed excerpts from three addresses that Woodruff later gave on the topic which make it clear that the church abandoned the Principle not because it considered it immoral or improper but because it was against the secular law of the land.

While Woodruff's Manifesto carries the weight of canon law

by its inclusion in the holy book, *Doctrine and Covenants,* the order calling for excommunication of polygamists does not. The excommunication order was a fiat handed down in 1904 by Woodruff's successor, President Joseph F. Smith, in response to questions raised when the U.S. Senate was investigating whether to seat Utah Republican Reed Smoot, the man whose ultimate political career as chairman of the Senate Finance Committee blazed the trail for today's LDS Sisterhood in Washington.

After testifying in Smoot's behalf, Joseph F. Smith issued the still standing order that polygamous Mormons "will be deemed in transgression against the church and will be liable to be dealt with according to the rules and regulations thereof and excommunicated therefrom."

Thus although the church remains adamantly opposed to the Principle for living Mormons, much of the dogma written by Joseph, Brigham, and the other pioneer lawgivers about the Celestial realm stands for the hereafter. Fundamentalists and mainstream church members alike find much in common when they reflect on polygamy's roots and its role in their beliefs. Those roots, of course, hearken back to the early days in Kirtland.

Today, thousands of Fundamentalists hold fast to that principle and scorn the mainstream for abandoning the true restored gospel as given by Joseph Smith. To these true believers, plural marriage is another of God's teachings that have been shunted aside by a church leadership overly concerned with material survival. To these zealots, Mormonism without polygamy is a hollow shell.

In the years Joseph and Brigham held sway, polygamy was the very heart of Mormon dogma. God and Heavenly Mother lived the Principle in the Celestial Kingdom and had taught it to Abraham, Jacob, Samuel, and the other prophets before They taught it to Joseph. Polygamy maximized fecundity and thus accelerated the passage across the veil of the last of the spirit babies whose transit would mark the Fulness of Times. Each resulting extended family of kindred produced by polygamous living would become the Godhead for its own universe just as the extended family of Father Adam rules the current one. Thus polygamy was the logical extension of all the other uniquely Mormon practices regarding baptism and sealing of the dead.

Wilford Woodruff gave up much more than just sensual license when he irrevocably committed the Saints to Christian monogamy with his Manifesto. Mainstream Mormons call it the Great Accommodation. To Fundamentalists like Vickie Singer and Addam Swapp it was the Great Sell-out, for which there was hell to pay.

John Singer, martyred patriarch of the defiant little clan that barricaded themselves in the mountain cabin, shared with other Fundamentalist Mormons an unwillingness to accommodate anyone on the Principle. His story illustrates much about the practice of latter-day polygamy in Mormon circles.

On January 28, 1988, with the whole world watching via the news media, the forces of law and order stormed a fortified compound in the Utah high country where Vickie Singer and Addam Swapp had barricaded themselves and their respective children claiming that the Endtimes had indeed arrived and that the One Mighty and Strong would save them from the surrounding police and then usher in the Millennium. It was decidedly unwelcome publicity for the church, but this tragic confrontation proved a stunning reminder to all that the Principle is far from dead. The story begins with John Singer in the depth of the Great Depression.

Singer was born in Brooklyn, New York, on January 6, 1931, to two German nationals, Hans and Charlotte Singer. The Singers took their new son, a U.S. citizen by virtue of his birth on American soil, back to Germany after the Nazi ascension and enrolled the boy in the Hitler Youth. Charlotte had been converted by LDS missionaries in Germany, and until she divorced Hans in 1945, the couple quarreled often over religion. John Singer later told friends of his father's lecturing him and a brother, Harald, "You are Nazis, not Mormons!" Ultimately John broke with his Nazi father and embraced Mormonism, but he never lost his thick German accent nor his belief in utter obedience to authority. Hans literally beat authoritarianism into John, and John, in turn, beat it into his own large brood.

After Hitler's surrender, the teen-aged Singer made his way to Utah via a harrowing train ride through war-scarred Europe, including a particularly dangerous night when he was forced to walk through bombed-out Leipzig, a city filled with foraging mobs of Russian soldiers and starving Germans. He crossed the city after meeting a soldier who told Singer to follow him. Later Singer taught his children that this soldier actually was one of the Three Nephites whom God let remain on earth after calling his Twelve New World Apostles home to heaven in the *Book of Mormon*. Like many deeply immersed in LDS culture, Singer saw the world as a place of ongoing miracles filled with evil spirits and angels alike. He believed not only that he was receiving ongoing revelations from God, but that Heavenly Father and Heavenly Mother were watching over and guiding his every move.

Because he was an American citizen, Singer quickly made his way from Europe to join relatives in Utah. He arrived in the mountains north of Salt Lake City in Kamas, Utah, a Mormon farm town of about 800 people. John moved in with Gustav Weller, an uncle and old-school Mormon Fundamentalist who owned a large farm just outside the hamlet of Marion two miles from Kamas. This area of extreme northeast Utah along the Wyoming border is a heavily Mormon part of the state with church membership reaching nearly 80 percent.

There was much for Singer's conservative LDS neighbors to admire in the young man who began attending ward meetings, tithed himself, and helped with more than his share of priesthood volunteer activities. After working for a few years for Gus, Singer moved onto a small tract given to him by his uncle.

John's property covered less than three acres but the location was prime ground just where the Uinta Mountains start to rise from the floor of the Kamas Valley. John built a log home almost single-handedly working only with an axe, an adz, and a rope. He foraged about Marion and Kamas and found discarded windows, doors, plumbing fixtures, pipe, glass, and other items that he used to complete it. He did all the carpentry, plumbing, and electrical work. He then set in a large vegetable garden and sunk a root cellar into the mountainside large enough to store food for an entire year, in keeping with church teachings on survivalism.

For John Singer the purpose of the nest building in the Uintas was to start a big Mormon family. He even picked a trade to earn enough money to support a brood. As a television repairman, he made a tolerable living moving up and down the string of Mormon towns along U.S. 189 in the mountains north of Salt Lake fixing sets and cracking jokes with his customers.

One summer day in 1961, he met eighteen-year-old Vickie Lemon, a dance student at the University of Utah. She had been voted beauty queen of the entire Kamas Valley the summer before. After a two-year courtship John and Vickie eloped and were wed in Idaho in 1963. The next year they went to the Salt Lake temple and solemnized the wedding vows that they had first given before a Nevada justice of the peace. They were sealed for time and eternity as man and wife in the church's eyes, but in their own eyes the sealing was nothing less than as patriarch and primary wife.

From the start they struggled for self-sufficiency on the small compound. She grew gardens and canned fruits and vegetables. They bought dairy animals and learned to churn butter, to make cheese, cottage cheese, and buttermilk. He hunted wild game in the uplands behind their house and each night they prayed together and read deeply in D & C, the *Pearl of Great Price, Book of Mormon,* and King James Bible. Vickie stopped wearing Levi's, pedal pushers, and skirts and went about in traditional ankle-length nineteenth-century Mormon dresses she sewed by hand from rude cloth. They stopped seeing dentists and doctors, professing that they had received "gifts of the Spirit" as described in D & C which include healing powers. They often told one another of receiving revelations from God, and each wrote them out in the comprehensive journals that they kept in observance of LDS teachings and which ultimately became court documents.

They set up a flagpole and flew a banner that Vickie had sewn by hand, a copy of the Mormon Ensign that Brigham Young had flown upon arriving at Salt Lake to symbolize that the place was Zion, the place for the final gathering of Saints. Vickie later explained that they believed from the start that their little farm would be the start of that gathering.

Their first child, Heidi, was born in a hospital in nearby Coalville in 1964, as were the next two, Suzanne (1965) and Timothy

(1966). By then, however, they were convinced that relying on hospitals was not "of God," and so John and Vickie learned midwifery from books. When pregnant, she exercised and walked a mile each day and watched her diet closely. In 1968, John helped Vickie deliver Charlotte in their log home. Three sons, Joseph, Benjamin and Israel likewise were delivered at home by their father.

During these same years, John and Vickie developed an intense friendship with the woman who would become his second wife, Shirley Black, a Kamas housewife originally drawn to Gus Weller by his fundamentalist preaching and reputation as a healer. Shirley and her husband, Dean Black, moved in and out of the Singers' lives for much of the 1960s before Shirley became John's second wife in a ceremony that John, Vickie, and Shirley performed together in 1978 near a baptismal font that John dug in a grove of trees on the farm.

Later Shirley was to describe how when she prayed for an answer to whether she should be sealed in the temple to Dean Black in 1965, God had told her that "I belong with John and Vickie, that some day I would be a member of their family. . ."

But her dream lasted for only a short while. Slightly more than a year after John Singer took his second wife, he was shot to death by law officers in his front yard in a confrontation over sending his children to a public school as is required under Utah law.

Singer's death had uniquely Mormon roots, but it turned the budding patriarch into a folk hero among Fundamentalist Christians of every stripe who also believe that public education fosters anti-God sentiments in children and that the Constitution guarantees parents the right to educate offspring in any way they choose.

Singer's fight with the Kamas school board made public one family's practice of modern-day polygamy and with it provided an opportunity to understand the approximately 50,000 practicing polygamists today who largely avoid the violent confrontations that cursed the Singers even as they share John's and Vickie's beliefs and goals.

On January 18, 1979, six years after he pulled his children from school in outrage at a picture of Dr. Martin Luther King

Jr. being treated as an equal of George Washington and Betsy Ross in their textbook, John Singer pulled a gun on law officers who confronted him as he went for his mail at the foot of his compound. The police insisted that they fired only in self-defense, but gripping photos taken at the morgue that afternoon show that Singer was hit repeatedly in the back. His daughter, Charlotte, who witnessed the shooting described in court how she saw her father running away from a band of law officers when he was shot from behind. When Singer fell to the ground, Vickie, Heidi, Shirley, and young Timothy all grabbed weapons and ran toward the scene. But when they found their patriarch had been killed, they offered no further resistance.

The agent of a second round of carnage on the Singer compound was a strange young fanatic named Addam Swapp. Addam's friends viewed him as a real Yankee Doodle Dandy of Mormonism. He was born on April 6, 1961, the same day that Joseph had founded the LDS church in Fayette, New York. Charlotte Singer, one of two of John and Vickie's daughters who would become Swapp's plural wives, said that April 6 was the true birthdate of Jesus Christ as well as of her husband and of the LDS church.

Like John Singer's sons, Addam was a typical freckle-faced boy who mowed the neighbors' lawns, pulled their daughters' pigtails, and loved baseball, track, and Dairy Queen soft ice cream cones. In 1973, when Addam was 12, his parents bought a small place in rural Fairview, south of Provo on the edge of the Manti-La-Sal National Forest.

Addam was a lousy student in Fairview but he loved to go hunting and fishing with his father, Ramon, in the mountains. In high school, Swapp became interested in various Fundamentalist Mormon issues such as the "Adam-God Doctrine," which, as the name implies, holds that as the father of the family that became the human race, Adam really is the God of the Old Testament and that Eve was merely his primary wife. Ramon provided a set of *Journal of Discourses* right alongside the family's volumes of *World Books* and the family scripture bundle, giving Addam access to many of the more startling pronouncements by Brigham Young.

Eventually Addam enrolled at the University of Utah and

spent a lot of time in the Salt Lake City library poring over "source" documents about pioneer Mormons and newspaper articles about neighbor John Singer's fight. He followed the Singer story on radio and television newscasts and was taken with Heidi Singer, by then an angelic 15-year-old with soft features and flowing blond hair. Obsessed by John's case, and by his daughters as well, Swapp dropped out of school and moved to Kamas from Fairview, where he took a job at a valley lumber yard to be closer to the Singer compound before he received his first invitation inside.

One afternoon in 1979, not all that long after John's burial, Swapp telephoned "Grandma Singer," John and Harald's mother, Charlotte, who then lived in the area, and asked her if she wanted a ride to the Marion farm for a visit. Once in the living room of the Singers' crude home, the obsessed Addam pawed eagerly through the books in the hand-built shelves and crowed in delight upon finding a passage that John had underlined, a page turned back at the corner for later reference. John's daughter, Charlotte, then 11, later recalled that she was put off by the fawning. "I didn't like him much at first. He acted goony—pulling Dad's books out of the bookshelves, real excited like."

But Charlotte's older sister Heidi was taken by the intense Addam, and when she turned 16 in September, 1980, she married him, first in the grove of trees where John, Vickie, and Shirley Black had consecrated their polygamous household and later on the steps of the Salt Lake Temple, where they sealed their vows after closing time and without official church sanction.

Two years later, in 1983, Addam took Charlotte as his second wife. She had just turned 14, a common age for polygamist females to become ancillary wives. In keeping with polygamy traditions, the Singer–Swapp group moved into four separate houses in the compound after John's death. Vickie and Addam lived in the big house together, although they adamantly denied that they were living as man and wife. Vickie insisted that she was sealed "for life as well as for eternity" to her dead husband.

Addam alternated among the big house and two other abodes, Charlotte's house and Heidi's house, for patriarchal conjugal visits. A fourth home was Suzanne's house, where John's other daughter lived with one of Swapp's cousins, Roger Bates, yet another excommunicated Kamas Valley Fundamentalist. There were many children moving in and out the doors of these scattered houses. Addam and Heidi had five children before the tragedy on the hillside that sent him to prison.

The drama started in the post-midnight hours of January 16, 1988, when Addam and Vickie walked across a mile of snow-filled crop lands from the Singer compound to the Kamas LDS stake center, the building where Vickie and John had received their excommunication notices after a brief trial in 1972. Addam and Vickie entered through an unlocked door and planted a bomb of eighty-seven sticks of dynamite and a crude timer along one wall. On the way back to the Singer farm, Addam left a spear planted in a snowbank with ten feathers to mark the tenth anniversary of John Singer's death. Once back in the big house they raised the Mormon flag and proclaimed it an "Ensign to all Nations," to signal the arrival of the Millennium.

The homemade bomb destroyed the LDS building when it exploded, causing more than $1 million in damages. The law officers who arrived at the scene had little difficulty identifying their suspects. Addam and Vickie's footprints still could be seen in the snow heading directly back to the Singer place from the ruined stake center. A thirteen-day siege ensued, during which law officers gradually escalated the pressure upon the embattled polygamists even as Addam, Vickie, and others seized the opportunity to broadcast their beliefs and their distrust of One Temple Square. When a team of law officers finally stormed the encampment, a young police dog handler named Fred House was killed.

There was a sad irony in that House's sister, Dawn, was a reporter for the Salt Lake *Tribune,* specializing in Mormon-related news. Putting aside her own grief, she wrote her brother's obituary for the next day's paper and in so doing revealed the anguish in Mormondom. She told how she, Fred, and four other brothers and sisters lost their hard-drinking Gentile father and how they had found Mormonism with their mother's second husband who brought them from California to Utah. She told of a brave young brother prone to strutting about the squad room and making sexist jokes but utterly devoted to his wife and three young children. He died trying to use a German shepherd guard dog to take away Swapp's rifle instead of firing a weapon. The piece ended, "Funeral services will be Monday noon at the LDS Windsor Stake Center, 1674 N. 200 West, Orem. I didn't want anyone else to write Fred's story. He was my brother. He was my dear, old friend."

Roger Bates later explained that House died because the compound dwellers had received a revelation that if they could provoke the police into attacking Vickie and John's children with deadly force, Singer would cross back through the veil to their rescue and, in so doing, usher in the Millennium.

While Bates acted briefly as an intermediary between the embattled polygamists and the law, the police preferred to work through Ogden Kraut, a self-described "independent fundamentalist," who had been both a friend of Singer's and a mentor to Addam Swapp.

Kraut, an occasional contributor to *Sunstone* and a frequent Utah radio and TV talk-show guest, provided a link between the bizarre and murderous Singer–Swapp group and various polygamy movements in Mormondom. According to Kraut, these more or less ordinary advocates of the Principle emphasize that church teaching always has said that the sole purpose of plural marriage is procreation, and that sexual gratification means nothing to those fully in the thrall of the Principle. Dorothy Solomon, a ranking daughter in the clan of polygamist Rulon Allred, writes in her book, *In My Father's House,* "the sexual activities of all partners are governed by the Law of Chastity, which states that sex is purely for procreation, not for lust." She added that there are only two occasions when a man can validly approach one of his wives in a sexual way: when he has received a direct revelation from God to attempt a mating and when the woman herself tells a suitor that she feels her cycle of fertility is at its peak.

The church has consistently refused to disclose information about the scope of the polygamy situation. Virtually every rebellious Mormon currently practicing polygamy has been excommunicated after formal hearings, but One Temple Square won't reveal its excommunication statistics. A common estimate by law enforcement officials and others who study the practice places the number of polygamists in Utah alone at about 30,000, with another 20,000 believed to be engaged in the lifestyle in other states such as Montana, Arizona, Wyoming, and California, as well as in the northern states of Mexico.

A number of settlements called "colonias" first were established across the Mexican border in the late nineteenth century by Saints fleeing prosecution. They found unanticipated tolerance among that heavily Catholic country's police establishment. At least a half dozen of these polygamous communes remain in Mexico along with three major colonias populated by mainstream Mormons who excommunicate polygamists just as quickly in Chihuahua as do the Saints in Utah.

One little-known aspect of today's polygamous families is the fact that there can be a lot of money in cohabitation on a relatively grand scale. In 1985 the Utah state welfare department, the Division of Recovery Services, filed suit in district court charging that followers of an immensely wealthy patriarch, John Ortell Kingston, then 65, had defrauded the government out of millions of dollars when polygamous wives had collected state and federal welfare benefits claiming to be unwed mothers of transient men, when in fact, they were part of an organized family. There were allegations that the Kingston clan numbering nearly a thousand members had grown wealthy on federal aid, from food stamps to Social Security payments netting millions.

The Utah welfare department case alleged that Kingston had at least four wives and twenty-nine children who collected hundreds of thousands in Aid to Families with Dependent Children payments. Meanwhile Kingston's federal income-tax returns for 1981 showed he had reported sales of $30 million from a string of enterprises that included a coal mine, a dairy, clothing and shoe factories, nearly a hundred pieces of real estate, an interstate vending machine company, and 40 percent ownership in a bank with assets of $21 million in the Salt Lake suburb of Murray, Utah.

While the Kingston clan is one of perhaps a dozen known polygamy cults that operate with varying degrees of fanaticism, experts believe that far more people practice the Principle in a more subdued fashion.

A prime example of the vast majority of Fundamentalists who

hew to the line on virtually every law except the one on Utah's books banning the Principle, is Royston Potter, a slim handsome man with two photogenic wives who went public after he was fired from the Murray, Utah, police department for practicing plural marriage. Potter fought his dismissal all the way to the U.S. Supreme Court where his final appeal foundered. He then started making appearances on television talk shows and in the pages of popular magazines arguing for the right to the Principle.

In a March, 1985, interview, Potter estimated that there are at least 20,000 men and women like his family, living as independent polygamists as contrasted to thousands more residing in sundry polygamy sects like the Kingston cult and patterned after the United Order concept that Joseph Smith and Brigham Young unsuccessfully tried to implement during their respective tenures.

Potter's wives each live in a different suburban house, and he compared running the households to operating a small business. Two households, of course, require much more spending on automobiles, mortgages, utilities, and the like than does living under a single roof. Potter said that he tried to make ends meet by such economies as always carrying the families' vacuum cleaner when he went from wife Mary's house to wife Vera's place twenty miles away. On vacations he often loads both wives and all their children into one car.

A common practice among less exotic polygamists is simply to rent a duplex and have the husband alternate between the two neighboring families. This is an effective arrangement not only because it cuts commuting costs and allows families to share appliances, but because it helps conceal the polygamous relationships from neighbors in Mormon country where rank-and-file church members are quick to shun anybody they suspect of practicing the Principle.

There are clusters of such polygamous duplexes in the Salt Lake south suburb of Taylorsville and in the town of Bluffdale, about halfway between Salt Lake and Provo on Interstate 15. Most of these people adhere to the principles of John and Vickie Singer and Addam Swapp, but they avoid angry confrontation, and in fact have tried to persuade a curious American public of the rightness of the Principle.

Take Tom Green, for example, who hands out videotapes of his polygamous home life and has made frequent TV appearances to explain the Principle. His suburban Salt Lake living room is graced by his latest wedding cake, a styrofoam and paste affair with a groom and three brides standing alongside. In 1988 at the age of 37, Green boasted that he differed from most patriarchs in that he didn't keep each of his wives and their children in separate houses. He said that the "joy of plural marriage" includes the pleasures of the family sharing the same roof enjoying each other. Thus, he took a different one of his four wives into the master bedroom each night.

While most sister wives each have a house of their own, Green's wives each had only a separate drawer in his dresser to store their "special nighties" and other essentials for the conjugal bed. The next morning the other wives and the family's thirteen children brought breakfast in bed to the pair in the master bedroom.

At chez Green sister wives post the monthly schedule on the refrigerator door. The unself-conscious adoration that Green displays to his womenfolk, and the affection they so openly return to him and to their sister wives underscores the power of plural marriage among consenting people (if not always adults) all across the face of Mormondom. But there are facts about the Greens that his videotape leaves out about the realities of the Principle.

Among the Green harem are two mothers and their two daughters from previous marriages, four females all of whom share the master bedroom on rotation despite their own cosanguinity—not to mention their parent-child emotional bonds. Green's version of the Principle illustrates that teen-aged brides and dangerous genetic mixings are commonplace in virtually every polygamous setting.

Numerous court cases in Utah take much of the bloom off of polygamy by disclosing that it is almost universal for men in the Principle to marry closely related women, sisters, cousins, aunts, and even the step-daughters produced by earlier husbands of their plural wives.

In an interview with the Los Angeles *Times* printed on May 13, 1988, Green made his case for plural wifery, telling reporter Bella Stumbo, "Just think how much easier it is for a teen-age mother here, than in monogamous marriage. Here, she's got three other women to help her out, to teach her what she doesn't know. You can't beat motherhood under conditions like these."

In fact, a patriarch needs these plural wives much more than they need him. A man can greatly enhance his standing among the rank and file in polygamous circles to the degree that he can control the doling out of wives to the remainder of the community's menfolk. The result is an intense pressure on females by each sect's patriarch to begin conjugal service soon after they reach sexual maturity.

Twelve- and thirteen-year-old mothers are routinely traded back and forth in such polygamous circles. To keep the babies coming, polygamous women live in an almost constant state of pregnancy from menarch to menopause. The trafficking in female progeny is polygamy's ultimate outrage. Try as they might, polygamists can never find as many women as they'd like in a Gentile-dominated world.

Tom Green found at least two of his young wives through what remains the Mecca of latter-day polygamy, the dusty but fecund village of Colorado City, Arizona. Previously known as Short Creek, Colorado City lies just down the road from "Cohab Canyon," named by the U.S. marshals who lost the trail of many a polygamist fugitive in those parched precincts of southern Utah and northern Arizona. Geography defines Colorado City. The north side of town straddles the Utah/Arizona border about fifteen miles due south of Utah's Zion National Park, a sanctuary of sandstone spires, desert fastness, and endless cliffs that makes the unforgiving landscape a national treasure in its own right. The south side of Colorado City lies entirely in the sovereign state of Arizona. The resulting isolation is splendid. It is impossible to approach Colorado City from the south because the Grand Canyon cuts across Arizona just forty miles away creating an uncrossable barrier. Entry is possible only from the north and then only via a single two-lane asphalt highway, making it easy for lookouts to spot any approaching traffic.

Skittishness is endemic in these Fundamentalist drylands to-day as always. Polygamous townsfolk who settled Short Creek in the early 1930s put wooden skids on their houses so they could drag them with horse teams across the state line into Arizona if the law descended from Utah as it often did while enforcing that state's anti-cohabitation laws. In fact, the Short Creek Saints never had to use those skids. Instead they produced a series of charismatic leaders, who with a few rather stunning exceptions, dealt admirably with the forces of Gentile law and order and kept these few Fundamentalist enclaves thriving in an unhospitable climate. Except for three federal raids over half a century, Short Creek has followed the Principle without pause since 1936 under the tutelage of some amazingly powerful patri-archs.

These zealots were men like LeRoy "Uncle Roy" Johnson, an uncompromising Fundamentalist who died at the age of 98 in 1986 as prophet, seer, and revelator of Short Creek's minions who call themselves quite simply The Church of Jesus Christ, the original name Joseph Smith gave his church.

"Our Father in Heaven," began the daily prayer at Short Creek's daily grade school sessions, "please bless Uncle Roy." In fact, "uncle" Roy was husband, father, uncle, father-in-law, or otherwise related to most of the 2,100 people who make up Short Creek as a result of polygamy. His own wives included thirteen women who gave him forty-four sons and daughters. These chil-dren continued in the polygamous lifestyle between the early 1930s when Johnson and another Fundamentalist visionary, John Y. Barlow, set up Short Creek with help from many other patriarchs.

Over the years Johnson and Barlow's heirs and patriarchs from a third major Short Creek family, the Jessops, have fought off lawsuits attempting to take over the town. Thus details are available about the inner workings of the commune that other-wise would be hidden forever.

Just as Joseph Smith made himself "Trustee in Trust" at Kirtland and held title to all surrounding lands, the Short Creek United Order owns everything in the entire town. All of the large houses were built by church members at their own expense, but are owned by the patriarchs under the trust. When men apostize, they quickly get an eviction note and often leave with little more than the clothes on their back.

As a result of past litigation, the controlling body today is named the United Effort Plan rather than the United Order, and it holds title to a major financial fiefdom in the Southwest, including two factories, one for making modular housing and another that produces wooden cabinets for the construction industry. A string of nursing homes, an egg farm, and other agricultural holdings round out the portfolio that various litigants have charged in lawsuits has a total value exceeding $60 million. The patriarch who replaced Uncle Roy in 1986, an octogenarian named Rulon Jeffs, maintains a luxury house in the Salt Lake City suburb of Holladay as well as houses for his families in Colorado City.

On the dusty streets of today's Colorado City girls dress in long pioneer gingham dresses, and boys wear Levi's and long-sleeved shirts. Unlike every other corner of rural America, there are no satellite TV dishes in Colorado City. The sect bans its members from watching television and reading periodical literature. Most homes have shelves with the five volumes of "discourses" by Uncle Roy as well as traditional Mormon scripture bundles.

There seem to be fewer males than females on the streets, and dissidents who have filed suit against the United Effort Trust charge that elders make an effort to keep the male population to a minimum to reduce the demand for wives which often are meted out to men deemed deserving by the patriarch. It is common to send young men out as "work missionaries," where they spend at least two years living frugally and performing manual labor to send the proceeds back to the United Effort.

It is considered all the better if these youths come home with a first bride and it's better still if they just keep sending money and eventually move into the outside world and never come home. Some of the girls likewise are sent out to earn money in places like the retirement community of Saint George, Utah, where they frequently take jobs in nursing homes owned by the United Effort Trust. The sect wants its girls back, however. The female missions involve only girls under 18, the age in Utah where a teen cannot be required by law to return to her parents.

One of these girls, a 17-year-old working in a Saint George, Utah, nursing home, told Ruth Terry of the Associated Press in May of 1985 that dating and courtship are forbidden for the town's teens. "When we think we're ready to get married the men will receive a revelation and tell us who to marry."

Court transcripts provided a glimpse into Short Creek's bedrooms in 1983 when Jack Cooke, one of the town's more popular men, was tried and convicted of sexually abusing his own teen-aged daughters. Cooke had been awarded much of the United Effort's fence-building business on its many agricultural properties by Uncle Roy and was an inner circle member.

The patriarch thus was generous in providing Cooke wives in the late 1940s and 1950s. Cooke asked for a 12-year-old, but Uncle Roy insisted that he first wed a 16-year-old and wait until his chosen was 13 when he did, indeed, marry her. When he was drafted into the army, Cooke took a 15-year-old bride before leaving for two years. He returned in 1953 and married a 16-year-old, his fourth and final wife. These women produced fifty-four children, twenty-seven girls and twenty-seven boys, and many of the daughters were "given" by Uncle Roy to other Short Creek men.

But on January 27, 1983, Cooke was arraigned in Utah's Washington County on charges of forcible sexual assault on four of his daughters. A plea bargain led to his conviction on two charges of forcible sexual assault, and he spent five years in prison before being released in 1988. While social scientists reacted to the case by noting that polygamists are no more prone to sexually abusing children than are monogamists, Cooke's aberrations did provide a rare glimpse at life in this strange town below the Vermilion Cliffs.

Of course much has changed for Colorado City in recent years. When it was founded in the early 1930s, America's sexual ethic was much different than it is today, when young men and women frequently cohabitate without a marriage license. Sheriff Chuck Ramsey, a monogamous Mormon in Sanpete County, Utah, acknowledged that he could arrest large numbers of people living

195

there in violation of Utah's antipolygamy laws, but added, "I'd be laughed out of town if I did. Besides, I'd have to arrest a number of our leading monogamous citizens too for living in sin."

During the heat of the 1988 presidential campaign, while he was still considered a viable candidate, former Arizona Governor Bruce Babbitt told the *Wall Street Journal* of Colorado City, "Talk about Americana. They're good people, hard-working people. Besides, I'm not in the business of condoning or commenting on people's personal lives" (*WSJ*, Jan 6, 1986).

In 1953, when the world at large first learned about Short Creek, the situation was markedly different. Arizona's governor at the time, Howard Pyle, arranged for a Salt Lake City detective to move into Short Creek posing as a Hollywood film scout looking for a location to shoot one of the many Westerns that have been filmed in the Canyonland environs around the town. Pyle also obtained a secret appropriation from the Arizona legislature for $30,000 to finance the raid by declaring a formal state of "insurrection" existed in the town.

A force of one hundred FBI agents, deputies, and state troopers moved on the town in a convoy. As they passed the cliffs outside town one car was hit by a bullet and roughly a dozen sticks of dynamite were set off in front of them. None of the invaders was hurt and when they reached town the men and women of Short Creek had gathered near the schoolyard to sing "America" while the children played volleyball.

A total of ninety-six townsfolk were fingered by the "movie agent" spy as known polygamists and arrested on the spot. Eventually, all of the women were released, and only twenty-seven men faced charges of conspiracy to commit adultery, bigamy, open and notorious cohabitation, and marrying the spouse of another. All received one year's probation.

In statements made at the time Pyle justified the raid because of the way Johnson and other patriarchs were treating women. Short Creek he said was "dedicated to the production of white slaves who are without hope of escaping this degrading slavery from the moment of their birth." Uncle Roy reacted to the publicity and the condemnation over "white slavery" by renaming the place Colorado City. Just as the patriarch hoped, the renamed commune quickly slipped from the public's mind, and residents smoothly resumed life in the Principle until lawsuits occasioned by the change of power after Uncle Roy died once again brought unwelcome attention.

It is clear that while Colorado City has become the best documented polygamous commune, the sect's beliefs are stranger than most Fundamentalist, excommunicated Mormons. Uncle Roy, for example, preached that the Grand Canyon and the Bonneville Salt Flats were formed by the great rending of the earth the day Jesus was crucified. He preached that Abraham Lincoln's body turned black in the grave because he didn't honor Mormon pleas for help in the early days of Deseret. And, almost predictably, he taught that Short Creek was built on the precise spot that would be the new Zion, the city prophesized in the Book of Genesis and the *Book of Mormon* where the final gathering of Saints will occur.

Chapter **10**

Friendly Foes and Mormon Haters

"We need not follow our researches in any spirit of fear and trembling. We desire only to ascertain the truth; nothing but the truth will endure; and the ascertainment of the truth and the proclamation of the truth in any given case, or upon any subject, will do no harm to the work of the Lord which is itself truth.

—Polygamist Brigham H. Roberts writing as
official LDS Church Historian in 1909

High in the Colorado Rockies where skiers flock each winter for the runs at Vail, local churches were forced by high land prices to build an ecumenical chapel overlooking the slopes. Members of the Catholic, Lutheran, Baptist, Episcopalian, Presbyterian, Christian Science, and Jewish congregations all worship there après-ski.

The centerpiece is a small cross fashioned out of two ski tips. When Jews hold services, the cross is easily moved aside, but when the Vail ward of the Church of Jesus Christ of Latter-day Saints applied to use the chapel for its services, the request was denied by a 7–3 vote in 1985 of the Vail Religious Foundation, which oversees the chapel.

"This is an interfaith chapel, not an intercult chapel," the Reverend Stephen A. Hoekstra, a Baptist minister, told the *Rocky Mountain News.*

In Jerusalem on Mount Scopus, a spur of the Mount of the Olives, where Christians believe Jesus Christ ascended into heaven, the $15 million LDS Study Center often is scarred by spray-painted slogans like "AIDS Mormons," and "Mormons Go Home." Ultraconservative members of Israel's parliament, the Knesset, have demanded since 1984 when construction started on the center that the government buy it and expel the Mormons inside. At one point, 7,000 anti-Mormon Jews demonstrated at a rally outside the building. Mormons are bound by Israeli law not to seek converts in the Holy Land.

Ironically enough, the Anti-Defamation League of B'nai B'rith felt compelled to come to the Mormons' aid with the observation that of all the peoples on earth Jews should realize the pain intolerance causes its targets.

In Idaho, a heavily Mormon state that long has been blighted by the fact that it serves as world headquarters of the neo-Nazi and white supremacist Church of Jesus Christ Christian/Aryan Nations, a 1988 poll by Boise State University on prejudice found 11.5 percent of respondents regarded their Mormon neighbors very unfavorably, a higher percentage of negative feelings than expressed for Hispanics, blacks, Jews, Japanese-Americans, and other minorities by poll respondents.

The Mormon teaching that other churches are preaching the word of the devil by using a trained clergy long has triggered extreme responses from non-Mormons. Likewise, the fact that the inner working of the church is kept secret even as Mormon doctrine compels clannishness makes it easy for Gentiles to fear and distrust the self-proclaimed Saints.

Within Mormon ranks, those same aspects—secrecy, authoritarianism, intolerance of dissent—create substantial friction between a growing number of Mormon intellectuals and their own elders with whom they clash over matters of theology and history.

Even as Mormonism is the fastest growing branch of Christianity, the church is in a state of siege, confronted by unfriendly Gentiles on the outside and clamoring intellectuals inside the pale. In other words, not much has changed since the days of Joseph Smith when the old settlers from without hurled hot lead while dissidents within Saintly ranks drafted heresies. Blessedly, those days are gone, but the foes remain strong and numerous. An influential group of scholars and writers seeking out historical vulnerabilities formed around the journal *Sunstone*. This magazine, brainchild of underground members including its longtime editor, Peggy Fletcher, great-granddaughter of the sixth LDS president Heber Grant, and an LDS version of a sixties liberal, became the sounding board for thousands of practicing Mormons who chafed at church censorship. Over the eight years Fletcher edited *Sunstone* its pages raged with Mormon controversies from Mother in Heaven to Joseph Smith's penchant for mystic incunabla.

The feisty magazine confronted elders with their intolerance for gay Mormons and their predilection for the Republican party and antifeminism. Importantly, this peculiarly Mormon journal published long and difficult monographs by scholars of the stature of Hugh Nibley or Yale-educated D. Michael Quinn, the one-time BYU historian whose book *Early Mormonism and the Magic World View* traced numerous *Book of Mormon* themes to various magical and occult legends of the era.

This modern strain of loyal opposition in Mormon life dates to the controversy that swept the church after one of its own, Fawn Brodie, stunned the world with *No Man Knows My History,* the devastating biography of Joseph Smith that first raised so many of the problems still confounding Mormon apologists almost fifty years later. The schism often is referred to by insiders as the "Iron Rod" Mormons versus the "Liahona" Mormons. Both the iron rod and the Liahona were devices that God gave to *Book of Mormon* people to guide them in various treks. The Iron Rod was grasped in the hand and the holder pulled it along exactly where God wanted him to go, to the tree of life. The Liahona was more of a compass that floated in the air. It gently pointed a way but the holder had to find the route. Iron Rod Mormons hew to the establishmentarian dictates; they follow the patriarchs without question. Liahona Mormons ask questions along the way. The metaphors for both types are taken from the *Book of Mormon* to underscore that both Iron Rodders and Liahonas remain faithful to the LDS church. When Peggy Fletcher married she did so as a loyal LDS wife in the sealing room of the Mormon Temple in Salt Lake.

As one scans the scholastic landscape, most of the Iron Rod versus Liahona tumult came not after the first edition of Brodie's book was issued in 1944 but after a second release in 1966, a time of great intellectual tumult throughout the American landscape so typified by the Viet Nam War protests, existentialism, and the civil rights movement championed by people like Fletcher on both sides of the Zion Curtain.

After Dr. Martin Luther King, Jr., was assassinated in 1967 the national mood turned militant regarding race relations and the Mormon ban on blacks joining the priesthood quickly became a major issue. The basketball and football teams of BYU often were greeted by protest marches when they traveled to play games at schools like Colorado State University and Stanford. At one CSU game a Molotov cocktail was tossed onto the court to protest antiblack LDS tenets.

The Western Athletic Conference nearly disbanded over the furor, and that meant a lot to rank-and-file Mormons who take a deep pride in the "Y" and its longstanding reputation for producing some of America's winningest football and basketball teams. More importantly, of course, the copious publicity given to protests against the Mormon teaching that a black skin was a curse from God made it even more difficult than before for missionaries to make progress in the field. Furthermore, even as the church was being attacked for rampant racism, Mormon elders had decided to move the missions into South America by establishing a temple in Brazil, a largely black country but key to the ultimate Mormon goal of converting the Lamanites in order to usher in the Millennium.

While the church ultimately rescinded its antiblack teaching through Prophet Spencer Kimball's 1978 revelation on the subject, the establishment's long resistance to change enlarged the ranks of the loyal opposition with Mormons of all ages who were more in tune with popular American values than were the elders at One Temple Square.

Although Peggy Fletcher and her colleagues involved with *Sunstone* tended to be young firebrands, an equally powerful knot of dissidents emerged around another nonsanctioned publication, *Dialogue: A Journal of Mormon Thought,* which tended to include more established—and older—members of the Mormon intelligentsia like the all-but-venerated Mormon historian Leonard J. Arrington. A man with flawless Mormon credentials and a more than impressive academic portfolio, Arrington pressed hard with his professional historian's view that unrestrained academic pursuit would only serve to strengthen Mormon positions, not undermine them. His 1958 book *Great Basin Kingdom: An Economic History of the Latter-day Saints* won him great acclaim among Mormon elders and academicians alike. The book was a rare critical success for a pro-Mormon writer because of its objective and insightful treatment of Brigham Young and other Mormon leaders as they converted what had been a dissonant minority religion into a major economic and political force on the Western frontier.

In his later book, *The Mormon Experience,* Arrington noted that underground groups like *Sunstone* and *Dialogue* were particularly helpful to thinking Mormons when they are faced with the need to "apply aspects of their secular education to their religion." In other words, banding together in this fashion, Mormons have tried to incorporate their training in scientific evolution, human archaeology and astronomy into a religion that teaches as fundamental truths that all history began seven thousand years ago, that the human race began in Missouri, and that the planet Kolob sits at the center of a universe that revolves once every thousand years.

Despite such quandaries for intellectuals, Arrington remained utterly committed to Mormon principles and thus worked from within to press the conservative elders to be more open with the all-important archives that Brodie and a handful of other scholars had used to produce truly groundbreaking scholarship about the faith and its origins.

Arrington, Brodie, and others made significant headway with the elders and throughout the 1960s gradually opened up access for genuine scholars to once-closed church archives. Along the way they established the Mormon Historical Association (MHA), a group that included not just Mormon scholars but also their counterparts from the Reformed Latter Day Saints church in Missouri and independent non-Mormon historians like Purdue University's Jan Shipps, whose book *Mormonism* was hailed by Mormons and outsiders alike as a powerful evocation of the Mormon way. Jerry Cahill, the longtime press spokesman for One Temple Square, praised Shipps book for having "a quality rare among those who observe and write about the Church of Latter-day Saints: she understands us."

In 1972 the underground was stunned when Arrington was named official Historian of the Church of Jesus Christ of Latter-day Saints, the first professional historian ever to receive carte blanche access to church archives. He responded with a public statement vowing not to be daunted by objections from above that a given piece of information might not be faith promoting and thus should be suppressed. Arrington said he would make that decision himself and indicated that he was inclined to think that the truth would never be anything but faith promoting and thus open to all Mormons.

At *Sunstone* and *Dialogue* they referred to Arrington's ascension as Camelot. Arrington announced plans to use core LDS source documents to produce a definitive sixteen-volume history of the church.

As it happened, Camelot was too good to last. The first two volumes of the project, *The Story of the Latter-day Saints* and *Building the City of God* drew angry responses from two members of the Twelve Apostles, Ezra Taft Benson and Boyd K. Packer. Benson charged that the books went out of their way to "humanize" church founders by exposing their failings and foibles "so that their human frailties become more evident than their spiritual qualities." Packer's criticism was even harsher. Arrington and his historians, said Packer, were "faith destroying."

The sixteen-volume project was abandoned and access to the Temple Square archives was cut off. Ultimately Arrington was removed as church historian in 1980, and that office was moved forty miles south to the campus at BYU, well out of reach of the Vault of the First Presidency. Camelot had been encircled by what angry undergrounders first called the "Zion Curtain."

In the ashes of that Mormon Camelot, however, a new zeal suffused the scholars. At BYU an alternative newspaper called *Seventh East Press* began publishing documents that had been purloined from closed archives and a brisk trade developed in photocopies of such material. Insiders called it the "Xerox Underground."

The crackdown from One Temple Square continued, and in 1983 the BYU trustees banned *Seventh East Press* from campus, a move that forced the paper to fold. Fletcher left *Sunstone* in

1986. Arrington remains a BYU professor emeritus but the fire is gone. Any future Camelot will have to patch up a lot of wounds, and advocates will have to convince the elders that just as the long-dead B. H. Roberts said at the turn of the century, the truth will do no harm.

A thirtysomething LDS Yuppie with tortoise-shell eyeglasses may have irreparably damaged the case of those who advocate airing Mormon historical controversies in public. Mark Hofmann, the Salt Lake forger-bomber, drew unwelcome attention to the church's seething in-house battles that will continue to haunt Mormons for years to come. A garment-wearing returned missionary who once had enrolled in pre-med at the University of Utah before starting a business selling rare coins and autographs, Hofmann followed closely as the loyal opposition at *Sunstone* and *Dialogue* brought the forces of modern-day scholarship to bear on such long-standing issues as whether Joseph Smith was a money digger, whether Sidney Rigdon played a hidden role in writing the *Book of Mormon,* whether the papyri printed in the Book of Abraham in *Pearl of Great Price* were authentic, and so on. Then Hofmann, a master forger, concocted seemingly authentic documents that not only addressed these hotly debated points but that almost invariably appeared to cast them in the worst possible light for the church. He then sold the bogus documents to One Temple Square, where elders promptly locked them away in the Vault of the First Presidency.

The Hofmann case blazed into the headlines on October 15, 1985, when Steven Christensen, a wealthy and well-connected Salt Lake investment counselor who had numerous dealings with Hofmann, arrived before 8:00 A.M. at his office in the Judge Building near Temple Square and found a package addressed to him leaning against his office door. Seconds after he touched the box, it exploded, killing him.

Kathy Sheets, the wife of Christensen's longtime business partner Gary Sheets found a similar package addressed to her husband leaning up against the garage door of their house in a wealthy Salt Lake suburb a short time after Christensen's life was blown away by nails and black powder. When she picked up the box out of curiosity she too died in the blinding flash and stench of cordite.

Hofmann himself was maimed the next day when a third pipe bomb exploded as he lifted it in his car just behind the church headquarters building on Temple Square, apparently en route to attack a third and still-unknown victim.

Ultimately Hofmann pleaded guilty to murder charges and acknowledged that the bombings were part of a plot to blackmail the church's ruling elders by selling them documents that appeared to undermine the church's position on key issues of history and dogma. He was sentenced to life in the Utah state prison. His father, Bill Hofmann, later was to lament to a reporter for the Salt Lake *Tribune* that Mark hadn't been executed. An execution order from the Utah governor would have allowed Mark to specify a firing squad and thus achieve blood atonement, Bill noted sadly.

In a remorseless jailhouse interview arranged as part of a plea bargain on the charges of murdering Sheets and Christensen, Hofmann told how he had held Mormonism in utter contempt through all the years of garment wearing, temple going, and food storing. He studied LDS scriptures and history deeply, but he did so with a secret agenda of destruction. Hofmann had lost his faith in Mormonism at age fourteen in a particularly eerie fashion considering his penchant for explosives that took two lives. As has many a precocious adolescent before him, Hofmann found the chemical recipe for gunpowder in the family *World Book Encyclopedia*—charcoal, saltpeter, sulphur—and mixed up a batch in his basement. During one experiment, apparently while young Hofmann was heating a beaker full of wood alcohol to produce a homemade bomb, it detonated in his face, seriously burning him and leaving a scar on his chin as a lifelong reminder of his ill-fated flirtation with matters pyrotechnical.

In his bed of bitter recuperation from the accident, Hofmann decided that if there were a God He wouldn't have allowed a mere boy to suffer so. Young Mark became an atheist and an anti-Mormon on the spot. To cheer up their badly burned and bed-ridden boy, Mark's parents gave him a book on coin collecting and brought him several rolls of pennies, nickels and dimes from the local bank to go through in search of rare specimens. Mark, however, quickly found that by using an electroplating kit he had been given earlier he could alter the date of certain coins and make them much more valuable than anything he was likely to find in the rolls of coins that mom and pop brought home from Zion's National Bank. He soon moved from forging coins to producing bogus Mormon pioneer currency, then autographs, and finally entire letters.

Hofmann never worked up the nerve to tell his fiercely devout father of his lost faith. Instead Mark lived an outwardly perfect LDS life. That lifestyle, in fact, became part of his scheme. Mark baldly lied and spoke of his testimony with other priests at ward meetings. He did temple work; he always wore the garment, and his basement was filled with stored food and 72-hour kits. But he did each of these things as a part of a grand charade. He kept a journal as most Saints do, but he later admitted that he filled the journal with the same lies he was telling his wife, his friends, his family, and his church elders about where he was getting his material. He later even used worms that he found in his basement food-storage wheat to help age a forged document. Hofmann made Mormonism itself his secret weapon.

Part of this genius for deception was that he usually concealed his historical expertise, casting himself in the role of a slightly greedy and even somewhat dense dealer in coins and other LDS arcania with little grasp of the great issues facing Mormondom that seemed to lie behind his various "discoveries." In one interview with *Seventh East Press* he stunned the eager would-be historians he often visited in the Underground by saying that he never made photocopies of the amazing documents he was finding and selling to the church and to well-heeled Saints like Christensen. The underground history buffs care much more about what a document says than in possessing the actual item. Hofmann's feigned lack of concern about the content of his wares disguised his historical awareness as part of the master plan. Hofmann was relying on the work of the Mormon Underground for his secret research. Each time he churned out a fake, he knew well the content and purported significance of each piece.

For example, when forging a fake letter in Joseph Smith's

hand he first performed enough historical research to find other evidence that Smith was in fact present at the time and place where the letter purportedly would be written. He then researched postal practices to make sure that his version carried the proper markings, routing notes, etc. He then found extant Smith writings of the time so that his version would reflect Smith's penmanship and spelling knowledge. Likewise, the content of the document reflected scrupulously researched details of Mormon lore. All of this knowledge was absorbed by avidly following the research of church historians and particularly of the Underground, whose work most often raised the sort of data and lurking issues that the church's representatives kept quiet. While his knowledge of LDS history deepened to that of a leading expert, Hofmann played the money-grubbing opportunist. It was a continuation of an assault on the faith of his fathers that had begun in a fourteen-year-old's sickbed and continued until Hofmann was on the verge of making his first million dollars peddling the bogus wares he created in the basement of his upscale house overlooking the Salt Lake Valley.

Many of the documents the strange young cynic produced early in his campaign had seemed to be what elders like to call "faith promoting." With them he won access to his targets in the First Presidency. These early items were doctored to confirm aspects of the official church view of history. For example, Hofmann's first big success was the so-called "Anthon Transcript," a bogus rendering of the "reformed Egyptian" alphabet, a set of strange markings that, according to the LDS scriptures, Joseph had copied from the golden plates of Lehi and that Martin Harris had taken to Professor Charles Anthon in New York with the request that, as one of America's leading linguists, Anthon confirm Smith's translation of the first 116 pages from the writings found in the Hill Cumorah.

Those 116 pages, it will be recalled, vanished after Harris, the upstate New York farmer who underwrote the first publishing of the *Book of Mormon* in 1830, took them home to show his Mormon-hating wife, Lucy. Transcribed in Harris's handwriting as Joseph translated from the storied plates, the pages were said to be the opening passages of the book of the ancient prophet

Lehi, the man who led his sons Nephi and Laman to the Americas six hundred years before the birth of Christ. Suspecting that Mrs. Harris had stolen the 116 pages and planned to use the pilfered document to discredit any retranslation of the Lehi passages, Smith told the world that he had been ordered by divinity to suspend the translation of the plates of Lehi and instead moved to the plates of Lehi's son and produced what was called the Book of Nephi. The *Book of Mormon* thus opens with the Book of Nephi rather than the lost book of Lehi.

Hofmann's forgery of the purported tiny fragment that Joseph Smith copied of the "language of the Egyptians" for Harris to carry to Professor Anthon, called the Anthon Transcript, was eagerly acquired by LDS elders in late 1980 because it seemed to be independent historical evidence corroborating Joseph's long-challenged version of how he received the restored gospel. Afterwards, it would be disclosed that Hofmann had concocted the bogus transcript with the deft strokes of a master.

He started with a 1668 Cambridge version of the King James Bible that he had bought from the bin of a bookshop in Bristol, England, while on his own two-year missionary tour in the 1970s. He then took a sheet of paper that he had sliced with a razor blade from the backing page of an early nineteenth-century book in the University of Utah's rare books collection and jotted the "reformed Egyptian" hieroglyphs in homemade iron gall ink mixed from an early nineteenth-century formula. He penned an emulation of Joseph Smith's own handwriting and pasted both pages into the back of the Bible, using Elmer's Glue that he had darkened with dust from the charcoal in his backyard barbecue. The brief Joseph Smith note said, "These caractors [*sic*] were diligently coppied [*sic*] by my own hand from the plates of gold and Given to Martin Harris who took them to New York City . . ." He added copies of many of the reformed Egyptian characters that had been floating around the Underground for years.

Using a process that he had invented, Hofmann placed the forgery in an "ozone chamber," and by flashing electrical sparks in the surrounding air, he was able to darken the ink just as it darkens over time. Then, using a vacuum cleaner and a specially constructed box, he applied suction to the ink, drawing it deep into the paper, just as happens with the mildly acidic ink when it eats into the page over time.

Historians called to authenticate the fake were particularly impressed that the note contained misspellings of several words that Smith apparently carried throughout life. These experts also commented that the writing was typical more of a young man's robust hand than were the many works of the older Joseph Smith at Missouri's Liberty Jail and in Nauvoo. Such early samples of the prophet's handwriting are extremely rare.

Selling the faked "Anthon Transcript" as his first major deal with the First Presidency, Hofmann received as payment a rare $5 Mormon gold coin dated 1850, a first edition of the *Book of Mormon,* and numerous bank notes printed by church elders in the early years in Utah. These items were worth at least $20,000.

A church press conference was called and Hofmann was showcased as the discoverer of the faith-promoting treasure. From that day onward, Mark Hofmann's credentials as a leading LDS documents sleuth appeared impeccable. He announced that he would abandon his pre-medical studies at the U. of U. and become a full-time dealer in antiquities both Mormon and non-Mormon. It was only after Hofmann's house of bogus cards collapsed when the third bomb blew up in his face that scholars gleaned the enormity of the strange loner's scheme. The Anthon Transcript was the opening gambit in a gargantuan campaign to produce eventually the ultimate Mormon forgery, the long lost 116 pages that Joseph first dictated to Martin Harris just months after opening the sacred vault at Cumorah, the opening of the never before seen Book of Lehi. Scholars would deem such a find priceless and even the hard-headed businessmen at One Temple Square would count its value in the many millions.

Hofmann won the elders' trust by cooking up the faith-promoting Anthon Transcript that they announced at a press conference. He then sold them perhaps a dozen documents that were decidedly non–faith promoting, documents that were promptly placed in the Vault of the First Presidency and kept secret. The documents in question included such bombshells as a land deed linking Sidney Rigdon to one Solomon Spaulding, the author of a novel called *Manuscript Story,* which deals with the ancient American Indians who make up the central characters in the *Book of Mormon,* bolstering the old suspicions that Joseph originally set out to write a novel instead of a scripture. Another Hofmann fake was a blessing from Joseph to his son, Joseph Smith III, stating that the son and not Brigham Young should have been Joseph's successor. Another cooked letter from Joseph Smith to Jonathan Dunham, the commander of Smith's militia, the Nauvoo Legion, ordered Dunham to storm the Carthage Jail and free Joseph and his brother Hyrum, a scenario that does violence to the long-standing church teaching that Joseph calmly accepted his martyrdom as the will of God rather than defending himself.

Hofmann later admitted that even while they brought him a substantial income, most of these fakes were part of the much larger fraud that he was working against the church, to "discover" the lost 116 pages. Meanwhile, in addition to selling the church forgeries for tens of thousands of dollars, Hofmann maintained a comfortable suburban lifestyle selling others around the country a prolific output of forgeries of everything from Charles Dickens manuscripts to a fake purported to be the earliest document ever printed in the American colonies.

It is difficult to imagine any other artifact of Mormon history that would be as valuable to the immensely wealthy church as would be the lost scripture written in Harris's hand that the prophet first translated with the sacred Urim and Thummim. Arguably, the lost 116 pages would be worth millions even if they were nothing more than a continuation of the sort of verses contained in the *Book of Mormon* proper. Of course their value would be greatly augmented if they were to contain material damaging to the long-standing LDS canon. For example, if those 116 pages were to indicate that Joseph was writing a mere novel rather than transcribing holy writ as scholars like Fawn Brodie had suggested, they would be devastating to the entire religion's underpinnings.

A major part of the scheme was to capitalize on the fact that there are virtually no genuine samples extant of Harris's own handwriting and few available of Joseph's penmanship early in his life when he was producing the *Book of Mormon*. So Hofmann concocted several examples of young Smith's and Harris's handwriting including a fairly lengthy letter from Harris to pioneer Mormon newspaper editor W. W. Phelps in which Harris discussed Joseph's own description of events surrounding the uncovering of the sacred cache on the Hill Cumorah. Because the letter was by far the longest sample ever found of Harris's handwriting, it also established Hofmann's version as the standard scholars would use to validate any future items purported to have flowed from the Harris pen. To boost its value, Hofmann made the salamander letter devastating. In the forgery Harris quotes Smith as saying that when he first approached the trove he was repulsed by an evil spirit that had taken the form of a white salamander, a commonplace motif among folk magicians of the day. The forgery also contains allusions to seer stones, money digging and "tricksters," all lending credence to the long-voiced suspicions that the *Book of Mormon* was part of a confidence scheme.

Christensen, a rising young bishop and successful investment counselor with close business ties to wealthy Mormon leaders in the Salt Lake Valley, bought the salamander letter for $40,000 from Hofmann and then donated it to the First Presidency in January of 1984, which placed it in the church's bank vault and kept its existence secret, just as the general authorities had hidden the existence of the other embarrassing documents that also turned out to be Hofmann fakeries. Experts now believe that Hofmann leaked a photocopy of the letter to the Los Angeles *Times,* and the content of the salamander letter became one of the raging sources of Underground and inner circle debate for several years.

Leaking the letter dramatized to the First Presidency just how controversial material could disrupt its usually obedient flock. The salamander debate likely added to the value of the next fraudulent package Hofmann cooked up. By the summer of 1985 Hofmann was negotiating with top church leaders for what was called the McLellin Collection, a major set of documents that were stolen from the Smith family by a defector named William McLellin. The centerpiece of Hofmann's rendition of the

McLellin documents was a sheet of Egyptian papyrus to capitalize on a long-standing allegation that the sacred papyri that Joseph had claimed to use in translating the Book of Abraham in the *Pearl of Great Price* were actually commonplace copies of the Egyptian "Book of the Dead," items that were widely sold in the 1840s in the United States by curiosity dealers. During negotiations for the collection, Hugh Pinnock, one of the Quorum of Seventy, arranged for Hofmann to receive an $185,000 bank loan and church officials demanded that Christensen serve as their representative in the transaction because they were happy with the way he had dealt with Hofmann over the salamander letter. Agreeing to represent the church with Hofmann a second time cost Christensen his life.

Before Christensen purchased the salamander letter from Hofmann he had brought in a well-known Boston documents expert named Kenneth Rendell to authenticate it. Rendell was fooled and testified to the letter's authenticity. He also met and developed a business relationship with Hofmann. In early 1985 Hofmann had made an arrangement with Rendell to take possession of a fragment of the "Book of the Dead" on consignment for an unnamed buyer. That papyrus, of course, was part of the faked McLellin package. But with the demand that Christensen be the church's purchase agent Hofmann knew that Christensen almost certainly would again call in Rendell and Rendell would immediately recognize his own papyrus. So Hofmann sent one bomb to kill Christensen and another one to the home of Christensen's business associate, Gary Sheets, hoping to make the police believe the murders were somehow tied to the two men's business problems.

The Hofmann case was particularly damaging to the church because it brought national headlines to bear on the raging controversies about the Mormon faith and the church's history. It also, of course, embarrassed the hierarchy with disclosures of efforts to keep embarrassing information secret. Worst of all, however, it gave substantial new ammunition to the wide variety of anti-Mormons who make no secret of their utter contempt for the Saints and their history. Here the players are diverse indeed. They include the Fundamentalist Baptists, bitter ex-

Mormons, and anti-Mormons Jerald and Sandra Tanner, who have fought for three decades to unmask what they consider Mormon heresy.

Sandra Tanner, a great-great-granddaughter of Brigham Young, spends business hours in the drawing room of her Victorian house just out of downtown Salt Lake. Here she sells anti-Mormon books, most of them published by Jerald and Sandra Tanner.

While Sandra handles business affairs, Jerald Tanner devotes much of his time to research, seeking out censored documents and working to further undermine the faith of his Mormon fathers. They share a born-again Christian faith and a belief that Mormonism is un-Christian.

As such the Tanners are part of a large conglomeration of anti-Mormons who base their attacks on their various views of Christian purity. They range from individual zealots to the prestigious Baptist-oriented Moody Bible Institute Press. Because Baptists tend to share many of the Mormons' Fundamentalist attitudes on questions like evolution and because they have similar views about proper moral behavior, a particular animosity has arisen between the two groups.

Mormons are particularly effective at winning converts among Baptists and allied Fundamentalists, a factor that many observers think greatly aggravates anti-Mormon sentiment at places like the Chicago-based Moody Bible Institute, which publishes numerous anti-Mormon titles including *Mormonism Mama, and Me,* a kiss-and-tell book by a former Mormon, Thelma "Granny" Greer, who devotes particular emphasis to the implications of treating God as a married entity with a wife and offspring. The book contains a challenge to any Mormon to prove that the strange dogmas that Greer alleges haven't been taught by church elders. The prize for proving Greer wrong is supposed to be a first edition copy of the *Book of Mormon.*

Commonly, groups like Moody, Saints Alive, and Ex-Mormons for Jesus produce literature attacking various Mormon teachings such as that the moon is populated by a particularly long-lived branch of Quakers, and that Adam and God are the same being. While Mormon spokesmen complain that Mormon teachings are cited out of context, the Tanners and other scholars continue to dig for such scandalous morsels.

Perhaps the greatest service these anti-Mormons have done for all who would study the Mormon way without joining the church is to acquire, often by apparent outright thievery, the various texts of the super-secret temple rituals, the core mystery at the center of Mormon circles where Gentiles forever are barred. These foes also have turned over copies of the standard temple recommend forms needed for access to the inner sanctum and samples of the sacred undergarments so key to temple Mormonism and otherwise hidden from all outsiders by the dictates of One Temple Square.

Today, when the more zealous among Mormon-haters picket temple open house ceremonies and other church events they frequently wear copies of the purloined garments with the specially sewn opening near the navel, the embroidered mason's compasses on the left breast, and the carpenter's square on the right that are so highly evocative of the secret ceremonies conducted in Masonic lodges all across small town America. To faithful Saints these protests are akin to burning a flag in front of the local VFW hall or spray painting a swastika on the walls of a synagogue.

Handing out scripts for the most holy of all Mormon rites, the endowment, these enemies note that both Freemasonry and LDS rituals involve the wearing of ceremonial garb and take the form of skits in which God, Adam, Satan, and other figures speak their lines while members of the audience participate. Likewise, both Masonic and Mormon ceremonies contain repeated blood oaths in which participants swear that they will never disclose the content of the ritual under pain of death in various violent ways, a concept scholars call "penalties."

The central Mormon ceremony, the all-important endowment, starts after each initiate goes through ritual washings and anointings and is led into the first of several rooms where the first of many speakers pledges them to secrecy under penalty of death. Then actors portraying Elohim, Jehovah, and Michael the

Archangel give a reprise of the seven days of creation and the great war in the spirit world. Moving to the Garden of Eden, Lucifer enters to tell Adam that his new home is like that he had in the preexistence. Adam replies he can't remember being on the other side of the veil. Satan lies to Adam, telling him that if he will eat the forbidden fruit he will see back across the veil. Adam knows better, but Eve succumbs and they are expelled after God tells her that because she, not Adam, ate first, woman must always be subservient to man. "Sisters," said Elohim, "arise, raise your right hand to the square. Each of you do covenant and promise that you will obey the law of your husband . . . Each of you bow your head and say yes."

Next the actors teach those assembled a series of secret handshakes and other signs that they can use in the future to identify one another when surrounded by Gentiles. After copious warnings that the penalty for betraying these secret signs is death in such gruesome ways as throat cutting or evisceration, the ceremony moves to a room representing "The Lone and Dreary World" where the audience is taught the unique Mormon belief that there is no hell in the traditional fire and brimstone sense.

Moving into a "Terrestrial Room," the women are pledged to chastity and the men are given the "First Token of the Melchizedek Priesthood or the Sign of the Nail," another secret handshake. Each then gets a secret name and vows to hold it forever inviolate.

The ceremony ends with rites symbolizing passage through the veil separating preexistence and the spirit world from human experience with volunteer "veil workers" showing the way. Following the endowment, those passing through the temple turn their attention to the day's real work, the never-ending round of vicarious baptisms, weddings, and other ceremonies on behalf of the dead that drives Mormons to a level of zeal that most other Christians can only covet. When one contrasts such striking tenets with the credos of mainstream American religion and then watches just how hard these Saints work to bring their strange beliefs about, the conclusion is inescapable. Just as Brigham Young said so long ago, these are a royal priesthood, peculiar people indeed.

Afterword

In 1990 the church hierarchy stunned many observers by ordering a number of changes in the endowment ceremony, that mysterious and essential component of Mormonism that has caused great criticism because of its striking similarities to the skits, garments, secret signs, bizarre "penalties," and other trappings of Masonry. Typically, while church officials confirmed publicly that changes had indeed been made in the endowment because of new revelations given to the First Presidency, they refused to discuss specifics because the rites themselves still remain secret under pain of excommunication. There were immediate reports, however, that among the cut material was most of the sexist language demanding that women obey men. Also reportedly excised were several controversial passages that cast all other religions, particularly Catholicism, as the direct work of Satan. Finally, much of the rigamarole about secret hand signs and "penalties" was reportedly dropped.

Thus, pushing harder than ever before for still more growth, the church entered the last decade of the twentieth century with a major concession to its critics and detractors about one of its most prized traditions, the temple rituals that had passed essentially intact from the Mormon Pentecost at Kirtland all the way to the present. Such compromises come hard for the gerontocracy at One Temple Square but come they do as was the case with the Great Accommodation to ban polygamy and the Second Accommodation that opened the church's ranks to worthy males of color. This Third Accommodation about the endowment came without the ballyhoo that accompanied the reversals on polygamy and blacks, but it amounted to a sea change of equal importance in the fabric of Mormonism and it came for the same reasons the other changes came. Leaders decided that without change the church couldn't continue to grow as quickly as it must. And in these latter days in Mormon circles nothing is as important as is growth.

One Temple Square decided in effect that the sexist and antisectarian language in Joseph's beloved temple rituals was alienating too many prospective converts, even as the last days of the last Dispensation were dawning with the final decade of what many Fundamentalist-thinking faithful members believe is the final "Kolob day" before the second coming of Jesus Christ. Time is running out in the sacred quest to bring the last denizens of the spirit world through the veil, and rumors of dark secrets behind temple walls were impeding the quest for converts.

Indeed, the Tanners and other anti-Mormons were quick to boast that the church was forced to redo the temple endowments because of recent widespread efforts to distribute the text and even to pass around secretly made tape recordings of the rites in an effort to slow down if not halt the church's phenomenal growth. The full text of the ceremony is contained in such Mormon-hating pamphlets as "What's Going On in There," published by church foes Dolly and Chuck Sackett, two longtime temple workers. The Sacketts also apparently hid microcassette tape machines under their garments and recorded the entire endowment ceremony. Those tapes have since been played on radio stations and passed around the Underground with glee.

The decision to rewrite the endowment ritual that Mormons had long been taught was itself an infallible revelation underscored the essence of Mormondom—pragmatism. The church is driven above all else by the quest to usher in the Millennium by completing the holy work of performing baptisms for all members' ancestors, by converting the "Lamanite" Indian and Hispanic peoples of South America, and by preparing through home food storage and other survivalist programs for the terminal Gathering of Saints in Utah when the end comes.

This enormous deadline pressure has defined America's most unique native religious movement almost from day one. The entire panoply of Mormon history, tradition, teaching, and culture carries an unshakable consistency when viewed from the perspective of preparing for a fast-approaching Millennium.

For example, a religion that sets as its prime purpose the fastest possible conversion of all Gentiles and the assimilation of all those Gentiles' forebears through vicarious rituals immediately establishes the "us" versus "them" climate that has defined

America's Saints throughout their often tragic and turbulent relationship with those outside Mormon circles. The separation is unavoidable, with the core LDS teaching revolving around the absolute need to bring across all those "special spirits" still waiting in the wings of the spirit kingdom as the Endtimes arrive.

Genealogy, of course, is essential to gathering the names needed to usher in the Endtimes and therefore another essential aspect of Millennarian Mormonism. The obsession with history, likewise, is part of the drive for genealogy. Polygamy is consistent with organizing human society to optimize birth rates thereby to provide bodies for spirit babies as the church drives to clear out the remaining "special" souls to populate the latter days. In the Principle's absence, the church's emphatic teachings urging the largest possible monogamous families and damning abortion are another way to meet the Dispensation's rushing baby-making deadline. Patriarchy thus becomes another millennial force by keeping a damper on church women who desire roles and careers much wider than just as makers of infant tabernacles for spirit babies.

In the same patriarchal mold is the church's adoption of American right-wing politics, with its acceptance of Christian Fundamentalist teachings, antifeminist tenets, acceptance of white male domination, and traditions of keeping government regulation at bay.

Like a millennial Ponzi scheme the church sends ever increasing numbers of young men and women out to work the missions, pumping the bulk of the funds realized from the new members they gather back into the quest for still more converts. That is why Mormon missions are exclusively dedicated to proselytizing rather than to operating hospitals, schools, and the other humanitarian services so favored by other Christian missionary drives. Meanwhile, as the new Mormon enclaves are created around the world the church moves quickly to supply each added stake and ward with the sophisticated communications equipment (satellite dishes, modems, computers, etc.) that both allow Salt Lake to be heard instantly throughout Mormondom and lay the groundwork for keeping Saintly circles intact when the rumblings and rumors of war arrive to usher in the Endtimes.

This selfsame sense of urgency is greatly amplified among the various extremists who display a common obsession with the looming Endtimes and the advent of the One Mighty and Strong predicted in *Doctrines and Covenants*. Whether it was Vickie Singer and Addam Swapp trying to bring John Singer back across the veil by forcing a gunfight with the police or demented Ervil LeBaron's blood-atoning hit missions, the Fundamentalists, survivalists, and polygamists of today are driven with even more passion than are mainstream Saints by the approach of the Seventh Day.

Meanwhile, bridging the gap between One Temple Square and the most remote polygamy commune are teachings of scholars like W. Cleon Skousen whose series of books on the various "days" of creation as outlined in the Old Testament and the *Book of Mormon* make it clear that many in this amazing church view the next few years as the climax of all human history.

In the months and years to come the entire church will have to deal with this millennial quandary in some formal way. To date, church general conferences and various sermons, monographs, and speeches by general authorities have shied away from discussing the actual advent of the twenty-first century as a millenarian event, but it's a topic that burns in Mormonism as it burns probably nowhere else.

Will the living prophets receive word from the Celestial Kingdom that the year 2000 is indeed the opening of the Endtimes? Or will the moves toward neo-orthodoxy such as purging sexism and religious intolerance from temple rites and downplaying the more exotic of Joseph's testaments propel the church into the next century as just another Christian sect, albeit a rather large one with a unique style and agenda? Certainly up to this point in their history the Mormons are a uniquely driven people unlike any other Christian subset of their size and stature.

One of the most impressive manifestations of their peculiar strength and solidarity is to watch a temple parking lot like the one at Manti, Utah, about one hundred miles south of Salt Lake and typical of outlying Mormon holy places around the world. Day and night the Manti parking lot is jammed full of cars as a steady stream of men and women move in and out of the sacred building carrying the small suitcases containing their temple clothes. They come in all ages, sexes, and sizes—old Saints hobbling on canes, middle-aged Mormons squinting at the lists of vicarious baptismal names through bifocals, and cocky young ones striding purposefully with a tennis racket sticking out of the same bag that carries their garments. They work together around the clock for the hordes of dead whose genealogies must be found so they can be given the vicarious baptisms that will add them to the coming kingdoms ruled over by beloved Joseph, Brigham, et al.

But now the names coming in from the field are arriving faster than ever before, and they include growing lists of Native American tribal peoples from Central and South America, the dark-skinned Lamanite heathens whose conversions will herald the beginning of the end and the end of the beginning in LDS lore.

As one Mormon eye scans these strange names on the ever-growing baptism rolls, however, the other eye is trained on the calendar. The task at hand couldn't be more urgent. The Millennium looms. For Fundamentalists there is a particular significance to the fast-approaching year A.D. 2000. As the century draws to a close the signs of the times are everywhere: sea changes in the Soviet Union, political transformations across Asia, social turbulence rumbling across Latin America. Can great land-wrenching upheavals be far off? Certainly this is not the time to wait and rest. Ever more missionaries must be sent to canvass the planet until the quakes come to signal the return of the fabled city of Zion to the surface of Earth. More temples still must go up. Ever more names must be gathered by the genealogists and joined for time and eternity via vicarious temple ordinances. Ever more babies must be brought forth to provide tabernacles for the few choice spirits that still linger beyond the veil. Newly established stakes and wards need to be joined by satellite uplinks. Food and medicine and survival gear must be stored for increasing numbers of new Saints who soon will flock to the great valley on the shores of America's Dead Sea. Above all, their gathering must go smoothly. Soon the trek will begin for Eden, or as most Americans know it, Kansas City.

Bibliography

Adams, Sherman. *First Hand Report: The Story of The Eisenhower Administration*. New York: Harper & Brothers, 1961.

Ahlstrom, Sydney E. *A Religious History of the American People*. New Haven: Yale University Press, 1972.

Arrington, Leonard J. and Davis Bitton. *The Mormon Experience*. New York: Vintage Books/Random House, 1980.

Beadle, J. H. *Brigham's Destroying Angel*. Salt Lake City, Utah: Shepard Publishing Company, 1904.

Benson, Ezra Taft. *An Enemy Hath Done This*. Salt Lake City, Utah: Parliament Publishers, 1969.

––––––. *The Constitution: A Heavenly Banner*. Salt Lake City, Utah: Deseret Book Company, 1986.

––––––. *The Teachings of Ezra Taft Benson*. Salt Lake City, Utah: Bookcraft, 1988.

Bradford, Mary L., ed. *Personal Voices: A Celebration Of Dialog*. Salt Lake City, Utah: Signature Books, 1987.

Bradlee, Ben, Jr. and Dale Van Atta. *Prophet of Blood: The Untold Story of Ervil LeBaron and the Lambs of God*. New York: G. P. Putnam's Sons, 1981.

Brodie, Fawn M. *No Man Knows My History*. New York: Alfred A. Knopf, 1986.

Brown, Robert L. and Rosemary Brown. *They Lie in Wait to Deceive*. 3 vols. Mesa, Arizona: Brownsworth Publishing Company, 1985.

Bushman, Richard L. *Joseph Smith and the Beginnings of Mormonism*. Urbana/Chicago: University of Illinois Press, 1988.

Campbell, Eugene E. *Establishing Zion: The Mormon Church in the American West, 1847–1869*. Salt Lake City, Utah: Signature Books, 1988.

Card, Orson Scott. *Saintspeak: The Mormon Dictionary*. Salt Lake City, Utah: Signature Books, 1981.

Church of Jesus Christ of Latter-day Saints. *Achieving a Celestial Marriage*. Salt Lake City, Utah: Church Education System, 1976.

————. *Teachings of the Living Prophets*. Salt Lake City, Utah: Church Education Department, 1982.

Coates, James. *Armed and Dangerous: The Rise of the Survivalist Right*. New York: Hill & Wang, 1987.

Collier, Fred C., comp. *Unpublished Revelations of the Prophets and Presidents of the Church of Jesus Christ of Latter-day Saints*. Salt Lake City, Utah: Collier Publishing, 1981.

Cowan, Richard O. *The Church in the Twentieth Century: The Impressive Story of the Advancing Kingdom*. Salt Lake City, Utah: Bookcraft, 1985.

Crockett, Barry G. and Lynette B. Crockett. *72-Hour Family Emergency Preparedness Checklist*. Salt Lake City, Utah: Publishers Press, 1988.

Drosnin, Michael. *Citizen Hughes*. New York: Holt, Rinehart and Winston, 1985.

Durrant, George D. *Get Ready, Get Called, Go!* Salt Lake City, Utah: Bookcraft, 1979.

Embry, Jessie L. *Mormon Polygamous Families: Life in the Principle*. Salt Lake City, Utah: University of Utah Press, 1987.

Fagan, Brian. *Elusive Treasure: The Story of Early Archaeologists in the Americas*. New York: Charles Scribner's Sons, 1977.

Firmage, Edwin B., ed. *The Memoirs of Hugh B. Brown: An Abundant Life*. Salt Lake City, Utah: Signature Books, 1988.

Fleisher, David and David M. Freedman. *Death of an American: The Killing of John Singer*. New York: Continuum Publishing Company, 1983.

Fuller, John G. *The Day We Bombed Utah*. New York: New American Library, 1984.

Gottlieb, Robert and Peter Wiley. *America's Saints: The Rise of Mormon Power*. New York: G. P. Putnam's Sons, 1984.

Bibliography

Greer, Thelma, *Mormonism, Mama, and Me.* Chicago: Moody Press, 1986.

Grey, Zane. *Riders of the Purple Sage.* New York: Pocket Books, 1980.

Hansen, Klaus J. *Mormonism and the American Experience.* Chicago: University of Chicago Press, 1981.

Heinerman, John and Anson Shupe. *The Mormon Corporate Empire.* Boston: Beacon Press, 1985.

Hilton, Hope A. *"Wild Bill" Hickman and the Mormon Frontier.* Salt Lake City, Utah: Signature Books, 1988.

Hinckley, Gordon B. *Truth Restored.* Salt Lake City, Utah: The Church of Jesus Christ of Latter-day Saints, 1979.

Hirshson, Stanley P. *The Lion of the Lord.* New York: Alfred A. Knopf, 1969.

Hofmann's Confession. Transcript of Mark Hofmann's interviews with Salt Lake prosecutors as part of plea bargain. 3 vols. Salt Lake City, Utah: Utah Lighthouse Ministry, 1987.

Hunt, Dave and Ed Decker. *The God Makers.* Eugene, Oregon: Harvest House Publishers, 1984.

James, William. *The Varieties of Religious Experience.* New York: The Modern Library, 1902.

Johnson, Sonia. *From Housewife to Heretic: One Woman's Spiritual Awakening and Her Excommunication from the Mormon Church.* New York: Wildfire Books, 1989.

Kelly, Tim, Neil Passy, and Mark Knudsen. *Utah: Gateway to Nevada!* Salt Lake City, Utah: Dream Garden Press, 1984.

Lindsey, Robert. *A Gathering of Saints.* New York: Simon and Schuster, 1988.

Martin, Thomas K., Tim B. Heaton, and Stephen J. Bahr. *Utah in Demographic Perspective.* Salt Lake City, Utah: Signature Books, 1986.

McConkie, Bruce R. *Mormon Doctrine.* Salt Lake City, Utah: Bookcraft, 1979.

Mecham, Evan. *Come Back America.* Glendale, Arizona: M P Press, 1982.

223

Miller, Ken. *What the Mormons Believe.* Bountiful, Utah: Horizon, 1981.

Morgan, William. *Freemasonry Exposed.* Chicago: Charles T. Powner, 1986.

Naifeh, Steven, and Gregory White Smith. *The Mormon Murders: A True Story of Greed, Forgery, Deceit, and Death.* New York: Weidenfeld & Nicholson, 1988.

Neal, Steve. *The Eisenhowers Reluctant Dynasty.* Garden City, N.Y.: Doubleday & Company, Inc., 1978.

Newquist, Jerreld L. *Prophets, Principles and National Survival.* Salt Lake City, Utah: Publishers Press, 1984.

Nielsen, Harold K. *Mapping the Action Found in the Book of Mormon.* Orem, Utah: Cedar Fort, 1987.

O'Brien, Robert. *Marriott: The J. Willard Marriott Story.* Salt Lake City, Utah: Deseret Book Company, 1987.

Peirce, Neal R. *The Mountain States of America.* New York: W. W. Norton & Company, 1972.

Porter, Roger B. *Presidential Decision Making, The Economic Policy Board.* Cambridge: Cambridge University Press, 1980.

Quinn, Michael D. "On Being a Mormon Historian," A lecture at Utah Lighthouse Ministry, Salt Lake City, Utah, 1982.

———. *Early Mormonism and the Magic World View.* Salt Lake City, Utah: Signature Books, 1987.

Richards, LeGrand. *A Marvelous Work and a Wonder.* Salt Lake City, Utah: Deseret Book Company, 1976.

Rosten, Leo. *Religions of America: Ferment and Faith in an Age of Crisis.* New York: Simon and Shuster, 1955.

Salsbury, Barbara. *Emergency Evacuation.* Salt Lake City, Utah: Deseret Book Company, 1986.

Scharffs, Gilbert W. *The Truth About the God Makers.* Salt Lake City, Utah: Publishers Press, 1986.

Bibliography

Schindler, Harold. *Orrin Porter Rockwell: Man of God Son of Thunder.* Salt Lake City, Utah: University of Utah Press, 1983.

Schlesinger, Arthur M., Jr. *The Age of Jackson.* Boston: Little, Brown and Company, 1945.

Scott, Latayne Colvett. *The Mormon Mirage.* Grand Rapids, Michigan: Zondervan Publishing House, 1979.

Shipps, Jan. *Mormonism: The Story of a New Religious Tradition.* Urbana/Chicago: University of Illinois Press, 1985.

Sillitoe, Linda, and Allen Roberts. *Salamander: The Story of the Mormon Forgery Murders.* Salt Lake City, Utah: Signature Books, 1988.

Skousen, W. Cleon. *Prophecy and Modern Times.* Riverton, Utah: Ensign Publishing Company, 1988.

Smith, Ethan. *View of the Hebrews.* (Reprint of the 1825 Edition), Salt Lake City, Utah: Utah Lighthouse Ministry.

Spencer, James R. *Beyond Mormonism, An Elder's Story.* Old Tappen, N.J.: Chosen Books, 1984.

Stegner, Wallace. *Mormon Country.* Lincoln, Nebraska: University of Nebraska Press, 1970.

Stewart, John J. *Mormonism and the Negro.* Provo, Utah: Bookmark Press, 1960.

Talmage, James E. *A Study of the Articles of Faith.* Salt Lake City, Utah: The Church of Jesus Christ of Latter-day Saints, 1987.

Tanner, Jerald, and Sandra Tanner. *Mormons and Negroes.* Salt Lake City, Utah: Utah Lighthouse Ministry, 1970.

———. *Mormon Spies, Hughes and the CIA.* Salt Lake City, Utah: Utah Lighthouse Ministry, 1976.

———. *Did Spaulding Write the Book of Mormon?.* Salt Lake City, Utah: Utah Lighthouse Ministry, 1977.

———. *Unmasking a Mormon Spy: The Story of Stan Fields.* Salt Lake City, Utah: Utah Lighthouse Ministry, 1980.

———. *Can the Browns Save Joseph Smith?*. Salt Lake City, Utah: Utah Lighthouse Ministry, 1981.

———. *Mormonism—Shadow or Reality?*. Salt Lake City, Utah: Utah Lighthouse Ministry, 1987.

———. *Tracking the White Salamander*. Salt Lake City, Utah: Utah Lighthouse Ministry, 1987.

———. *Mormonism, Magic and Masonry*. Salt Lake City, Utah: Utah Lighthouse Ministry, 1988.

———. *Major Problems of Mormonism*. Salt Lake City, Utah: Utah Lighthouse Ministry, 1989.

Turner, Wallace. *The Mormon Establishment*. Boston: Houghton Mifflin Company, 1966.

Twain, Mark. *Roughing It*. Facsimile, 1872, New York: Hippocrene Books, 1988.

Utah Governor's Commission on the Status of Women. *Utah Women and the Law*. Salt Lake City, Utah: Bonneville Books, University of Utah Press, 1986.

Van Wagoner, Richard S. *Mormon Polygamy: A History*. Salt Lake City, Utah: Signature Books, 1986.

Van Wagoner, Richard S., and Steven C. Walker. *A Book of Mormons*. Salt Lake City, Utah: Signature Books, 1982.

Vogel, Dan. *Indian Origins and the Book of Mormon*. Salt Lake City, Utah: Signature Books, 1986.

———. *Religious Seekers and the Advent of Mormonism*. Salt Lake City, Utah: Signature Books, 1988.

Walker, John Phillip, ed. *Dale Morgan on Early Mormonism: Correspondence and New History*. Salt Lake City, Utah: Signature Books, 1986.

Wallace, Irving. *The Twenty-Seventh Wife*. New York: Simon and Schuster, 1961.

Warren, Steve. *Drat! Mythed Again: Second Thoughts on Utah*. West Valley City, Utah: Altair Publishing Company, 1986.

Bibliography

Wasserman, Harvey, and Norman Solomon. *Killing Our Own*. New York: Delacorte Press, 1982.

West, Ray B., Jr. *Kingdom of the Saints*. New York: The Viking Press, 1957.

Young, Ann Eliza. *Wife No. 19*. Reprint, New York: Arno Press, 1972.

Index

Index

Hoover, Herbert, 123
Hoover, J. Edgar, 170
House, Dawn, 187
House, Fred, 181, 187–88
Hyde, Orson, 25, 78, 94

Idaho, 57, 66, 111, 112
Illinois, 41, 42, 48, 49, 51, 53, 54
Indian burial mounds, 4, 10, 11–13
Iowa, 54, 55, 59
Iron Rodders, 200
Israel, 172, 198–99
Israelites, 3, 11, 12. *See also* Lamanites;
  Nephites

"Jack Mormons," 64, 81, 115
Jeffs, Rulon, 194
Jerusalem, 10, 89, 198
Jesperson, Brent, 135, 139, 140, 141–42
Jesus, 9, 68, 108, 146, 152, 173, 174,
  185, 217; ascension of, 95, 198; body
  of, 81; in the *Book of Mormon*, 81,
  95–96, 137; death of, 90; as the first-
  born, 78, 93; Gospel of, 41; and Mary
  Magdelene, 77; and the Millennium,
  89, 151; and missionaries, 106; and
  money, handling of, 115; in Mormon
  movies, 112
Jews, 2, 3, 12, 51, 77, 80, 198; anti-
  Mormon, 198–99; Babylonian captiv-
  ity of, 12, 15; congregations of, in the
  U.S., number of, 126; and the Dispen-
  sation of the Law, 136; Jesus and, 96;
  Orthodox, and dietary laws, 102; and
  political activism, 126
Johnson, LeRoy, 193, 194, 196, 197
Johnson, Nicholas, 114
Johnson, Sonia, 121, 127–34
Jordon, Daniel B., 1, 162, 164
Journal of Discourses, 79, 85, 93, 167,
  185
Judeo-Christian tradition, 76, 78, 80

Kapp, Ardeth G., 91
Kennedy, David, 122
"Keys to the kingdom," 107–8, 140, 141
Kimball, Heber C., 25, 52, 56, 107, 167
Kimball, Spencer, 94, 107–8, 110, 119,
  129, 201
King, Martin Luther, Jr., 184–85, 201
Kingston, Ortell, 189, 190
Kirtland, 21–27, 28, 32, 40, 43, 72, 155;
  Mormon Pentecost at, 216; polygamy
  in, 175, 180; restorations in, 150; and
  Smith's notions of urban planning,
  33; Young in, 52–53

Knapp, Ricky, 157
Kraut, Ogden, 188

Lafferty, Allen, 154, 156
Lafferty, Brenda, 1, 154, 156, 157
Lafferty, Daniel, 152–58, 159, 165
Lafferty, Erica, 1, 154
Lafferty, Ronald, 152–58, 159, 165
Laman, 28, 208
Lamanites, 3, 9, 10, 11, 28, 92, 201, 217,
  220
Law, William, 49
Law of Enoch, 23
Law of Jacob, 41, 44, 45. *See also* Po-
  lygamy
Law of Sarah, 44, 45
LeBaron, Ervil, 161–65, 219
LeBaron, Joel, 164
LeBaron, Verlan, 164
Lee, George P., 108
Lee, John, 36, 67, 69, 71, 72
Lee, Rex E., 128
Lehi, 10, 17–18, 28, 207, 208, 209
Longo, Bruce, 158–61, 165
Longo, Dean, 158
Lucifer, 93, 97, 112, 157, 215
Lyman, Amasa, 57

McConkie, Bruce, 81, 93, 94, 97, 98,
  107–8, 152; and the geological time-
  scale teaching, 171; on revelations,
  165–66
McKay, David O., 151
McLellin, William, 211–12
Marks, William, 49
Marriage, 83, 85, 128, 140, 156, 215;
  Catholic, 86; celestial, 25, 136, 175;
  dates, in Mormon archives, 87; patri-
  archal order of, and God, 1; planned,
  and revelation, 98; and "temple rec-
  ommends," 85, 86. *See also* Polygamy
Marriott, J. Willard, Sr., 123
Marston, Eddie, 164
Marston, Ramona, 163
Mary Magdelene, 77
Masons, 4, 41, 46, 48–50, 105, 214, 216
Maxwell, Neal A., 80
Michael the Archangel, 78, 93, 97, 156,
  214–15
Millennium, 11, 21, 88–91, 187, 188,
  201, 217–20; and the appearance of
  the "One Mighty and Strong," 157;
  Jesus and, 89, 151; and survivalism,
  155, 166–74; tradition of "gathering"
  for, 22
Miracle of the Sea Gulls of 1848, 56